BIBLICAL
ERRANCY

BIBLICAL ERRANCY

An Analysis of its Philosophical Roots

Norman L. Geisler, Editor

ZONDERVAN
PUBLISHING HOUSE

OF THE ZONDERVAN CORPORATION
GRAND RAPIDS, MICHIGAN 49506

BIBLICAL ERRANCY: AN ANALYSIS OF ITS PHILOSOPHICAL ROOTS
Copyright © June 1981 by The Zondervan Corporation
Grand Rapids, Michigan

Library of Congress Cataloging in Publication Data

Main entry under title:

Biblical errancy.

    Includes bibliographical references and indexes.
    1. Bible—Evidences, authority, etc.—Addresses, essays, lectures. 2. Philosophy,
Modern—Addresses, essays, lectures. I. Geisler, Norman L.

BS480.B4753   190   80-28486
ISBN 0-310-39291-8

Copy edited by Diane Zimmerman and Gerard Terpstra
Designed by Paul Hillman

Printed in the United States of America

83   84   85   86   87   88 — 10   9   8   7   6   5   4   3   2

CONTENTS

PREFACE

A number of contemporary evangelical writers have pointed to the epistemological roots of the current denial of the inerrancy of Scripture, but few have attempted to identify and elaborate them. This book is an effort in that direction. Each essayist is trained in both philosophy and theology and writes out of an expertise in the specific philosophies discussed.

Perhaps the primary scriptural exhortation prompting this work is that of the apostle Paul: "See to it that no one takes you captive through hollow and deceptive philosophy" (Col. 2:8). Indeed, in this book, to quote the apostle again, "we demolish arguments and . . . take captive every thought to make it obedient to Christ" (2 Cor. 10:5). But we believe that to "beware of philosophy" we must first be *aware* of it. We must be aware of its subtleties and of its liabilities in view of the Christian's fundamental commitment to the inerrant Word of God.

It is often naïvely assumed that because contemporary theologians are evangelical in doctrine and practice they are somehow immune from adverse philosophical influence. This fallacy is tantamount to claiming that doctors and nurses never get sick. Indeed, often in the history of Christianity some of the most philosophically and theologically unorthodox writers believed themselves to be defending and preserving "true" Christianity. Spinoza, who was an unequivocal pantheist and uncompromising antisupernaturalist, doggedly denied that his view undermined confidence in Scripture. He wrote, "I have said nothing unworthy of Scripture or God's Word. . . ."[1] A tragic current example of how one can be blind to the subtle but erosive influences of philosophy on his own thinking is Stephen T. Davis, a contemporary denier of inerrancy. He ironically points a finger at "liberals," saying, "What leads them to liberalism . . . is their acceptance of certain philosophical or scientific assumptions that are inimical to evangelical theology. . . ."[2]

The purpose of this book is to expose some of these philosophical assumptions we believe to be inimical to evangelical theology. In this regard an explicit disclaimer is necessary. We do *not* claim that all contemporary errantists are directly and consciously influenced by any or all of these philosophers. Many

7

have been influenced only indirectly and unconsciously by only some of these views. Philosophical assumptions are often "caught" rather than taught. They are picked up unawares in the culture and through education. They are contracted almost like a common cold, simply by breathing the contaminated "air" of our age. But like the undesirable virus, these unacceptable assumptions are to be both guarded against and treated when caught.

The philosophical "air" is alive with everything from Bacon's inductivism to Heidegger's mysticism: with Hume's skepticism, Kant's agnosticism, Hegel's transcendentalism, Kierkegaard's existentialism, Nietzsche's atheistic relativism, and Wittgenstein's linguistic noncognitivism. Few errantists may admit the influences of most of these men on their thinking, but only the naïve and untrained can miss the marks of these philosophers in their writings. We hope that, by exposing these alien presuppositions, these essays will alert evangelicals to the philosophical roots of biblical errancy.

INDUCTIVISM, MATERIALISM, AND RATIONALISM: BACON, HOBBES, AND SPINOZA

Norman L. Geisler

Norman L. Geisler is Professor of Systematic Theology at Dallas Theological Seminary. He is a graduate of Wheaton College (B.A. and M.A.), Detroit Bible College (Th.B.), and Loyola University, Chicago (Ph.D.). He has held the positions of Christian Services Director for Northeast Suburban Youth for Christ; Pastor, Dayton Center Church, Silverwood, Michigan; Assistant Pastor, River Grove Bible Church, River Grove, Illinois; Pastor, Memorial Baptist Church, Warren, Michigan; President, Alumni of Detroit Bible College; and first president, Evangelical Philosophical Society. His teaching experience includes that of the following positions: Assistant Professor of Bible and Apologetics at Detroit Bible College; Assistant Professor of Bible and Philosophy at Trinity College, Deerfield, Illinois; Associate Professor of Philosophy at Trinity College; and Professor of Philosophy of Religion and Chairman of the Department of Philosophy of Religion, Trinity Evangelical Divinity School, Deerfield. Among his books are General Introduction to the Bible; Ethics: Alternatives and Issues; Philosophy of Religion; To Understand the Bible: Look for Jesus; Popular Survey of the Old Testament; Introduction to Philosophy: A Christian Perspective; A Christian Ethic of Love; Christian Apologetics; Inerrancy *(editor); and* Options in Contemporary Evangelical Ethics. *He has also contributed articles to numerous journals and periodicals. Dr. Geisler is a member of the Evangelical Theological Society, American Philosophical Society, Evangelical Philosophical Society, and the Council of ICBI.*

CHAPTER SUMMARY

This chapter traces the early modern roots of biblical errancy to the philosophies of Bacon, Hobbes, and Spinoza. Once the inductive scientific method was assumed to be the means of obtaining all truth, it was a natural step to assume that Scripture dealt only with religious truth. Such was the separation of science and Scripture set up in the wake of Bacon's inductivism. The materialism of Hobbes led to some of the earliest naturalistic and negative higher criticism of the Bible. But the full force of antisupernaturalism and negative criticism was set in motion by the rationalism of Spinoza. Thus within a little over one hundred years after the Reformation the philosophical seeds of modern errancy were sown. When these seeds had produced their fruit in the church a century or so later, it was because theologians had capitulated to alien philosophical presuppositions. Hence, the rise of an errant view of Scripture did not result from a discovery of factual evidence that made belief in an inerrant Scripture untenable. Rather, it resulted from the unnecessary acceptance of philosophical premises that undermined the historic belief in an infallible and inerrant Bible.

1 *Norman L. Geisler*

INDUCTIVISM, MATERIALISM, AND RATIONALISM: BACON, HOBBES, AND SPINOZA

IT IS NOT uncommon to mark the modern departure from biblical authority and inerrancy from the early nineteenth century. In 1804 Johann Eichhorn issued a critical introduction to the New Testament. F. C. Baur in the 1830s applied a dialectic to Peter and Paul that resulted in dating several of their books in the second century. Julius Wellhausen (1876) popularized the documentary hypothesis of the Pentateuch. Before this (ca. 1866) K. H. Graf laid down the basis of the JEPD theory. And even before these men, other scholars had in effect denied the inerrancy of Scripture. H. B. Witter (1711) believed in two accounts of creation, and Jean Astruc used divine names to identify some dozen different writers in Genesis (1753).

However, as important as these men were to the denial of the inerrancy of Scripture, the truth is that over one hundred years earlier the philosophical roots of biblical errancy had been firmly laid in the philosophies of Bacon, Hobbes, and Spinoza. From these philosophical roots, the seeds of errancy spread to Richard Simon in France. He is called by many the "Father of Biblical Criticism." Like Spinoza, he denied the Mosaic authorship of the Pentateuch and is said to have been the first to introduce the word *critique* into the discussion of the Bible (1678).

We will begin our survey almost two generations before Simon with the Englishman Francis Bacon. We will see that the roots of modern errancy are to be found in the philosophical soil of the seventeenth century.[1] From here the errancy position has spread gradually down through the centuries to our own day.

FRANCIS BACON—INDUCTIVISM*

About one hundred years after the Reformation, Francis Bacon (1561–1626) published his famous *Novum Organum* (1620) in which he set the stage for modern biblical criticism and the denial of the full authority and inerrancy of the Bible. Inerrancy is undermined in several ways in this work.

Bacon claimed that all truth is discovered inductively. After tearing down the "idols" of the old deductive method of discovering truth, Bacon argued that "the best demonstration by far is experience."[2] The inductive method, he said, is the true way to interpret nature. One can understand how Bacon could consider inductive logic a valid method for scientific inquiry, but he went far beyond reasonable bounds when he claimed universal applicability for this method. He wrote:

> It may also be asked . . . whether I speak of natural philosophy only, or whether I mean that the other sciences, logic, ethics, and politics, should be carried on by this method. Now I certainly mean what I have said to be understood of them all; and as the common logic, which governs by the syllogism, extends not only to natural but to all sciences, so does mine also, which proceeds by induction, embrace everything.[3]

Science is the true model of the world. In view of the exaltation and extension of the inductive method, it is not surprising to hear Bacon say, "I am building in the human understanding a true model of the world, such as it is in fact, not such as a man's own reason would have it to be." This new and true model, Bacon dared to claim, would discover "the creator's own stamp upon creation." He even went so far as to identify it with "the Ideas of the divine."[4]

Truth is known pragmatically. Bacon saw clearly that his method implied a pragmatic test for truth; namely, If it works, it is true. "Truth and utility," he wrote, "are here the very same things."[5] For "of all signs there is none more certain or more noble than that taken from fruits. For fruits and works are as it were spon-

---

*The first part of this chapter (pages 12–19) is a substantial reproduction of material on pp. 312–320 of *Inerrancy*, ed. Norman L. Geisler (Grand Rapids: Zondervan, 1979).

sors and sureties for the truth of philosophies."[6] In short, all truth is tested by its results. This is pragmatism some three centuries before William James or John Dewey.

Bacon separated science and the Bible. Some have mistakenly claimed that Thomas Aquinas was responsible for separating faith and reason. This view is unfounded. Aquinas did make a formal *distinction* between the two realms but never an *actual separation.* For Aquinas, human reason at its best is finite and fallible, and can never attain the content of the Christian faith.[7] Reason is only the servant of the theologian, a tool in the discovery and expression of one's faith.[8] But what Aquinas did not do, others like Bacon did: Bacon completely separated the realm of reason and science from the realm of faith and religion. He wrote, "It is therefore most wise soberly to render unto faith the things that are faith's," for from the "absurd mixture of matters divine and human" proceed heresies and "fantastical philosophy." It is for this reason that "sacred theology must be drawn from the word and oracles of God, not from the light of nature, or the dictates of reason." Bacon went so far as to say, "We are obliged to believe the word of God, though our reason be shocked at it." And therefore, "the more absurd and incredible any divine mystery is, the greater honour we do to God in believing it; and so much the more noble the victory of faith."[9]

Science is excluded from Genesis and Job. In view of Bacon's complete separation of faith and science, one is not shocked to hear him debunk a hermeneutic that considers the biblical affirmations in Genesis and Job to be factually true. He said, "Some have endeavored to build a system of natural philosophy on the first chapter of Genesis, the book of Job and other parts of Scripture; seeking thus the dead amongst the living."[10] Now certainly it is one thing to read modern scientific theory into ancient poetry,[11] but it is another to exclude space-time affirmations from the book authored by the Creator of the physical universe. Surely Bacon went too far here.

It is not difficult to see how Bacon set the stage for the view that the Bible is infallible only in "spiritual matters" but does not speak to us inerrantly of historical and scientific matters. If we must render to science what is science's (namely, *all* truth), then what is left for religion? For Bacon, and even more clearly for Hobbes who followed him, the Bible serves a religious and evocative function—it leads us to honor and obey God—but it does not make cognitive truth claims about God nor affirmations about the physical universe.

THOMAS HOBBES—MATERIALISM

Thomas Hobbes (1588–1679), like Bacon, appeared to be a professing Christian. But in view of the lack of religious toleration in those days (and the natural fear one would have to speak openly against religion) it may be better to understand Hobbes as a tongue in cheek believer. He is considered by many to be the father of modern materialism. There are numerous ways in which Hobbes's views directly and indirectly undermine the traditional doctrine of scriptural authority.

Hobbes advocated materialistic sensationalism. In Hobbes's materialism, the forerunner of Hume's skeptical empiricism, all ideas in one's mind are reducible to sensations.[12] "There is no conception in a man's mind, which hath not at first, totally, or by parts, been begotten upon the organs of sense. The rest are derived from that original."[13] Hobbes was very explicit when he spoke of this. He boldly declared that

> the world (I mean not the earth only . . . , but the *universe*, that is, the whole mass of all things that are) is corporeal, that is to say, body; and hath the dimensions of magnitude, namely, length, breadth, and depth: also every part of body is likewise body, and . . . that which is not body is no part of the universe: and because the universe is all, that which is no part of it is nothing, and consequently nowhere.[14]

God-talk is evocative but not descriptive. Hobbes argued that "there is no idea or conception of anything we call *Infinite*. . . . And therefore the name *God* is used, not to make us conceive him . . . but that we may honour him."[15] In this Hobbes was a forerunner of the logical positivists and linguistic analysts who deny the cognitivity of revelational language. As A. J. Ayer later claimed, all God-talk is literally nonsense.[16] Of course if there is no meaningfully descriptive God-talk, then none of the propositions in the Bible are meaningful descriptions of God. Needless to say, if Hobbes were right, it would play havoc with any divinely inspired propositional revelation that purports to inform us about God.

Miracles are brought into question. Hobbes discredited the belief in natural religion by claiming that it is based on such things as opinions about ghosts, ignorance, and fear.[17] Supernatural religion, according to Hobbes, is based on miracles. But the credibility of these miracles is seriously weakened, he said, by false miracles, contradictions, and injustice in the church that claims them to be true. Furthermore, miracles actually weaken faith in that "miracles failing, faith also failed."[18] Hobbes undermines the credibility of miracles by placing them in such a poor light. He thus opened the door for later deists and naturalists to deny the miraculous altogether. Of course, if Hobbes's implication is right and miracles do not occur, then obviously the Bible cannot be a supernatural revelation from God.

The Bible has absurdities we must accept by blind faith. Some have mistakenly held that Kierkegaard taught that we must make a blind leap of faith into the realm of the rationally absurd. But what Kierkegaard did not teach, Hobbes did. He explained that our "natural reason" is the "undoubted word of God," which is "not to be folded up in the Napkin of an Implicit Faith." Hobbes claimed that there are "many things in God's Word above Reason; that is to say, which cannot by natural reason be either demonstrated, or confuted. . . ." These are "not comprehensible" and we must live by the "Will to obedience" to "forbear contradiction; when we so speak, as by lawful authority we are commanded; . . . and Faith reposed in him that speaketh, though the mind be incapable of any Notion at all from the words spoken."[19] Elsewhere Hobbes spoke of the deity of Christ and the Trinity as untranslatable "absurdities."[20] If these words are taken seriously, it is one of the most blatant forms of blind fideism ever proposed. What is significant to this study is the radical separation of faith and reason and the apparent relegation of matters of faith to the unverifiable and paradoxical realm of the absurd and contradictory.

Hobbes engaged in higher criticism of the Bible. Hobbes was one of the first modern writers to engage in explicit higher criticism of the Scriptures. In one passage he boldly suggests that "the Scriptures by the Spirit of God in man, mean a man's spirit, inclined to Godliness."[21] After claiming that the story of Jesus healing the demon-possessed man was simply a "parable," Hobbes announced: "I see nothing at all in the Scripture, that requireth a belief, that demoniacs were any other thing but madmen."[22] In brief, the miracles of the Gospels must be understood as spiritual or parabolical, but not historical.

Hobbes completely separated religion and science. In view of this kind of hermeneutical desupernaturalization of Scripture, it is little wonder that Hobbes could claim that "the Scripture was written to show unto men the kingdom of God, and to prepare their minds to become his obedient subjects, leaving the world, and the philosophy thereof, to the disputation of men, for the exercising of their natural reason."[23] In short, he proposed a complete separation of divine revelation and human reason, in which the latter has a monopoly on all cognitive truth and the former demands only blind obedience to its "spiritual" truths. In this respect Hobbes not only precedes but also goes beyond both Kierkegaard and Barth!

BENEDICT SPINOZA—RATIONALISM

Higher criticism of the Bible manifested itself more fully in the Jewish pantheist, Benedict De Spinoza (1632–1677). Using a strict deductive rationalism, Spinoza constructed a system of higher criticism.

All truth is mathematically knowable. Spinoza limited truth to what is self-evident or what is reducible to it.[24] He claimed that all truth—even religious truth—is mathematically knowable.[25] Anything not subject to his deductive geometric reason was rejected.

The Bible contains contradictions. It is not surprising that Spinoza concluded that there are contradictions in the Bible. Samuel denies that God ever repents (1 Sam. 15:29), and Jeremiah declares that God does repent (Jer. 18:8–10). "Are not these two texts directly contradictory?" asked Spinoza. "Both statements are general, and each is the opposite of the other—what one flatly affirms, the other flatly denies."[26]

The Bible merely contains the Word of God. Spinoza affirmed the classic liberal formula of Scripture—the Bible *contains* the Word of God—centuries before it became the byword of modernism. Speaking of the "Scripture," he wrote: "Insofar as it contains the word of God, it has come down to us uncorrupted." And not unlike later liberal Christians, he claimed that readers "will find nothing in what I have written repugnant either to the Word of God or to true religion and faith . . . ; contrariwise, they will see that I have strengthened religion. . . ."[27] Surely with such "defenders" as this Christianity needs no enemies!

The Bible is not propositional revelation. Spinoza denied propositional revelation and attacked what in the twentieth century Emil Brunner termed the "paper-pope theory." "I will show," Spinoza boldly claimed, "wherein the law of God consists, and how it cannot be contained in a certain number of books." If anyone should object that "though the law of God is written in the heart, the Bible is nonetheless the Word of God," Spinoza would reply: "I fear that such objectors are too anxious to be pious, and that they are in danger of turning religion into superstition, and *worshipping paper and ink* in place of God's Word" (emphasis added).[28]

The Bible is authoritative only in religious matters. Like Bacon and Hobbes before him, Spinoza relegated the authority of the Bible to purely religious matters. He claimed, "I have neither said anything against the Word of God nor given any foothold to impiety." Why? "Because," he continued, "a thing is called sacred and Divine when it is designated for promoting piety, and continues sacred so long as it is religiously used; if the users cease to be pious, the thing ceases to be sacred."[29] So as long as the Bible is used for religious purposes, it is a sacred book. Of course, a religious purpose is the only purpose of Scripture for Spinoza, for faith and reason are entirely separate domains. As to the question of "whether the meaning of Scripture should be made to agree with reason; or whether reason should be made to agree with Scripture," Spinoza replied, "Both parties are, as I have shown, utterly in the wrong, for either doctrine would require us to tamper with reason or with Scripture." The conclusion is clear: "Scripture does not teach philosophy, but *merely obedience,* and . . . all it contains has been adapted to the understanding and established opinions of the multitude" (emphasis added).[30] In other words, the Bible has nothing to say to reason. It is an accommodation to the false opinions of men who use their senses rather than their minds for thinking. Philosophy, on the contrary, is for those who think rationally (i.e., geometrically and pantheistically). True science is the domain of the intellect; religion is for the obedient will.

Moral criteria are used to determine the truth of the Bible. Commenting on the authenticity of the great love command in Matthew 22, Spinoza confidently concluded:

This cannot be a spurious passage, nor due to a hasty and mistaken scribe, for if the Bible had ever put forth a different doctrine it would have to change the whole of its teaching, for this is the

cornerstone of religion, without which the whole fabric would fall
headlong to the ground.[31]

Spinoza applied the same moral criteria for determining the authenticity of Scripture as a whole. "The only reason," he argued,
"which we have for belief in Scripture or the writings of the
prophets, is the doctrine we find therein and the signs by which it
is confirmed," for "the prophets extol charity and justice above
all things, and have no other object. . . ."[32] In short, if the passage teaches love and justice, it is authentic; if not, then it is not.
Spinoza did not seem to recognize the circularity of this reasoning. How are the biblical teachings of love and justice even
known, unless they are derived from authenticated Scripture?

The miraculous is categorically denied. Spinoza is one of the most
strongly antisupernatural writers in the history of philosophy.
The major premise of his pantheistic philosophy is that God and
nature are identical.[33] The belief in miracles, he insisted, is
based on ignorance and is used by religious authorities to preserve faith. Spinoza reserved severe words for those who thus
believed in the miraculous.

> Anyone who seeks for the true causes of miracles and strives to under-
> stand natural phenomena as an intelligent being, and not gaze
> upon them like a fool, is set down and denounced as an impious
> heretic by those, whom the masses adore as the interpreters of
> nature and the gods. Such a person knows that, with the removal
> of ignorance, the wonder which forms their only available means
> for proving and preserving their authority would vanish also.[34]

So dogmatic was Spinoza in his naturalism that he proudly proclaimed, "We may, then, be absolutely certain that every event
which is truly described in Scripture necessarily happened, like
everything else, according to natural laws."[35] Why can one
make such an absolute assertion? Because, answered Spinoza,
"nothing comes to pass in contravention to her [Nature's] universal laws, nay, nothing does not agree with them and follow
them, for . . . she keeps a fixed and immutable order."[36] Spinoza
even appealed to the Bible for proof of his incurably naturalistic
presupposition. "Scripture," he declared, "makes the general
assertion in several passages that nature's course is fixed and
unchangeable."[37] Spinoza did not mince words when it came to
miracles. He flatly declared, "A miracle, whether a contravention to, or beyond nature is a mere absurdity."[38]

The Bible is subjected to systematic higher criticism. In light of such a radical antisupernatural bias, one is not surprised that Spinoza is the father of much modern biblical criticism. His *Tractatus* was one of the best-selling books in Europe in the late seventeenth century, going through numerous pseudonymous editions.[39]

Spinoza began his higher criticism with the Pentateuch. Because of certain names, locations, and third-person references to Moses, he concluded that someone after Moses' time must have been the author. Hence, "as there are many passages in the Pentateuch which Moses could not have written, it follows that the belief that Moses was the author of the Pentateuch is ungrounded and irrational."[40] Who wrote it? The same person who wrote the rest of the Old Testament, namely, Ezra.[41]

Higher criticism was not reserved for the books of Moses alone. "I pass on, then, to the prophetic books," wrote Spinoza. "An examination of these assures me that the prophecies therein contained have been compiled from other books . . . but are only such as were collected here and there, so that they are fragmentary."[42] Daniel did not write all of the book that bears his name, only chapter eight to the end.[43] The Old Testament canon was determined by the Pharisees.[44] The prophets did not in general speak "from revelation"; and "the modes of expression and discourse adopted by the Apostles in the Epistles, show very clearly that the latter are not written by revelation and Divine command, but merely by the natural powers and judgment of the authors."[45] As to the Gospels, "it is scarcely credible that God can have designated to narrate the life of Christ four times over, and to communicate it thus to mankind."[46] As to the crucial doctrine of the resurrection, Spinoza omitted it from the apostles' preaching, saying, "The Apostles who came after Christ, preached it to all men as the universal religion solely in virtue of Christ's passion."[47]

It is clear from this that over a century before Johann Semler (1725–1791), and two centuries before Julius Wellhausen (1844–1918), Spinoza engaged in systematic antisupernatural criticism of the Bible. Indeed, virtually all of the central emphases in modern liberalism—"the Bible contains the Word of God . . ." issue, the accommodation theory, rationalism, naturalism, the religious-only view, the moral criterion for canonicity, and even the allegorical interpretation of Scripture[48]— are found in Spinoza.

EVALUATION AND CRITIQUE

The real problem at the base of the contemporary drift from the historical and biblical position of inerrancy is philosophical. To be sure, not all errantists would admit the specific influence of one or more of these philosophers (or those to be discussed in later chapters) on their thinking. One modern errantist has, however, pinpointed the problem very well. Stephen Davis wrote:

> What leads them to liberalism, apart from cultural and personal issues, is their acceptance of certain philosophical or scientific assumptions that are inimical to evangelical theology—e.g., assumptions about what is "believable to modern people," "consistent with modern science," "acceptable by twentieth-century canons of scholarship," and the like.[49]

The irony of Davis's statement is that it is unwittingly self-descriptive. This ought to be a warning to "see to it that no one takes you captive through hollow and deceptive philosophy" (Col. 2:8). In this connection it should be stressed that the contemporary evangelical flirtation with the errancy position is not the result of new factual finds that undermine a belief in inerrancy. In fact, just the opposite is the case. There is probably more factual evidence in support of biblical inerrancy than ever before.[50] *The problem is not new facts but old philosophies.*

In the case of each philosopher examined above there are central philosophical presuppositions that are incompatible with an evangelical view of Scripture. I will briefly evaluate some of these.

Bacon's inductivism. Two problems emerge in Bacon's philosophy. First, Bacon assumes that the only method for discovering truth is the inductive method. This is the grandfather of the once-popular belief that "if you can't put it in a test tube, then don't believe it." Fortunately, few believe this any more, but contemporary thinkers are still heirs to the Baconian legacy. Much of modern "scientism" or the semideification of the scientific method is a delinquent grandson of Bacon's inductivism. Actually the contemporary "Baconian problem" is a kind of *methodological category mistake.* It assumes that a method adequate in physical science should be applied to social science (and ethics), to metaphysics (if there are any metaphysical realities), and to the biblical doctrine of inerrancy.[51] But it simply does not follow that the inductive or experimental method should be universally applied.[52] Taking a method that is sufficient for the practical use of humankind's natural environment and extending it to biblical doctrines is equally disastrous. Doctrines are not based in the data or phenomena of Scripture; they are *based* in the teaching of Scripture and *understood* in the light of the phenomena of Scripture.

Second, Bacon (and Hobbes as well) radically disjoins the realms of religion and reason, the spheres of faith and fact. This is called *separationism*. Of course, if there were no factual aspects to our faith (only obedience and worship being required), then biblical errancy would follow. However, Evangelicals believe that God's great redemptive acts are spatio-temporal. We believe that the birth, life, death, and resurrection of Christ are events of space and time. And not only these but also the Old Testament events affirmed by Christ and Scripture to be historical[53]—events such as the creation of man, the Fall, the Flood, and the Exodus from Egypt—are part of our faith. In fact, Jesus said, "I have spoken to you of earthly things and you do not believe; how then will you believe if I speak of heavenly things?" (John 3:12). Hence, Evangelicals cannot look at historical and scientific affirmations in Scripture as purely symbolical or mythical.[54] In short, we cannot separate science and Scripture. When the Bible declares that Jesus was born of a virgin, then it affirms a *biological* truth as well as a spiritual one. And when Jesus answered the question about divorce by saying, "Haven't you read that at the beginning the Creator 'made them male and female'" (Matt. 19:4), He not only laid down a moral principle but made a *scientific* pronouncement as well. The scientific cannot be separated from the spiritual without doing violence to the spiritual.

Hobbes's materialism. Not much time is needed to expose the presuppositions of Hobbes; they are hardly hidden. His materialism and antisupernaturalism are clear from the quotations above. For the Christian, "God is spirit" (John 4:24); hence, not all is matter. Materialism is really a reductionistic fallacy. There are few strict materialists today. Much has happened even in modern science to expose the clay feet of materialism. In fact, we are told there really is not much "matter" in matter; most of it is empty space. Also, the things that are most valued in life (love, persons, beauty, truth) are not reducible to matter: they have an unmistakably spiritual and transcendent dimension.

Hobbes also had a *naturalistic* presupposition in his thinking. As the above quotations show, this naturalism led him to desupernaturalize some of the miraculous accounts in the Gospels. Antisupernaturalism is more explicit in Spinoza, so my comments on the position will be held for the critique of Spinoza.

Spinoza's rationalism. Two presuppositions in Spinoza led to his conclusions: rationalism and antisupernaturalism. The first of these—deductive or geometric rationalism—is also a methodological mistake, as was Bacon's presupposition. While Bacon took the inductive method from the experimental sciences and made it *the* method for discovering all truth, Spinoza took deductive (Euclidian) geometry and developed a rigid rationalism. Here again, there are perfectly legitimate applications for geometric reasoning. But to assume that *all* truth can be deduced from self-evident axioms is far from self-evident. Few philosophers today accept either Spinoza's axioms or his philosophical method, and there is no reason why an evangelical Christian should do so either. If the basis for Spinoza's pantheistic rationalism is invalid, then his basis for biblical criticism fails too.

Spinoza's antisupernaturalism is blatant. He defines miracles out of existence a priori by designating natural law as "inviolable." Scientists today would not agree. Natural law is a description of the way things do occur *regularly;* it does not dictate the way they must occur *universally.*

For the Christian a "natural law" is the way God *usually* works in the physical realm and a miracle is the way He works on *special* occasions. In any event, if the God of the Bible who created the world exists and is in sovereign control of the universe, then miracles are *ipso facto* possible. And if miracles are possible, then no one is obligated on philosophical grounds to engage in antisupernatural attacks on the inerrancy of the Bible.

In summation, the denial of the inerrancy of Scripture is not primarily a factual problem, though it has factual dimensions, to be sure. The root problem of modern errancy is philosophical. And the apostle Paul has urged us to "demolish arguments and every pretension that sets itself up against the knowledge of God" (2 Cor. 10:4, 5). In view of this it seems to me that the best *refutation* of biblical errancy is a clear *exposition* of the premises on which it is built, whether these presuppositions be grounded in inductivism, materialism, rationalism, or naturalism.

SKEPTICISM: HUME

Gary R. Habermas

Gary R. Habermas is Associate Professor of Apologetics and Philosophy of Religion at William Tyndale College (formerly Detroit Bible College). He is a graduate of Detroit Bible College (B.R.E.), University of Detroit (M.A.), and Michigan State University (Ph.D.). He has served as pastor at Beech Park United Brethren Church, Detroit, and at Kalamazoo United Brethren Church, Kalamazoo, and taught for three years at the Montana Institute of the Bible, Lewiston, Montana. Dr. Habermas has written two books–The Resurrection of Jesus: A Rational Inquiry *and* The Resurrection of Jesus: An Apologetic—*and numerous articles for periodicals. He is a member of the Evangelical Theological Society, the Evangelical Philosophical Society, and the Conference on Faith and History.*

CHAPTER SUMMARY

The Enlightenment period was characterized by differing strains of intellectual thought, from which emerged the skeptical philosophy of David Hume (1711–1776). He held that many accepted philosophical and theological beliefs were devoid of epistemological proof and therefore could not be known with certainty to be true. His twofold attack against the inerrancy of Scripture consisted initially of denying the particular evidences in the form of miracles by holding to the superiority of man's experience for the laws of nature. Also, he further posited empirical standards of judgment against the Christian belief in the inspiration of Scripture as a whole. By these specific means, in particular, Hume possibly exercised the greatest influence on the rejection of inerrancy by critical philosophers and theologians of various schools of thought from his time to the present.

In spite of the immense influence of his critique, both Hume and those who have generally followed him in these endeavors are refuted on several accounts in their attempts to dismiss either miracles or the inerrancy of Scripture as a whole. In particular, they failed by not ascertaining if there is a God who chose to act in history by temporarily suspending the laws of nature and in written revelation in Scripture. Since both Hume and his followers have failed in their endeavor to dismiss the truthfulness of such beliefs, the possibility of a Christian theistic world view certainly remains.

2 *Gary R. Habermas*

SKEPTICISM: HUME

 T HE ENLIGHTENMENT was a particularly significant period in the formulation of modern thought. The seventeenth century marked the development of three strains that later dominated Enlightenment philosophy. The chiefly Continental movement known as rationalism received its impetus from René Descartes (1596–1650). This philosophy was further developed by such scholars as Benedict Spinoza (1632–1677) and Gottfried Leibniz (1646–1716). Deism emerged from the teachings of Herbert of Cherbury (1583–1648) and was popular in England chiefly among such scholars as Matthew Tindal (c. 1655–1733) and John Toland (1670–1722). British empiricism grew out of the thought of Francis Bacon (1561–1626). Within the empirical tradition were John Locke (1632–1704), George Berkeley (c. 1685–1753), and David Hume (1711–1776). These three philosophical traditions are often grouped because their methodologies are closely related to one another.

Enlightenment philosophers espoused concepts that have had great influence on twentieth-century epistemology. For this reason, a brief overview of these three movements that arose during the Enlightenment will provide background for identifying and evaluating David Hume's influence on the denial of biblical authority.

BACKGROUND OF HUME'S THOUGHT

The rationalists' epistemology was based on the theory that reality is essentially rational and that by making the proper deductions, an individual could achieve knowledge of self, others, and the world. Reason and particularly deductive logic were emphasized. Even God could be known, at least to some extent, by the exercise of reason.

Descartes started with the reality of doubt and the ability to think. His well-known dictum "I think, therefore I am" is a good example of rationalism's stress on reason. Beginning with the truth that we doubt and are therefore not perfect, he reasoned to the existence of God as the Perfect Being, using the ontological and cosmological proofs. Since a Perfect Being would not deceive lesser beings, whatever we can deduce by means of clear and distinct reasoning concerning the reality of the world must therefore be true.[1]

Spinoza also held that the universe is structured on rational principles and that it can be known through the proper exercise of reason. However, dismissing Descartes's mind-body dualism in favor of pantheism, he maintained that reality is composed of one substance. Because God, the world, and human beings are rational, worship is also to be expressed rationally. Ideas such as these are expressed in his major work, *Ethics,* published post-humously. Especially noteworthy for our study of Hume is that Spinoza held that miracles, if understood as violations of nature, do not occur.[2] Some of the beginnings of biblical criticism can thus be seen in the work of this philosopher.

Leibniz was another thinker in the tradition of rationalism. In his key work, *Monadology,* he described reality in terms of monads—metaphysical units of force. This theory contrasts with the view of materialism, in which the atom is the basic compo-nent of reality. Leibniz spoke of a hierarchy of monads, cul-minating in God, the Monad of monads. Accepting some of the arguments set forth by other rationalists to prove the existence of God, Leibniz maintained that God ordered the monads in such a way that the universe is completely rational and that this is "the best of all possible worlds."

Contemporary with the rise of Continental rationalism was English deism. Herbert of Cherbury is considered the founder of this movement. In *De Veritate* Herbert delineated five "common notions" about religion: the existence of a supreme God, the worship of God, the need to live a moral life, repentance from sin, and an eternal life of either reward or punishment.[3] He offered these as principles that are the foundation of world religions and that constitute the essence of true religion. These five principles, Herbert claimed, are based on mankind's common reason.

The major endeavor of the deists was to formulate a natural religion based on reason as the primary authority. For some scholars, including Herbert of Cherbury, reason could support the orthodox understanding of the Christian faith. There were discrepancies between this approach and revealed Christianity, but this form of deism was not an outright attempt to disprove Christian belief.

Other deists, however, presented their positions as alternatives to revealed religion. Matthew Tindal, for example, considered "true" Christianity to be synonymous with natural religion. In his view, all doctrines not conforming to reason were to be rejected. Miracles were dismissed and morality was stressed. John Toland also believed that nothing in the Bible could conflict with reason. Therefore, miracles were given natural explanations. To these deists, comparative religion and critical investigations of Christianity were popular studies. In fact, deism had a major influence on biblical criticism. The stress on reason led to close similarities to rationalism, but the deists were also affected by the British empiricists.

Rebuttals to those deists who were critical of Christianity were offered by such philosophers as John Locke (see below), Thomas Sherlock (1678–1761), Joseph Butler (1692–1752), and William Paley (1743–1805). The work of Butler, in particular, is thought to have been a major factor in the fall of deism.[4] These scholars argued for the rationality of revealed religion and also wrote in defense of miracles. Some of their works are appreciated even today as well-reasoned defenses of Christianity.

About the same time that deism and rationalism were developing, British empiricism was emerging in England. The British empiricists were convinced that argumentation based on deductive reasoning (the scholastics) or on innate principles of the mind (the rationalists) is not valid. Rather, these scholars based their epistemology on verification of sense experience. Empirical investigation is thus the chief test of truth claims.

Francis Bacon was one scholar who rejected the methodology of scholastic theology. In *Novum Organum* he proposed that inductive logic replace Aristotle's deductive logic. (Aristotle's deductive approach had greatly influenced Western thought since the late Middle Ages.) Bacon helped to develop the experimental method, in which data are gathered and organized inductively so that conclusions can be drawn. His methodology was very influential for subsequent empirical systems.

John Locke also challenged the thinking of the past. In *Essay Concerning Human Understanding* he rejected Descartes's theory that there are innate ideas in the human mind. Instead, Locke maintained that the mind is an "empty slate" at birth. Knowledge is obtained by the accumulation of sensory data—this is the basis of all learning—and by reflection on that data. Thus Locke rejected the logic of the rationalists in favor of knowledge gained through the senses. Interestingly enough, Locke also defended the tenets of Christian theology. In *The Reasonableness of Christianity* he argued that miracles validate Christian doctrine and point to God's activity in the world.

George Berkeley took Locke's theory of knowledge one step further. In *Principles of Human Knowledge* and other works he taught that learning is a mental process. We do not actually know the material world. All that can be said to exist are other minds (spirits) and their mental perceptions (ideas). For something to exist, it must be perceived. However, reality does not cease to exist if it is not observed by a human being, for reality is still perceived by God, the Eternal Perceiver. Berkeley saw in this approach a new argument for the existence of God.

In summary, three major Enlightenment schools of thought—rationalism, deism, and empiricism—provided the background for the philosophy of David Hume. While often categorized as an empiricist, Hume was critical of each of these movements. In much of his work he questioned the epistemological bases of philosophical beliefs, and in so doing he attempted to establish that some longstanding assumptions were devoid of epistemological proof.

Hume's Epistemology

Though often placed in the tradition of British empiricism, Hume arrived at more radical conclusions. He continued the emphasis on sense experience by distinguishing between impressions—that is, sense perceptions—and ideas—memories or recollections of these impressions. The validity of an idea can be tested by tracing it back to the impression. If the idea consistently conforms to the impression, then it is valid. If it does not conform, then it must be rejected.

However, this explanation implies that Hume was much less skeptical in epistemological matters than he actually was. Hume went beyond Locke in asserting that the external world cannot be verified with absolute certainty. He went beyond Berkeley in concluding that spirit also cannot be verified and therefore is not empirically knowable. Here, where he differs with Locke and Berkeley, we can see Hume's major effect on empiricism. He postulated that commonly accepted beliefs such as the reality of the external world and even the existence of the self cannot be proven to be true. As will be shown below, Hume pointed out that certainty will more likely come from abstract reasoning (such as mathematics, logic, or tautologies), while knowledge is derived from empirical data. Even then, we must rely on probable knowledge and not proven certainties.

One of Hume's best-known teachings was that cause and effect cannot be proven to be true, in spite of the long-held belief on the part of most men that certain effects follow naturally from certain causes. In Hume's thinking, we observe these successive events, but we cannot find the necessary link between them. Cause and effect can only be accepted by instinct or by faith.

Hume directed stern rebukes at rationalists and deists who believed that reason could penetrate metaphysical issues such as the existence of God and other theological truths. In *Dialogues Concerning Natural Religion* he voiced doubts concerning some aspects of the traditional theistic proofs. In *The Natural History of Religion* he asserted that the earliest religion of humankind was not a monotheism characterized by fundamental rational principles, but rather a polytheism that evolved into monotheism. This view challenged a cornerstone of deistic thought. In denying the supremacy of reason, Hume called into question the very basis of rationalism and deism.

Hume also rejected much of the ethics developed by the rationalists when he denied that natural law provides any basis for morals. In yet another critique he maintained that immortality cannot be proven because there is no way to demonstrate the existence of an immaterial soul.

Hume agreed with Spinoza and some of the deists in rejecting miracles and special revelation. Few thinkers have created more doubt concerning the tenets of Christianity than Hume.

In short, Hume believed that there are definite limits in epistemology, and these limits even affect areas that had come to be regarded as truth or knowledge. Throughout it is important to note his usage of probability. Although many have held that Hume *denied* such concepts as cause and effect, theistic arguments, absolute ethics, and immortality, it is more likely that he proclaimed such could not be *known* to be true in the sense of proof. Thus, while such teachings *could* be true (and they can be accepted by instinct, habit, or faith), the crux of the matter is that we cannot *know* them to be true. Although this appears to be less of a frontal assault, herein lies much of Hume's influence.

Basic Premises in Hume's View of Scripture

Hume rejected the claim that Scripture is inspired and is thereby an authoritative revelation of God to humanity. There were at least two reasons for this denial of inspiration. One concerns the *particulars* in Scripture, and the other has to do with Scripture as a *whole*. Hume denied the *particular evidences* for Scripture when he asserted that, according to the canons of probability, miracles and prophecy cannot be used as supernatural indications of the inspiration of Scripture. He rejected the inspiration of Scripture as a *whole* by judging that it was not a work of abstract reasoning, and that it could not be verified by empirical testing. Therefore, according to Hume, the Scriptures "contain nothing but sophistry and illusion."[5] Thus, since neither particular evidences nor the Scripture as a whole can be accepted as inspired, the Bible cannot be considered a reliable basis for knowledge. There is no way to know that Scripture contains God's words for humankind.

We will examine these two premises in more detail. This is not to say that Hume's other views are not relevant here. However, in these two ideas Hume was taking direct aim at the veracity of Scripture. These two premises have been a major factor in the rejection of the inspiration of Scripture in the twentieth century.

Concerning Miracles

Hume's essay "Of Miracles" is part of *An Enquiry Concerning Human Understanding* (1751), one of his major works. In this essay he defines a miracle as *"a transgression of a law of nature by a particular volition of the Deity, or by the interposition of some invisible agent"* (Hume's emphasis). Hume asserts that the laws of nature are themselves proof against miracles:

> A miracle is a violation of the laws of nature; and as a firm and unalterable experience has established these laws, the proof against a miracle, from the very nature of the fact, is as entire as any argument from experience can possibly be imagined.[6]

Not only would the occurrence of miracles entail a breaking of nature's laws by the will of God (or some other invisible agent), but such occurrences are extremely improbable. The twofold evidence supplied by the laws of nature and man's experience of these laws provides a proof against a miracle. To state it another way, Hume believes that miracles have not occurred, for they are disproven by the superior evidence of the uniformity of nature's laws, as witnessed by the experience of mankind.[7]

To support this major argument, Hume introduces four subsidiary points.[8] First, he asserts that no miracle has ever been attested by a sufficient number of competent witnesses who are beyond reproach, suspicion, or delusion.

Second, people like to speak of extraordinary and unique events and to spread tales about them. In fact, even if a story is false, people will continue to lie about it in order to promote their own vanity or some personal cause.

Third, miracles usually occur among barbarous and ignorant peoples. And lying is a possible explanation in these cases also.

Fourth, the miracles in the various world religions supposedly support the teachings of that religion. But since such miracles and teachings conflict with those of other religions, they oppose and cancel out each other, leaving no instances of valid supernatural events.

Hume sought in this way to remove the evidential basis for all miracles and to show that reports of miracles are untrustworthy. He realized that by casting doubt on miracles and prophecy, a form of miracle, he was also destroying Christianity's claim that Scripture is an inspired revelation from God, since no evidence would then remain to support such beliefs.

In the concluding paragraphs of his essay, Hume adds that Christianity is founded on faith and cannot be defended by reason.[9]

Concerning Scripture as a Whole

Hume ends the *Enquiry* with a brief and almost entirely un-explained but very important statement:

> If we take in our hand any volume—of divinity or school metaphysics, for instance—let us ask, *Does it contain any abstract reasoning concerning quantity or number?* No. *Does it contain any experimental reasoning concerning matter of fact and existence?* No. Commit it then to the flames: for it can contain nothing except sophistry and illusion (Hume's emphasis).[10]

For Hume, then, theology is not a subject concerning which we can gain verifiable knowledge. Only assertions that involve abstract reasoning—such as mathematics, logic, and statements that are true by definition—or assertions that correspond to empirical data can be said to be knowable. If something is not true by definition or by evidence based on human experience, it cannot be known to be true.

Therefore, the Scriptures cannot be used for drawing objective epistemological conclusions. Hume insisted that theological matters cannot be known to be true. The Scriptures can be believed by faith alone. This belief was very influential in later philosophical discussions.

HUME'S INFLUENCE ON THE DENIAL OF BIBLICAL AUTHORITY

The Rejection of Miracles

Hume published the best known and most influential attack against miracles in the history of intellectual thought. According to John Herman Randall, Jr., this philosophical protest was so influential that it was the determining force in causing religious liberals from Hume's time to the present to reject miracles.[11] Wilbur M. Smith contends that Hume's work was the strongest argument ever raised contrary to belief in miracles.[12] Nineteenth-century liberalism and twentieth-century existentialism and postexistential trends relied on Hume's critique as the reasoning behind the rejection of miracles.

The nineteenth-century theological school of thought known as liberalism depended heavily on Hume's reasoning for the rejection of the miraculous. Perhaps the best example of this is found in the ideas of the German theologian David Strauss

(1808–1874). In his hotly debated work *A New Life of Jesus*, Strauss claimed that because Hume's essay had completely disproven the possibility of miracles, there was no longer any question in his mind that events that contradict nature's laws do not occur.[13]

Friedrich Schleiermacher (1768–1834), often referred to as the father of liberalism, followed Hume's assertion that miracles are reported most often in areas where there is little knowledge of nature's laws. Supernatural occurrences must be rejected because they destroy the concept of nature and because there are no known examples of them.[14]

Heinrich Paulus (1761–1851), a German rationalist who desired to judge theology by the criteria of reason, also denied that miracles were actual supernatural events. He held that the eyewitnesses of such events in Scripture were not aware of the laws of nature. For those who know these laws, the actual event remains, but not the miraculous element in it. Scholars must therefore discover the natural causes of so-called miracles.[15]

German theologian Bruno Bauer (1809–1882) agreed with Strauss that nature would be mocked if miracles occurred, since its laws would be violated. Therefore, such events must be rejected, for nature's laws cannot be denied.[16]

French scholar Ernst Renan (1823–1892) stated that Jesus accepted miracles as common occurrences, believing that they were not at all out of the ordinary. Jesus' belief was conditioned by the thought of His day and He was simply not aware that nature followed certain laws. In this sense, Jesus fell prey to ancient assumptions.[17]

For German theologian Otto Pfleiderer (1839–1908), science had made great strides in its pursuit of knowledge over the past centuries. One of its achievements was recognizing that nature's laws have such regularity they cannot be changed or violated.[18]

Adolf Harnack (1851–1930), one of the last major scholars of nineteenth-century liberalism, held a view similar to that of his contemporaries. For ancient peoples miracles appeared to be common occurrences, because these people did not know about the existence of the laws of nature. But modern people cannot accept any events that interrupt these laws. Such events simply do not occur, and we cannot believe accounts of them.[19]

In documenting this influence of Hume's essay, it is not being asserted that no other Enlightenment thinkers before him ever used similar arguments. Rather, as asserted by Randall, Strauss, and others, liberals followed Hume's thought as the definitive statement on this subject.

In rejecting miracles, nineteenth-century liberal theologians not only followed Hume's insistence that the laws of nature cannot be violated, but they also accepted Hume's suggestion that naturalistic alternatives to miraculous events are more probable than the actual miracles.[20] These theologians explained accounts of supernatural intervention in one of two ways.

Some scholars, following views such as those of Paulus, offered rationalistic alternatives to "supposed" miracles. The most common technique was to accept the general framework of the circumstances and surroundings of a miracle as being historical, but then to provide a naturalistic explanation for the actual miraculous element. Others, following Strauss, treated the entire account, including the nonmiraculous circumstances, as having little or no basis at all in history. Almost the entire account was believed to be an expression of mythology meant to convey a message.

Although Paulus's views gained acceptance by nineteenth-century liberals, Strauss's mythological explanation was deemed to be more sophisticated by later critical scholars. In the twentieth century the mythological approach found a strong proponent in Rudolf Bultmann.

This dismissal of miracles, revealing a definite reliance on Hume's essay, is not only a characteristic of nineteenth-century theological thought. As already mentioned, twentieth-century existentialism and contemporary postexistential trends reveal a similar dependence.

For German New Testament scholar Rudolf Bultmann (1884–1976), modern man is too advanced to accept any literal concept of miracles. In this day of increased knowledge, the ancient world view cannot be comprehended literally. Because of the contemporary understanding of the laws of nature, what used to be considered miraculous is so no longer. Miracles should therefore be demythologized, or reinterpreted existentially, in order for modern man to grasp the truth being expressed by the myth.[21]

According to Paul Tillich (1886–1965), events that are supernatural interferences with nature's laws cannot be accepted. Such a view, he claimed, distorts the workings of God. A miracle

may be interpreted as an unusual or astonishing event as long as
it is not believed to contradict natural laws.[22]
English theologian John A. T. Robinson (1919–) concurred
with the idea that the modern world view has no place for
mythological concepts. Accordingly, miracles and other myths
must be rejected as being contrary to nature's laws. Supernatural intervention is just not comprehensible in literal terms to
modern man. The truth embedded in such concepts is what
should be grasped.[23]

American theologians Harvey Cox and Lawrence Burkholder
directly cite Hume's essay as the major reason for the twentieth-
century rejection of miracles. Burkholder expresses some reser-
vations about a total acceptance of Hume's thesis but admits its
strong influence on his own views. Cox notes that he and other
scholars have been so profoundly affected by Hume's essay that
they are unable to accept the literal reality of miracles.[24]

This brief survey has shown that both nineteenth- and
twentieth-century critical scholars as a whole utilized Hume's
essay to reject and reinterpret miracles. Several explicitly mentioned Hume's work as the key reason for this rejection. Without
doubt, Hume's essay rejecting miracles on epistemological bases
has exerted more influence on the scholarly world than has any
other writing on this subject.

The Empirical Testing of Scripture

Hume's application of his epistemology to Scripture as a
whole also exerted much influence on nineteenth- and
twentieth-century philosophy. To Hume, a statement must contain abstract reasoning or empirical data in order to be known to
be true. Theology is subject to this empirical testing. The development of this empirical test became a chief inspiration for
twentieth-century logical positivism and linguistic analysis.

Immanuel Kant (1724–1804) further clarified Hume's
twofold distinction between abstract reasoning and experimental
reasoning. Statements that are true by definition he termed
analytical. Assertions that are true by empirical observation he
termed *synthetical*.[25] Like Hume, Kant also concluded that
metaphysical issues cannot be known, since they cannot be
tested by empirical methods. Religious beliefs can be established, to be sure, but by the exercise of practical reason and not
by sense data.

French philosopher Auguste Comte (1798–1857) agreed with
Kant that religious beliefs cannot be established by empirical
verification. But Comte went further in insisting that traditional
metaphysics be eliminated. For Comte, history is characterized
by three major periods of thought. Ancient man utilized *theological* reasoning, endeavoring to lean on God and supernatural
interferences for an understanding of the world. Then man
passed through the *metaphysical* period, when abstract reasoning
was believed to be the chief means of acquiring knowledge.
Modern man, however, has reached the *positive* period, when
scientific methodology is the key to knowledge. Humanity thus
has reached the point where reliance on metaphysical speculation is no longer needed. Rather than waste time on theological
issues, concerning which we cannot really gain knowledge, we
should concentrate on what is scientifically verifiable. In this
way, then, Comte said, religious issues are outdated and illegitimate avenues of inquiry.[26]

In the early twentieth century empirical verification became
an even more crucial issue. Austrian philosopher (and later
Cambridge University professor) Ludwig Wittgenstein (1889–
1951) stressed the importance of the study of language. In his
famous *Tractatus* he argued that a careful analysis of language
and thought is the chief occupation of philosophy. Many philosophers dealt with meaningless issues that are not open to
verification, such as metaphysical questions. For Wittgenstein,
we can only speak of what we know and otherwise we must
remain silent.[27]

Another Austrian philosopher, Moritz Schlick (1882–1936),
shared similar views. Schlick was the founder of the Vienna
Circle, a group of philosophers who were convinced of the need
to analyze language. According to Schlick, the major goal for
philosophy is to clarify the meanings of assertions, thereby
providing an empirical reference point for knowledge. Many
meaningless debates in philosophy could thus be solved because
of their lack of an empirical criterion of meaning.[28]

The teachings of Wittgenstein, Schlick, and the Vienna Circle
influenced the development of the school of thought known as
logical positivism. Logical positivism was popularized by the
English philosopher A. J. Ayer (1910–), especially through his
work *Language, Truth and Logic* (1936). Ayer held that a sentence
can be said to be significant in any factual way only if it can be

either verified or falsified according to empirical criteria. If such a conclusion is not possible and if the sentence is not tautological, then it is meaningless.[29]

Emerging from this discussion was the concept known as the *verification principle*. Factually meaningful statements are either analytical, and thereby true by definition, or they are synthetic, that is, capable of empirical validation. Analytic statements include assertions of pure logic, mathematics, and other tautological statements. They provide no new knowledge concerning the factual world. Synthetic statements are capable of experiential verification (or falsification). If statements fall into neither of these two categories, then they are pronounced factually meaningless.[30] Ayer states that his verification principle is an outgrowth of Hume's thoughts on this subject.[31]

The verification principle was not designed to be a test of truth, as such, but rather an indicator of the *meaningfulness* of statements. By applying such criteria to philosophy and clarifying both the purpose and methodology of the philosopher, Ayer concluded, many of the traditional debates could be by-passed as meaningless. Theological and ethical assertions, according to this standard, are literally meaningless because they cannot be verified or falsified. However, such statements were sometimes granted an emotive (but not factual) value.

Interestingly enough, Ayer used his standard also against the statements of atheists and agnostics. Since any proposition about God is said to be nonsensical, no meaningful statement can be made to affirm God's nonexistence or even to assert that knowledge about God is impossible. In short, all statements of any sort concerning God are nonsense, since they cannot be true by definition or by empirical verification.[32]

Moral assertions are likewise said to lack any means by which they may be experientially tested, since they are not factual propositions. Rather, they express the speaker's personal sentiments. For instance, the statement "murder is wrong" is not factually testable and therefore cannot be proven to be either right or wrong. It only relates that the one making the statement believes that murder is wrong.[33]

Ayer's verification principle is rejected by philosophers today, but many scholars still believe that the concept of verifiability or falsifiability is quite crucial. From such a concern developed the principle of falsification. Popularized by Antony Flew, this prin-

ciple has the advantage of being flexible while still providing a
means of testing assertions.

According to Flew, whenever a statement is made, the conditions under which it would be false should be ascertained. In
other words, before we can really know if a statement is valid, we
must also know what facts would make it invalid.[34] Only after
we know that no such probable negation exists can we contend
that the original assertion is valid, providing there are also reasons to accept it as being true.

In spite of the popularity of logical positivism in the early
twentieth century, it was plagued by several inherent weaknesses
discussed in the Evaluation and Critique section below. Indeed,
strictly speaking this school of thought no longer exists.[35] Philosophers of the last few decades have turned from logical
positivism to a less rigid usage of related principles—linguistic
analysis. It has modified the stricter and more dogmatic assumptions of its predecessor and has turned more attention to the
subject of language analysis.[36]

Along with the development of less rigid standards of verification, many linguistic analysts also became convinced that God-
talk was not so meaningless after all. For instance, today many
linguistic analysts are convinced that certain areas of theology
are open to verification. Topics such as God's existence, immortality, and even miracles are discussed in a congenial light and
are defended by some of these scholars.[37] This school of thought
no longer presents a unified front against metaphysics. Analytic
philosophers are divided over the question of whether such pur-
suits are verifiable.

To summarize: The ideas of David Hume have had a tremendous influence on the denial of biblical authority. His rejection of
particular evidences for the inspiration of Scripture—miracles
and prophecy—was accepted by the religious liberals of the
nineteenth century and by the existential and postexistential
scholars of the twentieth century. Hume's assertion that theological works must be judged according to whether their statements are true either by definition or by empirical investigation
influenced a number of philosophers, especially the Vienna Circle and logical positivists of the first half of the twentieth century.
Following logical positivism, linguistic analysis has developed
and, although less rigid in its evaluation of metaphysics, it still
bears the stamp of David Hume's ideas.

EVALUATION AND CRITIQUE

The Rejection of Miracles

In spite of the continuing influence of Hume's essay "On Miracles," I am convinced that there are at least five valid criticisms that invalidate Hume's entire argument. The first criticism is that in his definitive statements concerning miracles and in his subsequent comparison of these events to humankind's experience of the laws of nature, Hume commits a number of errors in logic. For instance, he states:

> There must, therefore, be a uniform experience against every miraculous event, otherwise the event would not merit that appellation. And as a uniform experience amounts to a proof, there is here a direct and full *proof*, from the nature of the fact, against the existence of any miracle (Hume's italics).[38]

It is evident that Hume does not begin his study with an impartial look at the facts. Earlier we saw that he defines miracles so that they are totally opposed from the outset by what he terms "firm and unalterable experience" and "uniform experience." In this quotation he continues to postulate that *all* experience favors the absence of miracles. In addition, he *specifically* states that if all experience does not oppose such events, then they cannot even be called miracles. He concludes by stating that this is a proof against the miraculous.

In his book *Miracles* C. S. Lewis notes that Hume can know that all experience favors his argument only by knowing in advance that all evidence in favor of miracle claims is false. But since he refuses to investigate miracles, he can know that these claims are false only by assuming that they do not happen. This is clearly circular reasoning, for Hume's position is certainly not evident a priori.[39]

The alternative to the approach taken by Hume is to examine miracles that claim strong experiential support. While speaking of Christ's miracles, Hume fails to investigate the exceptionally good evidence for the chief miracle claim of Christianity—the resurrection of Jesus Christ. It is not valid to rule out an opponent's view by defining one's own position to be true while ignoring evidence to the contrary.

Strangely enough, he even refers to his argument as a proof against the miraculous when, once again, he assumes that which he neglects to prove, namely, that uniform experience and all other data rest against all miracles. He cannot annul experiential claims for such events by utilizing faulty definitions, by assuming the evidence needed to prove one's view (and by doing so circularly), and by not examining the empirical, evidential claims in favor of the miraculous.

Hume's position is an unproven assumption and cannot disprove miracles. It is most noteworthy that even critical theologians admit that Hume argues circularly in this essay.[40]

The second criticism is that Hume's conclusion that humankind's experience of the laws of nature provides superior evidence against miracles in no way eliminates the possibility of the occasional intervention of a power still superior to these laws.

At the outset it must be agreed that there are natural laws. But although these are known by scientific inquiry to exist, such laws do not dictate whether occasional abnormalities can occur. In other words, the mere existence of such laws proves nothing concerning whether there is a God who is capable of temporarily suspending them. Thus, Hume should be less concerned with nature itself and more concerned with whether such a Being has indeed broken into nature from the outside.

Hume's concept describes what would happen *if* there is no intervention into nature by God. However, since it is *possible* that God exists and that He has sufficient power to temporarily suspend the laws of nature, no amount of arguing from naturalistic premises inside a system can ever disprove the possibility that God has performed a recognizable event in nature from outside of it. Therefore, the proper question here is not the internal query of the strength of the laws of nature. Rather, the proper question concerns the possibility that God, by utilizing superior strength, temporarily suspended nature's laws in order to cause such events to occur. It is readily evident that no matter how strong this natural system is, it is useless to rest one's case on it if there is a stronger Force.

A valid means of arriving at an answer to this issue of whether miracles have occurred would be to establish the validity of a theistic universe. By whatever means this is established, the endeavor would assign much importance to an investigation of the historical facts surrounding a claimed miracle—such as Jesus' resurrection—in order to ascertain the probability of that event occurring in history and being performed by God. It follows that if the evidence points to a probable miracle, recognized as being performed by God, then such evidence is actually *superior* to the laws of nature *at that moment*, for it would reveal that natural law can be temporarily set aside by a superior Force. This is simply because, in order to occur, a miracle would involve God's temporary suspension of those laws.[41]

It should be noted here that it has *not* been concluded that miracles have occurred. It is not the purpose of this essay to provide such an apologetic. It has only been pointed out that historical investigation of a miracle claim in a theistic universe might provide evidence that such an event may have happened. As such, an interference with the laws of nature might be the most probable solution.

The third criticism of Hume's thesis is that he ignores a group of purported miracles that even he admits have outstanding evidence in their favor, namely, the alleged miracles of the Jansenists of eighteenth-century France. After introducing the case for the Jansenist miracles, Hume evaluates the type of evidence they offer, seemingly according to his four supportive criteria.[42]

In answer to the first criterion—that miracles must be attested by an adequate amount of witnesses in order to insure their validity—Hume admits that many of these Jansenist miracles "were immediately proved upon the spot, before judges of unquestioned integrity, attested by witnesses of credit and distinction."

Concerning the second criterion—that people like to gossip and even lie about wonderful events—Hume admits that among these witnesses were "determined enemies to those opinions" who were not able to disprove the Jansenist claims.

Although the third criterion states that miracles occur among ignorant and barbarous nations, Hume explains that the Jansenist miracles occurred "in a learned age, and on the most eminent theatre that is now in the world."[43]

Hume's fourth criterion states that the miracle claims of many different religions cancel out rival ideologies. But such a criterion would be valid only if all miracle claims were *true*. That one religion may back its revelation claims with invalid "miracles" is no reason to reject a religion possessing valid claims. Inept systems cannot cancel a religion that may be supported by evidence that is shown to be probable. Since obviously not all miracle claims are valid, historical investigation into evidential claims in a theistic universe is needed to ascertain if any religion has a probable basis.

Hume himself felt that the Jansenist claims had very strong positive evidence in their favor. How, then, does Hume respond to the concluding evaluation of the Jansenist miracles? He states:

> Where shall we find such a number of circumstances, agreeing to the corroboration of one fact? And what have we to oppose to such a cloud of witnesses, but the absolute impossibility or miraculous nature of the events, which they relate? And this surely, in the eyes of all reasonable people, will alone be regarded as sufficient refutation.[44]

It is evident that Hume dismisses these claims not because of an insufficient basis of testimony, but because of the assumed impossibility of all miracles. Therefore, even such claims that are judged to have strong evidence are simply ignored. Again, in a clear example of circular reasoning, Hume assumes a conclusion because he has already decided in advance that "no testimony is sufficient to establish a miracle. . . ."

The fourth criticism of Hume's argument is that his four supportive criteria are invalid on historical grounds and cannot be applied to historical investigation.

How many accepted historical events were established by such unquestionably good witnesses as to guard against all error and suspicion? How much history is prejudiced by the fact that the one reporting had much to gain, such as Julius Caesar's accounts of his military victories? Are the Roman wars with the Gauls to be judged fictitious? How much history took place among ignorant and barbarous nations? Do we rule out all of ancient history on this account?

Clearly, by the standards that Hume used to judge miracles, history itself would be in question. However, it is well recognized that historical events can be known to a good degree of probability in spite of such questions. In fact, few scholars of the eighteenth century recognized this better than Hume, who is quite well known as a historian[45] as well as a philosopher. Yet, Hume did not subject his historical endeavors to these philosophical criteria. The criteria he described as being applicable to records of miracles he would not apply to history as a whole. The results would obviously be self-defeating for such a scholar who was also involved in the writing of history. But it is equally reasonable to reject the application of these criteria to historical accounts of miracles as well.

The fifth and last criticism of Hume's stance on the question of miracles is that, although Hume rejected the knowledge of cause and effect, his argument against miracles clearly depends on the uniformity of the laws of nature. C. S. Lewis notes that such a concept of uniformity rests on some form of causal argument. Hume must assume that the small part of nature that man does know is the same as that part of nature that man does not know. He must also assume that nature in the future will follow its past pattern and vice versa.[46] But how can these principles be known to be true? Thus, the fact that miracles may not be occurring at this present time does not indicate that they have not happened in the past or that they will not happen tomorrow.

It is interesting that Hume fully realized that this was the case, since he taught in other works that the past can provide no basis (other than custom) for statements concerning the future. Nothing can be known to be true concerning the future on the basis of past conformity. Certainly no proof from past experience can provide a knowledge of such a transition to the present or future.[47]

However, Hume abandoned this belief when he asserted that the uniformity of nature's laws could be used as a *proof* against miracles. He thereby violated both his own philosophical principle and the need to ascertain if this is a theistic universe in which miracles occur in history. Therefore, his argument can by no means rule out present or future miracles, to say nothing of any evidence for past miraculous events.

We thus conclude our overall critique by asserting that Hume's method of rejecting miracles must itself be rejected.

As noted above, Hume's essay was also the chief inspiration for the modern rejection of miracles. Updating Hume's reasoning and placing it in contemporary garb, it became popular to argue, for instance, that no evidence is sufficient to establish a miracle, since anything occurring in nature must be a natural event. Related approaches are taken by scholars such as Alastair McKinnon[48] and Patrick Nowell-Smith.[49] Another example is Flew's position that miracles are nonrepeatable events, whereas the scientifically established laws of nature are repeatable and therefore more readily verifiable. Therefore, the scientific is given precedence over the historical, and whenever an event

suspends the laws of nature, the law is simply expanded to include such events, therefore leaving only nonmiraculous, natural
occurrences.[50] Such scholars additionally argue that a miracle
could not be recognized as such even if one did occur. But it must
likewise be concluded that those who reject miracles based on
Hume's reasoning (including such modern renditions) must also
be said to have done so invalidly. Although not following
Hume's exact arguments, there are at least three points at which
the critique given above also applies generally to these approaches today.

First, it is an improper procedure to define miracles incor-
rectly or to arbitrarily attempt to mount up the facts against
them so that no evidence could establish their occurrence. It is
thus clearly invalid to automatically state that any event in nature must be a natural event. That conclusion can be reached
only if the possibility that God caused the event has already been
ruled out. And that can only be established by an investigation of
the facts. As remarked by C. S. Lewis, when such has not been
done, the naturalist can only *assume* his position by arguing circularly, for such a position is certainly not evident a priori.[51]
Thus, one cannot assume that naturalism is the correct position
by such circular reasoning any more than theists can state the
case so that all such occurrences in question could be called
miracles. Such approaches cannot properly solve this issue.

Such naturalistic theses also fall prey to the second critique of
Hume. It was pointed out that one cannot determine, even by
viewing the scientific evidence for the laws of nature, whether
God intervened by a superior power to perform miracles. It
should be obvious here that if a miracle has occurred, it cannot
be called a natural event just because it happened in nature or
because science has established these laws. Indeed, miracles *must*
normally happen in nature if men are going to know of them at
all. But the crucial question of the *cause* of the event, which is the
most important factor, is not determined by such naturalistic
approaches. *God* could still have *caused* such an event to occur in
nature by exerting power superior to that of the natural laws.
Therefore, our earlier point should be remembered—if probable
evidence does indicate that a recognizable miracle has occurred
in a theistic universe, then it provides *superior* evidence because it
indicates that the laws of nature, however strong or scientifically
verified, were temporarily suspended.

We noted above that Hume neglected to examine the possibility that God exists and that He acted in history to perform a miracle. This criticism also applies to the nineteenth- and twentieth-century reworkings of Hume's thesis, because if there is probable evidence for a recognizable miracle having occurred in a theistic universe, it cannot be dismissed simply by calling it a natural event. Neither can these events be dismissed by referring to the scientific verification of the laws of nature and then by expanding or adjusting these laws accordingly. This has already been shown in our previous two points and we will now present a third point against these naturalistic approaches.

It is true that if a miracle repeatedly occurs in a predictable manner under certain conditions, then it is probably more appropriate to attempt to adjust the law than to continue to call it a supernatural event. There are, however, several indications that an original law is correct and that a real miracle may have occurred and that it is recognizable as such. For instance, if a given law applies in all instances except the one in question, we have a good indication that the law is valid, especially since science relies so much on repeatability. Additionally, it may be virtually impossible to arrive at a new law that allows for the event, since it is so contrary to known reality. Also, a new law may endeavor to account for an event at the expense of allowing so many abnormalities that the original purpose behind the law is lost—in other words, it is no longer workable, due to its being qualified to such a large extent.[52]

Therefore, if a probable event had certain characteristics, a good case could be made for it being a miracle. The strongest example would be an event that had at least four features. First, this occurrence would be nonrepeatable; second, it would be contrary to at least one law of nature; third, this would be the only known exception to this law; fourth, there would be no viable means by which to change the law without losing the law's purpose or workability, especially when the event is so contrary to known reality.

This is not to say that occurrences without such characteristics cannot be miraculous. Rather, it is being asserted that events that do have all four features present a much stronger case, as well as providing additional pointers as to its recognizability as a miracle.

This brings us back to our major critique, which asserts that

the facts must be examined in order to determine if such events
have actually happened. I suggest that a strong refutation of
both Hume and those who generally accept his thesis is that the
resurrection of Jesus can be said, according to probability, to be
an actual historical event performed by God in a theistic universe. Jesus' resurrection fulfills the four criteria listed above.
The raising of Jesus was a nonrepeatable event and was
definitely contrary to the natural laws governing the process
called death. This event is the only probable exception to these
laws and there is no known means to modify or change them.
The universal law of death is that a dead person does not rise
by any known natural means, especially in a glorified body, as
reported by the eyewitnesses. Interestingly enough, Hume
explicitly stated that the resurrection of a dead man would be
a true miracle, necessitating the involvement of supernatural
powers.[53]

The purpose here is not to present an apologetic for Jesus'
resurrection and for a Christian theistic world view, but to show
that, as a probable historical event, this thesis offers a final and
substantial criticism of Hume's position and also disproves those
who have followed Hume's thesis. It is obvious that if a miracle
has occurred, then the laws of nature *were* temporarily suspended, and positions to the contrary are incorrect.

Here we conclude our critique of Hume's essay against miracles and the views of those who have followed along similar lines
of thought. Five criticisms were leveled at Hume and three criticisms were reapplied to contemporary approaches which follow
Hume. In conclusion, it was found that miracles cannot be ruled
out a priori. The possibility must be allowed that in a theistic
universe God could have temporarily suspended the laws of nature by a superior power in order to perform a miracle; therefore,
we must investigate the evidence to ascertain if such an event has
occurred.

The Use of Empirical Criteria

Hume not only greatly influenced the rejecting of particular
miraculous evidences for the inspiration of Scripture; he also
doubted inspiration as a whole by suggesting that any theological work, such as the Bible, should be tested to see whether it
contains abstract reasoning (and is thereby true by definition) or
experimental reasoning (and is true by empirical data). If

neither test applies, then the work is said to be factually meaningless. This testing by means of empirical criteria also
influenced philosophers, especially the logical positivists of the
early twentieth century. In spite of the popularity of various
types of empirical testing, we will note three criticisms that reveal that strict applications of this methodology are invalid.

The major problem for logical positivism was that the verification principle could not be verified. In other words, it failed its
own test. This principle obviously cannot be true by abstract
reasoning. First, such a position cannot be defined to be true.
Second, tautological statements are said to reveal no real information about the world, whereas the verification principle is
plainly intended to communicate a standard of meaningfulness.
Nor can this principle be true by empirical testing, because sense
data cannot prove that the only valid way to gain knowledge is
by empiricism. In short, there was no way to verify the verification principle itself. Thus, positivism failed by its own epistemological standard. By endeavoring to show that theology was
factually invalid, positivism factually invalidated itself.

It is interesting that Ayer agreed with this criticism and
modified the verification principle in later years.[54] This criticism
is generally accepted today, so that, strictly speaking, logical
positivism no longer exists as a philosophical school of thought.[55]

This criticism applies not only to Hume and to logical
positivists but also to other philosophers who advocate that,
except for statements that are true by definition, only empirically
verifiable truths are meaningful. This includes the views of
Comte, Schlick, and the Vienna Circle. In fact, this critique
applies to any view that asserts that the only (or the chief) means
of acquiring knowledge is by sense data. Briefly stated, there is
no way to demonstrate that this is the only (or major) approach
to epistemological issues. There is no way to prove that empirical
investigation occupies such an exclusive (or semiexclusive) position.

Our second major criticism of these positions is that the possibility of miracles is often still rejected through the influence of
Hume's essay. In other words, these philosophers have followed
Hume in dismissing miracles not only because of the empirical
criteria just discussed (criticism number one) but also because of
man's experience of the laws of nature as seen earlier in this
chapter. An example has already been noted above in the ap-

proach of Flew. However, it has been shown how Hume's reasoning against miracles (and those who follow him) is a second
failure to explain away the miraculous. It should now be obvious
that such attempts are still invalid for reasons such as those set
forth earlier.

The third major criticism of such naturalistic hypotheses is
that, once the strict application of empirical criteria is found to
be faulty, theological issues can no longer be judged to be
meaningless. Even Ayer admits that statements that cannot be
said to be true either by definition or by empirical data may still
be meaningful. In fact, he explicitly asserts that metaphysical
statements cannot be eliminated without in-depth analyses of
particular supportive arguments.[56]

Once again, establishing a theistic universe relegates much
meaning to an investigation of history to ascertain if recognizable
miracles have occurred. Such is a meaningful endeavor. Interestingly, if the resurrection of Jesus was shown to be historically valid, this would be a decision in favor of an empirical
event, established by the sense experience of the earliest eyewitnesses. Thus, even by the standards of a strict empiricism, there
would be a solid miraculous basis for Christianity. If this or
other miracles were shown to be historically (and empirically)
valid, they would also constitute a final refutation of such views,
as noted earlier.

Therefore, Hume's empirical criterion of testing is also not a
valid procedure. Strict applications of such empirical standards
of verification are clearly invalid. Indeed, some linguistic
analysts do believe that metaphysical issues are not only meaningful but verifiable, as mentioned above.

To be sure, the philosophy of David Hume has been instrumental in causing many of the contemporary doubts concerning
the inerrancy of the Scripture. His twofold support of errancy in
the form of his essay against miracles and his proposal for empirical testing especially influenced nineteenth- and twentieth-
century philosophical and theological schools of thought. It is
possible that his influence in this area is unparalleled in the
history of philosophy. Yet, it is plain that both of these lines of
argument, having been themselves disproven, have failed to disprove either the inspiration of the Scriptures or the miraculous
element contained in it.

Thus we conclude this essay by asserting that both Hume's

position against miracles and his strict use of empirical testing are invalid. Several criticisms have been applied to each concept, revealing that they are abortive attempts to dismiss the inspiration of Scripture, as are modern renditions of similar argumentation. It was not our purpose here to construct a positive apologetic for inspiration or for God's existence, miracles, eternal life, or other aspects of theology that have been called into question by such methods. Yet such an apologetic is a distinct possibility, especially when such critical attempts fail.[57]

AGNOSTICISM: KANT

W. David Beck

W. David Beck is Associate Professor of Philosophy and Chairman of the Philosophy Department, Liberty Baptist College, Lynchburg, Virginia. A graduate of Houghton College (B.S.), Trinity Evangelical Divinity School (M.A.), and Boston University (Ph.D.), he also did graduate work at the University of Rhode Island. Besides a review article, "Is God Lost?" in Christianity Today, *he has written a chapter, "A Letter of Bugenhagen to Luther," in* Principalities and Powers, *edited by J. W. Montgomery. Dr. Beck is a member of the American Philosophical Association and the Evangelical Philosophical Society.*

CHAPTER SUMMARY

This chapter identifies the results of Kant's philosophical system on the contemporary discussion concerning an inerrant revelation. Knowledge, for Kant, is possible only as the forms and categories of the mind organize the raw data of the senses. Beyond this phenomenal world, the mind can only postulate what must or ought to be. It cannot know what is. The first postulate of this practical reasoning is freedom. The individual is autonomous, knows the good, and is capable of willing and doing as he ought.

Within such an epistemological framework, revelation becomes unnecessary, useless, and unverifiable. Inerrancy is not only false but incomprehensible in such a system. Since Kant's theory of knowledge largely dominates contemporary theology, it is inevitable that inerrancy cannot be seen as an option.

3 *W. David Beck*

AGNOSTICISM: KANT

$\mathbf{T}$HERE IS FAIR agreement among historians of thought that Immanuel Kant (1724–1804) must be regarded not only as the great creative genius of the modern period but also as one of the most important framers of the contemporary mind. His significant contributions to epistemology have secured him wide fame, while his influence on the development of theology has been unparalleled.

Part of Kant's greatness lies in the fact that he was able to synthesize the two dominant but conflicting modes of thought of the Enlightenment, empiricism and rationalism, into an integrated whole. That, however, should not blind us to the originality of his thought, in which the other part of his greatness is to be found. This two-sidedness—a synthesizer, yet original—forces us to study Kant against the background of his historical and cultural setting. He is as much a culmination of preceding thought as he is a foundation for what was to follow.

Having said all of this, I must hasten to add that Kant's influence has not been regarded as salutary in all corners, especially among evangelical theologians. A few examples will suffice. John Gerstner states that it was Kant who began "the philosophic revolt against reason which for contemporary man has made any sort of rational apologetic impossible."[1] Clark Pinnock, in a similar vein, refers to Kant's "repudiation of rational religion,"[2] the result of which has been that "the objectivity and rationality of divine revelation have been philosophically questioned."[3] Francis Schaeffer claims that "with his work, the hope of a unified knowledge was on the threshold of splitting into two parts, neither having a relationship with the other."[4] Schaeffer is referring here to the isolation of metaphysics, and with it religion, from factual knowledge. This split, and the placing of religion in the realm of the *postulated* but not *known*, is for Schaeffer the source of contemporary "autonomous" man[5] who determines for himself the God in whom he will believe.

As these quotes might indicate, most theologians have focused on Kant's epistemology. In this essay, therefore we will spend some time developing this foundation of his thought and will return to it in the closing critique. However, most of the essay focuses on Kant's views on revelational religion, as he presents them in *Religion Within the Limits of Reason Alone* (1793).

This study is divided into four sections. The first is a brief history of Kant's life. Second, we look at the basic structure of Kant's system, in particular the possibility of knowledge. We turn then to the question of religious knowledge and the implications of his epistemology for revelation. The concluding section presents critical remarks and shows the importance of Kant's influence on contemporary theology.

A BRIEF HISTORY

Most of Kant's biographers have noted—sometimes to the point of exaggeration—that his life was singularly uneventful. Certainly in comparison to many other philosophers Kant had a rather ordinary life. On the other hand, the productivity of his last twenty years is extraordinary to say the least. But let us start at the beginning.

Immanuel Kant was born in 1724 in Königsberg. His father was a saddler and quite poor; his grandfather was an emigrant from Scotland. Königsberg, and with it Kant's family, had felt the influence of the Pietist movement. Without doubt, the Pietist renewal within the Lutheran church was a major influence in Kant's life, particularly in the person of Franz A. Schultz, the family's pastor. The young Kant attended the Pietist Collegium Fredericianum from 1732 to 1740. Schultz became the director there the year after Kant entered.

Pietism had been founded by Philipp Jakob Spener (1635–

1705). His mantle fell on his student August Franke. The key to Pietism was its concentration on experience, including an insistence on a clear, sometimes exaggerated, conversion experience. Pietism also emphasized the practical rather than dogmatic use of Scripture—that is, the purpose of Scripture is to nourish and sanctify. Many commentators have stressed the negative results of this view of Scripture—particularly on Kant—but that ought not to blind us to the positive aspects of this renewal movement. German historians trace the beginnings of social programs for the needy, including orphanages and missions, to Spener and Franke. There is no doubt that Pietism also brought about a concern for a disciplined and separated life on the part of the believer.

At the Collegium Fredericianum this concern developed into a regimented, regulated routine that impressed Kant as being superficial and led to his total—and lifelong—rejection of religious practice in general. Though Kant retained a permanent respect for Pietism, he consistently refused to attend church or take part in any sort of church activity.

At age sixteen Kant became a student in the faculty of theology at the University of Königsberg. Here he encountered the second major theological influence that molded his philosophy: Wolffian rationalism. Though Königsberg had previously been staunchly Pietistic, it had, in the decade before Kant began his studies, come under the influence of English "free thinkers" and deists and especially that of Christian Wolff's (1679–1754) theological development of Leibniz.

Whereas Pietism stressed revelation and the experiential, Wolff looked to the rational and metaphysical. He held that reason is capable of developing the doctrines of Christianity without the assistance of, though perhaps at the instigation of, revelation. Wolff deduced, with geometric precision, a complete theology beginning from the ontological argument for God's existence.[6]

Kant learned most of his philosophy during these years from Martin Knutzen, a Wolffian, though a favorite pupil of the Pietist Schultz. Knutzen introduced Kant to the broad scope of his knowledge from mathematics to astronomy, but particularly physics. Kant's earliest writings were in physics, including his dissertation in 1755, and he remained interested in the work of Newton throughout his life.

During the eight years between the completion of his studies at Königsberg and the dissertation, Kant earned a meager living as a family tutor. For the fifteen years that followed, Kant was unsuccessful in securing a professorial appointment at the university. He was forced to remain in relative poverty as a private lecturer, despite the fact that he quickly gained a reputation as a brilliant teacher and attracted students from far beyond Königsberg.

In this period, from 1755 to 1770, Kant was strongly influenced by Rousseau and Hume. The former gave Kant the importance of the concept of freedom; the latter awakened him from his "dogmatic slumbers" as Kant himself put it. The Kant who emerged from these years had shed his Wolffian rationalism and come to grips with empirical skepticism at the other extreme.

Having rejected appointments at two renowned universities, Kant was finally offered the chair of logic and metaphysics at Königsberg in 1770, a position he held until poor health forced him to retire in 1797. He died in 1804.

The years following 1770 were marked by unbelievable productivity. During the first ten years he carefully worked out his system. In 1781 his chief work, *The Critique of Pure Reason*, appeared. *Prolegomena to Any Future Metaphysic* was published in 1783, followed by *Fundamental Principles of the Metaphysic of Morals* in 1785 and *Metaphysical First Principles of Natural Science* the following year. In 1788 Kant published the second great critique, *The Critique of Practical Reason*, and in 1790 the third, *The Critique of Judgment*. The last of the great works of this period, and the main source for this discussion, is his *Religion Within the Limits of Reason Alone*, published in 1793.

This last-named work, *Religion Within the Limits of Reason Alone*, precipitated the only real "event" of Kant's life. In 1786 Frederick William II had ascended the Prussian throne. His officials imposed rather stringent censorship on religious publications. The first section of the *Religion* passed without much problem. The other sections were not approved at Königsberg; Kant was forced to gain the *imprimatur* from the faculty at Jena. Outraged, the king demanded that Kant no longer publish on matters of religion, a demand to which Kant assented, though the *Religion* itself was frequently published and revised in following years.

KANT'S THEORY OF KNOWLEDGE

Kant's epistemology begins with the rejection of the two major options that faced him: Humean empiricism and Wolffian-Leibnizian rationalism. Nevertheless, Kant does make use of many of the insights of each. With Hume he agrees that knowledge is of sensations, but with Leibniz he recognizes that knowledge is possible only when the mind determines the nature of its data.

The problem in Hume is that limitation of the mind to the passive reception of impressions makes knowledge impossible. Kant argued that if Hume were correct, there could never be anything beyond the impressions. Knowledge presupposes the recognition and comparison of causal, spatial, and temporal relations, and much more. None of this, however, is provided by the senses. They give us only tastes, odors, color patches, and so on. If there is knowledge, and Kant never doubted that there is, then Hume must be wrong.

We should note here Kant's method for philosophy. He does not begin with definitions, as did Wolff, nor does he attempt a psychological analysis of knowledge, as did Locke and Hume. Rather, Kant asks for the logical prerequisites of what we know to be the case. There is knowledge. How then is it possible? What must be the case for it to occur? This is the "critical" or "transcendental" method, the first method designed specifically for philosophy.

How then is knowledge possible? Kant begins the introduction to *The Critique of Pure Reason* with the following statement:

> There can be no doubt that all our knowledge begins with experience. . . . In the order of time, therefore, we have no knowledge antecedent to experience, and with experience all our knowledge begins.[7]

Kant accepts, then, the view of the empiricists regarding the senses. The senses are passive receptors of isolated and atomic sensations—sounds, color patches, and so forth. They are also the only means by which any content can be provided for our minds to process.[8]

Kant is equally adamant, however, that sensation by itself cannot be knowledge. Without the operations of the mind, there can be no determination of the data. The impressions do not identify, coordinate, or categorize themselves. We do not necessarily know what we are seeing when the mechanism of the retina registers light impulses. Knowledge begins with sensation, but it does not end there. Kant himself puts it this way: "Thoughts without content are empty, intuitions without concepts are blind."[9]

Just what is it that the mind adds to the sensations so that knowledge results? First, the sensations *are* always sensed, and *can* be sensed, only within the structures of time and space. If the impressions were not put in sequence, arranged in relationship to each other, and determined in size, extension, and so on, we could not know at all. Since time and space are not actual impressions yet are presupposed by the possibility of knowing, they must be *forms* of intuition for the mind. They are not part of the data, but are rather the ways in which our minds conceive the data.

There is, further, a "transcendental logic," that is, the necessary *categories* whereby the mind judges the nature of sensations in respect to their quantity, quality, relations (this includes, for example, causal dependence), and modality. Together, the forms and the categories are the filters that give order and determination to the data of the senses.

Knowledge, then, is the mind's conceptualization of the data. When there is no sensory input, there can be no knowledge. As we shall see, the initial conclusion of Kant's epistemology is significant for his treatment of revelation.

Kant is convinced, however, that there is another type of judgment that we can make. The judgments that we make regarding the contingent data of the senses are, to use Kant's term, *a posteriori*. But, Kant asks in the *Critique,* how and in which disciplines is it possible to make judgments that are *necessary* and *universal?* Such judgments would have to be a priori, that is, before and independent of the sensory data. The judgments that we make on the basis of the senses could never meet the criteria. They cannot be universal since no one could ever observe every possible instance of a judgment. The geometric judgment that the shortest distance between two points is a straight line— universally—cannot be known from observation. Perhaps it will turn out differently the next time! Likewise, our observations cannot establish the necessity of any judgment. The senses, says Kant, can only tell us what is, in fact, the case. They cannot support a judgment about what necessarily is the case.

In fact, we have already come across the source of universal and necessary judgments. The forms of intuition (time and space) and the categories are concepts that govern *every possible* sensation and thus meet the criteria. Kant considers these to be the foundations of mathematics and the sciences. These disciplines are thus firmly based. Their principles are known as universal and necessary truths.

Is there metaphysical knowledge? We can now ask if, and how, it is possible for an individual to know anything about the ultimate nature of reality—the existence and nature of God, the condition and destiny of man, the status and source of values, and so on. At this point it is important to restate the essential conclusion of Kant's epistemology: While sensation provides the data of knowledge, it is the mind that actually makes the knowing possible by forming and categorizing. Furthermore, it is only the "pure" understanding of the concepts of the mind that is universal and necessary.

Kant argues that there can be no knowledge of metaphysics because an attempt at such knowledge takes the concepts of the mind beyond their proper use. In the section of the *Critique* titled "The Antinomies of Pure Reason," Kant claims to demonstrate that when reason is applied to the ultimate, that is, the absolute or infinite, a curious fact ensues: both sides of a contradiction can be proved. The best known of Kant's four examples is the third antinomy. He states it this way:

> *Thesis:* Causality in accordance with laws of nature is not the only causality from which the appearances of the world can one and all be derived. To explain these appearances it is necessary to assume that there is also another causality, that of freedom.
>
> *Antithesis:* There is no freedom; everything in the world takes place solely in accordance with the laws of nature.[10]

Kant takes the antinomies to be proof that our rational abilities are meant to function only in relation to the realm of sensible data. We cannot know reality in itself. We know only the appearances, not what is really out there. We cannot get beyond our agnosticism by extending the use of the categories to the metaphysical realm of freedom, God, and values; nor can we ever have direct acquaintance with the objects of our world. The possibilities of knowing are limited by the forms of intuition and the categories of judgment in their *proper function.*

Kant's discussion, however, does not end here. While it is true that we have exhausted the realm of pure reason and knowledge proper, Kant discovers a second use of reason. Reason in relation to experience can find only purely causal relations between physical objects. Nevertheless, reason knows that there must be an initiation of causal chains by the will. Knowledge of the "phenomena," to use Kant's term for the appearances as ordered by the mind, could never include the freedom of the will as an agent of events. Yet the chain of natural causes cannot be thought of as going back infinitely. For no link in the chain provides a complete ("sufficient"[11]) explanation. There must be an absolute beginning, a "prime mover."[12]

There can be only one solution to the third antinomy. Freedom is not part of the phenomenal world but of the un*know*able "noumenal" world—the world as it really is, not as it appears to us to be. Freedom *must be* the case, but we do not *know* it. This precisely is the second use of reason, namely, in relation to what ought to be, not what is. Kant refers to this function as *practical reason*, the subject of his second major "critique." Practical reason is to be identified as *will* in its intellectual function of determining action.

Thus, in the *Critique of Pure Reason* Kant has determined the possibility of freedom and the noumenal. But this, of course, does not give us actual evidence for the reality of freedom. For this step there must be experience.

In the case of freedom there can be no empirical evidence. The data of the senses give us no clue. We experience desires, emotions, and feelings; but these could all exist without the freedom to fulfill them. Kant holds that there is experience of the moral law. It is at this point that we turn to the *Critique of Practical Reason*.

> The moral law shows its reality, in a manner which is sufficient even from the point of view of the *critique* of theoretical reason, in adding a positive characteristic to a causality which so far has been conceived only negatively and the possibility of which, although incomprehensible to theoretical reason, had yet to be assumed by it. This positive characteristic is the conception of reason as immediately determining the will (through the condition that a universal form can be given to its maxims as laws). Thus, for the first time, the moral law can give objective (though only practical) reality to reason which always hitherto had to tran-

scend all possible experience when it put its ideas to a theoretical
use. . . .[13]

For Kant this experience is unassailable. The conclusion of the
Critique of Practical Reason begins with the oft-quoted statement of
the two things that "fill the mind with ever new and increasing
admiration and awe. . . : the starry heavens above and the moral
law within."[14] The moral law is apprehended as a sense of *duty*.
Duty, in turn, implies an obligation that is necessary (it does not
depend on how any individual *in fact* behaves) and universal (it
applies to all human beings). It has a "categorical imperative,"
to use Kant's term. That is, maxims or principles of action con-
front me as applications of a moral law.

Kant concludes that there can be only one possibility for a
moral law that is necessary and universal and therefore unconditional. The categorical imperative is: "Act only according to that
maxim by which you can at the same time will that it should
become a universal law."[15]

From this position we can derive all the great ideas of
metaphysics: freedom, immortality, and God.[16] Freedom is, for
Kant, the immediate postulate of the moral law. The very notion
of a moral duty is senseless unless I am free to perform it. The
concepts clearly imply each other. Without freedom there could
be no moral law. Apart from the moral law I would not know
that I was free.

Again, as a reminder, we are not dealing with the realm of
knowledge. Freedom is a postulate of practical reason, not an
item of knowledge of pure reason.[17] Moreover, freedom is an
immediate postulate. My apprehension of duty is senseless without it.

The second postulate of Kant's ethical religion is immortality.
This postulate follows, Kant says, from the necessity of the moral
law and the principle that what is in fact a duty is also achiev-
able.[18] The moral law demands perfect holiness. This is possible
only with infinite progress. Thus the soul must be immortal in
order to achieve this perfection.

The third postulate is the existence of God. In the first *Critique*
Kant had argued that pure reason is incapable of establishing
any argument for God's existence.[19] Thus the existence of God
cannot be *known*, but it can be *postulated*. This is, however, the
weakest even of the postulates; it is third in line. Practical reason

must assume that happiness is coincident with obedience to the moral law. Happiness, however, is the condition of man in the world, that is, the *causal* world. But a person is not able to ensure such harmony of the noumenal will and the phenomenal world. Thus, if perfection is attainable, then there must be an infinite God who harmonizes morality and nature and ushers in the final state of perfect existence. Christian doctrine refers to this state as the kingdom.

In this way practical reason gives us not only the main elements of metaphysics but also leads to religion: an *ethical* religion. That is, its only content pertains to how I ought to act, how free action is possible, and what the conditions are under which obedience is attainable. Religion, Kant says, is "the recognition of all duties as divine commands, . . . as essential laws of any free will as such."[20] We turn next, then, to Kant's development of religion by practical reason and the position and possibility of revelation.

The Possibility and Value of Revelation

In *Religion Within the Limits of Reason Alone* Kant works out his natural theology. That is, practical reason is allowed to fully work out its postulates in relation to the major themes of religious knowledge. The work is divided into four sections. In the first section Kant explores the subject of man's natural inclination to evil. In section 2 he discusses the conflict between good and evil and the nature of salvation. Section 3 is concerned with the nature of true religion and especially the contrast between rational and revealed systems. It is this part that occupies most of our attention as we discuss directly the possibility of revelation. The final section provides the meaning of service and the general mode of life under a rational religion.

On the Radical Evil in Human Nature

Is man innately good or evil? Kant's answer to this question is two-sided. On the one hand he holds that there is no reason to think that any of man's original predispositions are aimed in any other direction than toward the good. Kant divides these original predispositions into animal (preservation, sex, community), human (equality), and personal (respect for law, consciousness of law). On the level of these natural instincts man is directed toward the moral law.

On the other hand Kant considers it obvious that man's will is inclined toward evil. In fact, he offers no argument for the position; it is self-evident. How, then, is this propensity to evil to be explained? What is corrupt is not man as man, but the "subjective ground" of his will.[21] That is, the maxims or rational principles of choice are no longer pure. Man is still conscious of the moral law, however, and thus practical reason as such is not destroyed. Evil has become, as Kant says, subjectively necessary. It is not innate to the species.

What accounts for the origin of subjective evil? Kant's response to this problem is vague at best, and at this point we begin to see the difficulties with his rational and nonhistorical, or even antihistorical, religion. Since evil's origin is not related to the species, it cannot have a single, temporal nature. Kant says that historical accounts such as that in Scripture have a *moral* use in helping us understand the nature of a subjective change; but if the change is, in fact, related to the will, then its event is not phenomenal—that is, having historically identifiable causes— but rather noumenal. Thus Kant adds in a footnote to this discussion that the "historical knowledge which has no inner bearing valid for all men belongs to the class of *adiaphora*, which each man is free to hold as he finds edifying."[22] He even tells us that as far as our ordinary awareness is concerned, each evil act is to be viewed as directly and individually a fall from innocence.[23]

If a temporal explanation fails, then what explanation will do? Evil must have originated in a rational act of will to incorporate improper maxims into—that is, alongside of—the categorical moral law, which it continues to know. Kant's difficulty at this point is that the rational origin of evil maxims is inscrutable.[24] Evil acts can come only from an evil will, but there is nothing that might explain the subjective choice of an evil maxim of will on the part of a good individual. How should a good man with a good will come to act out of selfishness or cruelty?

Nevertheless, Kant is convinced of the radical evil of man, though man remains accountable because he remains rational and free. We are always able to do what we ought to do.[25] This leaves Kant in a second difficulty. Just as the initiation of discordant maxims is inscrutable yet obvious, so also the condition of an evil will is irreversible yet restorable. It is irreversible for the same reason that its origin is incomprehensible: it is noumenal, not phenomenal, and there is no cause that can explain the reversing of the will, understood as practical reason.

Much of Kant's predicament here results from identifying the will with reason in its practical function, and from placing the will in the noumenal realm. There can be neither causes nor independent reasons for choices of maxims, except for the moral law itself. The universal law is the only maxim that conforms to freedom and it is, therefore, a reflection of man's true autonomous nature. To obey it is thus the only choice conceivable for the rational will. Yet it is just this radical autonomy that makes possible the rejection of the freedom to be good. There remains no explanation for the adoption of irrational and evil maxims, nor for the return to rational functions—except that man is *free* to do so.

> Man *himself* must make or have made himself into whatever, in a moral sense, whether good or evil, he is or is to become. Either condition must be an effect of his free choice; for otherwise he could not be held responsible for it and could therefore be *morally* neither good nor evil.[26]

Salvation must also share this noumenal nature. It must be possible to return to purity of maxim, but we cannot understand how. It must be possible because duty demands it, not because revelation tells us. Salvation, Kant says, consists of a simple, yet radical change of will, even though the actual change in a man's life is gradual. Nevertheless from God's viewpoint (that of timeless reason), regeneration and sanctification, to use more traditional theological language, are a simple unity.

What role does God play in salvation? We again face a dual answer. From the point of view of rational freedom any work of grace or divine assistance is contradictory in Kant's system.

> For the employment of this idea would presuppose a rule concerning the good which (for a particular end) we ourselves must *do* in order to accomplish something, whereas to await a work of grace means exactly the opposite, namely, that the good (the morally good) is not our deed but the deed of another being, and that we therefore can *achieve* it only by *doing nothing*, which contradicts itself.[27]

Theoretically, then, Kant considers grace a useless concept. A free will must correct its own principles of choice. Nevertheless, Kant knows that this is impossible:

But does not this restoration through one's own exertion directly contradict the postulate of the innate corruption of man which unfits him for all good? Yes, to be sure, as far as the conceivability, *i.e.*, our *insight* into the possibility, of such a restoration is concerned.[28]

Faced with these difficulties, Kant concludes that while we cannot adopt the notion of a work of grace into our maxims of reason, we do know that much is beyond our comprehension and we can, therefore, choose to accept it by *reflective faith*.[29]

Concerning the Conflict of the Good With the Evil Principle for Sovereignty Over Man

In the second section of *Religion Within the Limits of Reason Alone* Kant deals with the actual nature of salvation. The first section begins to give, however indirectly, a picture of Kant's view of the function of revelation. It is clear that individual autonomous reason, functioning "practically" in relation to the moral law, must be the ultimate source of knowledge. This now becomes much clearer, particularly in Kant's discussion of the role of Christ in salvation. Kant has already dismissed the rational function of a redemptive act of grace, but what about the *revelational* role of Christ? While Kant deals with other problems as well in this section, it is this topic to which he repeatedly returns.

In the course of section 2 Kant offers at least five reasons why revelation—in the form of a model—is unnecessary. The first is perhaps the most obvious. There is nothing to be known from revelation that practical reason cannot postulate by itself. (We must remember that practical reason, strictly speaking, does not *know*.) What is required of man, why it is required, that he can perform it—all of this is already present to each individual.

The second reason follows from the first. If man already has what he needs, then the search for an example or any sort of verification is precisely an act of unfaith, not faith. The very act of believing in Christ rather than relying on free autonomous practical reason is an act of disbelief.

Third, Kant argues that a living example, known only as a phenomenon, could never disclose what is really necessary, namely, the purity of maxims of the will. The latter is of course a noumenal act of reason. Kant states it thus:

According to the law, each man ought really to furnish an example of this idea in his own person; to this end does the archetype reside always in the reason: and this, just because no example in outer experience is adequate to it; for outer experience does not disclose the inner nature of the disposition but merely allows of an inference about it though not one of strict certainty.[30]

Fourth, if any man can achieve purity of maxims, then Christ, even if it could be proved that his origin was supernatural, can be of no benefit to us. There is nothing Christ could reveal to us by way of example that is not already understandable by the natural man.

Finally, Kant argues that it is already difficult enough to follow the moral law known to us. It only makes matters worse to bring in an outside example. Kant argues in the following way:

And the presence of this archetype in the human soul is in itself sufficiently incomprehensible without our adding to its supernatural origin the assumption that is hypostasized in a particular individual. The elevation of such a holy person above all the frailties of human nature would rather, as far as we can see, hinder the adoption of the idea of such a person for our imitation.[31]

Salvation, then, is found in reason, in conformity to the archetype known to the mind.

Now it is our universal duty as men to *elevate* ourselves to this ideal of moral perfection, that is, to this archetype of the moral disposition in all its purity—and for this the idea itself, which reason presents to us for our zealous emulation, can give us power.[32]

Kant does have a high regard, however, for the person of Christ. At one point he even affirms that we find salvation through a *"practical faith in this Son of God."*[33] Kant makes one suggestion as to how the archetype known to reason can also be faith in the Son of God. The mind itself, he says, cannot be the source of the moral law as a universal and necessary ideal. It can only *"come down* to us from heaven"[34] and is thus a "humiliation."

Kant's ethical religion, then, as shown in the reasons given above does not find itself in need of revelation in the sense of a historical model. While Kant acknowledges and respects the historical Christ, the statements of Scripture that refer to Christ are to be understood *existentially,* to use a contemporary term. That is, the christological statements are to be understood as statements about *my* self. The revelation of the ideal man in Christ is, in fact, the rational apprehension by man's reason that duty is identical to the will of God. Scripture's language is "figurative,"[35] or "vivid,"[36] or pictorial.[37] For example, Kant says the following concerning Scripture's use of "evil spirits" to signify the enemies of the archetype:

> This is an expression which seems to have been used not to extend our knowledge beyond the world of sense but only to make clear *for practical use* the conception of what is for us unfathomable.[38]

Another example of Kant's use of Scripture can be seen in his examination of the concept of sacrifice as necessary for payment of debt. Kant can say that it is the archetype that bears the penalty for sin. What that means, however, is roughly the following existential translation.[39] The sacrifice is the giving up of selfish maxims by the rational will. It constitutes *"punishments* whereby satisfaction is rendered to divine justice."[40] In fact, each man must do this for himself.

We turn next to Kant's remarks directly concerning revelation. This involves us in the question of the actual nature of religion.

The Victory of the Good Over the Evil Principle,
and the Founding of a Kingdom of God on Earth

In section 3 Kant is concerned to show how a universal religion is possible. That is, how can all individuals be brought to recognize the need to adopt a purity of maxim? The answer is simply that revelation cannot achieve this recognition, while rational faith can—and has done so. We must seek the truth within us, not in an external revelation. Kant allows for revelation only in a subservient sense. It may show what "has hitherto remained hidden from men through their own fault."[41] I count in this section thirteen reasons why rational faith is superior to revelation. This section, then, applies Kant's epistemology to revelation and clarifies revelation's status in relation to religion.

1. Rational faith is ethical. As we have seen, Kant concludes that religion is ethical in nature. Its tenets are postulates of practical reason. Thus the purpose of revelation, says Kant, can only be to serve practical reason. The principle of biblical exegesis shifts in Kant from Luther's explicit christocentrism to ethicocentrism: What does the Bible tell me to do?[42] Clearly, rational faith is superior, since it admits of direct cognizance of the moral law. Revelation is indirect at best.

2. Rational faith is necessary. The religion of practical reason is a necessary postulate. It *must be* true if we are to make sense of our knowledge of moral law. Revelational propositions merely *are* true.

Revelation would have to be verified by reason to be of any use. This would have to occur in one of two ways. Either reason directly determines the truth of the *propositions* of revelation or it verifies the *source* of that revelation. In the former case revelation is, of course, uselessly repetitive. It is necessarily true, but only because of its verification, line by line, by reason. In the latter case, revelation may provide us with additional information hitherto undiscovered by reason. However, it cannot be known with necessity. Any verification of source, Kant says, must involve historical or factual considerations.[43] As a result, our knowledge will be a posteriori and contingent, not necessary.

3. Rational faith is universal. The problem with revelation as a means of providing man with information on how to act is, according to Kant, that it can never reach everyone. Revelation is empirical in nature and thus bounded by social, linguistic, and practical conditions. As a result, individual revelation can be the source only of localized, dogmatized *faiths*, not the universal true *religion*.

> *Pure religious faith* alone can found a universal church; for only [such] rational faith can be believed in and shared by everyone, whereas an historical faith, grounded solely on facts, can extend its influence no further than tidings of it can reach, subject to circumstances of time and place and dependent upon the capacity [of men] to judge the credibility of such tidings.[44]

4. Rational faith is prior. Any revelation, Kant argues, is immediately posterior to reason in that it must first be verified or authenticated by reason.[45] Reason must interpret revelation.

Kant is forced to deny any notion of a self-authenticating knowledge of revelation. There is no knowledge without the operation of pure reason. All else is superstition. In the *Critique of Judgment* Kant explains that rational religion prevents theology from becoming theosophy (the use of transcendental concepts above reason) and it prevents religion from becoming theurgy (the belief in feeling or direct contact with the supernatural).[46] The general epistemological principle cannot be broken, even for a supposed divine revelation.

5. Rational faith is an act of free will. It is thus not only ethically prior, but also ontologically prior, to revelation.[47] Revelation may assist the less thoughtful, but any faith that relies on it denies the nature of man.

Revelation can produce only an ecclesiastical faith. It cannot, by itself, give a person true understanding of what is required of him. It can tell him, but this is always for Kant an external source of knowledge. Thus it indicates a reliance of the will on heteronomous sources. This is, of course, a denial of man's autonomous freedom.

Of all of Kant's reasons, it seems to me that this one strikes at the heart of what is important to him. Whereas the others indicate mostly epistemological inferiorities of revelation, this reason concerns the very being of man. Rousseau's influence on Kant is quite apparent here. But it is also true that Kant's doctrine of freedom is firmly grounded in his epistemology. Nothing can be known without the operation of pure reason. Nothing can be postulated without the uncaused adoption of practical reason.

6. Rational faith is self-promoting. Closely connected to the above is revelation's dependence on a "learned public" that is related to the origin of the revelation by a tradition of scholarship.[48] In a sense, revelational faith is thus elitist. It cannot continue without highly skilled exegetes and theologians who verify and interpret the revelation to the common man. Rational faith needs no such assistance. It promotes itself. Every person is capable of full comprehension of the dictates of practical reason.

7. Rational faith is an end. Ecclesiastical or revelational faith, because it is not fully rational, can only be a means to an end and not an end in itself.[49] It serves as a vehicle for rational faith but it can never function as a goal. Rational faith embodies the fulfillment of human existence. Man's ultimate goal is found in free moral conformity to the categorical imperative.

8. Rational faith is complete. A truly saving faith must accomplish two purposes, Kant holds.[50] It must first provide "atonement"; that is, it must undo sin and return a person to purity of maxim. Second, it must provide morality. It must give a person a new life and tell him how to live.

The atonement of revelation is incomplete. It does not tell a person how to live a new life but tells him simply that he is forgiven without first improving his life. No thoughtful person can bring himself to believe this. The best proof of this, says

Kant, is that if it were true then surely people would universally respond. This is clearly not the case, but Kant is certain that universal response would be so for the ethical religion of reason.

9. *Rational faith is productive.* Revelational faith, and Kant includes Christian revelation here, is not universally effective in changing men's lives.[51] Some will choose to obey it—and even that is, of course, a decision for heteronomy—but many will not alter their conduct. Rational faith, however, never fails. Recognition of the moral law always converts the free will that sees there the fulfillment of its being.

10. *Rational faith is private.* Revelation produces actual, local ecclesiastical faiths. These are external and public congregations. Rational faith, at least until the goal of universality is achieved, "has no public status."[52] It is purely an inner change, an invisibly developing church.

11. *Rational faith is ultimate.* Kant's theology is specifically goal-oriented. The title of one of his shorter works is translated *Perpetual Peace* (1795). The German title is *Zum ewigen Frieden*, that is literally, *To Eternal Peace.* Kant outlines here how his ethical religion works itself out in political policies. He is convinced in the *Religion* that the religion of reason will lead to universal peace and harmony. Revelational faiths may accomplish limited peace. The ultimate stage of human history, however, will not be ushered in until rational faith has become universal.[53] Ultimacy is thus tied to universality.

12. *Rational faith is permanent.* Since rational faith will usher in the ultimate end of history, and since a will with pure maxims cannot corrupt itself, the results of such faith are permanent. Reason's victory is eternal.[54]

13. *Rational faith is identical with revelational faith.* After all that has been said, this final point may seem contradictory. Kant's point, however, is important to the question of *inerrant* revelation. Kant seems always to assume that despite all of the inferiorities of revelation, if it could, in fact, be shown to be authentically divine in origin—by prior reason—that would constitute proof of its truthfulness.

We have already seen, however, that Kant interprets the nature of truthfulness in a moral or existential rather than a descriptive and historical sense. Thus a literal sense of inerrancy cannot apply in Kant's view of revelation. *Genuine* revelation must be identical in content to purely rational faith. In both the content is the archetype of human conduct, "lying in our reason, that we attribute to [Christ] (since, so far as his example can be known, he is found to conform thereto)."[55]

When we, then, properly understand a verified revelation, its content will coincide with the product of reason alone. This is the proper function of religion. Kant says, "It concerns us not so much to know what God is in Himself (His nature) as *what He is for us* as moral beings (emphasis added)."[56]

Concerning Service and Pseudo-Service Under the Sovereignty of the Good Principle

While Kant's stated subject in this section deals with the organizational aspects of religion, the section serves also as a summary statement on the relationship between reason and revelation. I am commenting on it here for just that purpose.

Kant's position on revelation begins, of course, with his epistemology, which requires that religion in general be ethical in content. Religion is simply the understanding of the moral imperative, no longer abstractly, but as God's will. As Kant phrases it, religion is "the recognition of all duties as divine commands."[57]

Since religion is concerned only with *individual behavior* (it is in that sense *existential*), it is not the imparting of true propositions either of fact or metaphysics.

> As regards the theoretical apprehension and avowal of belief, no assertorial knowledge is required (even of God's existence), since, with our lack of insight into supersensible objects such avowal might well be dissembled; rather it is merely a *problematical* assumption (hypothesis) regarding the highest cause of things that is presupposed speculatively. . . . The *minimum* of knowledge (it is possible that there may be a God) must suffice, subjectively, for whatever can be made the duty of every man.[58]

Religion, however, is not simply a list of particular duties and services. It would then offend man's autonomy. Religion is simply the recognition that duty, apprehended in the moral law, is related to God as postulated by practical reason.

Religion, so defined, must rest on universal human reason. Any revelation will lead to an individual and local church because of its empirical character. It cannot command unconditional allegiance because its authenticity and authority must first be determined by reason. Kant says this of revelation's claim to authority:

> Since assurance on this score rests on no grounds of proof other than the historical, and since there ever will remain in the judgment of the people . . . the absolute possibility of an error which has crept in through their interpretation or through previous classical exegesis, the clergyman would be requiring the people . . . to confess something to be as true as is their belief in God. . . .[59]

Our belief in God rests on a postulate of practical reason. Belief in the truth of revelation could never be more than possible and contingent. Thus Kant warns us of the problem when we "seek religion without and not within us."[60]

EVALUATION AND CRITIQUE

There can be little doubt that Kant's epistemology figures largely in the contemporary discussion concerning the possibility and actuality of inerrant revelation. Many of the characteristics of the positions of those who deny authoritative and inerrant revelation are drawn directly from Kant. In many cases the reliance on Kant is explicit and admitted. And, while it is true that some elements of this position are prior to Kant, it seems evident that it was Kant who first put them into a coherent whole and introduced them into the mainstream of Christian (particularly German) theology. From Kant the line of influence is not difficult to trace through Schleiermacher to nineteenth-century liberalism, and then to contemporary neoliberalism. Schubert Ogden, perhaps the most prominent interpreter and critic of Bultmann in the late 1950s, is the spokesman of those who are currently working out a "process" theology, following Whitehead and Hartshorne, on top of an existential epistemology.[61] I will use Ogden as a source throughout the Evaluation and Critique.

The Value of a Revelation

We will examine two aspects of Kant's philosophy that show his influence: first, the bifurcation in Kant's epistemology between facts and values and the effect of that bifurcation on arguments for the existence of God and on the value of an inerrant revelation; second, the view of salvation and human nature and

Kant's emphasis on choice—the free act of the will—and the implications of that view for the necessity of revelation. The bifurcation between facts and values shows itself in Kant as the two functions of pure and practical reason. While contemporary theologians may use different terminology, the result is the same: the source of science is different from the source of values. There is a difference not only in source, and thus in the mode of verification, but also in status. Facts are *known;* values are not, even though they are considered important. This bifurcation is clearly seen in the many variations of existential theological epistemologies as the distinction between "objective" knowledge known by the senses and "existential" awareness. (The latter is the direct, intuitive confrontation with the inner self and its possibility of authentic existence.)

The existence of God is included in the list of what ought to be, not of what, in fact, is. This goes hand in hand with the summary rejection of the arguments for God's existence. In existential theology this becomes the denial of God as "an object among objects." Ogden's only argument, if that is the correct term, for God's reality is a strictly moral one, similar to Kant's. God must exist, says Ogden, or else our trust in the value and meaning of life makes no sense.[62] There is no argument based on the objective data but only on the demands of existentialist awareness.

Kant's position and influence are curiously two-sided at this point. There is, on the one hand, no denying the fact that Kant believed there is a God and that Kant was pious and religious, at least in an ethical sense. Kant is clearly not intentionally a naturalist. On the other hand, Kant's position leads to a rejection of supernaturalism as a *rational* option. God's existence cannot be known, only postulated. Following Kant there have been, not surprisingly, a series of noncognitive, subjective or practical attempts to justify belief. Feeling, experience, encounter, precognitive choices of categories or language games, and many other options have been suggested. They all agree on one thing: they concede with Kant's agnosticism that a truly rational approach is impossible. The specific objections that Kant raised to the theistic arguments have long been countered from many quarters. Nevertheless, the opinion that the arguments are unreliable and that religion is nonrational has continued as the majority view, frequently even among conservative theologians and evangelicals in philosophy.

This influence of Kant seems to me to be one of the primary factors that have led many contemporary theologians to deny the real value of an inerrant revelation. If the truly important matters of life, such as God and the possibility of authentic existence, are not to be known by ordinary knowledge, then they will not be known by propositional communication, particularly not that of historical events. The language of facts is well suited for science and ordinary activities, but it will not do for the inner and the subjective. Thus any revelation in objective language, the Bible in particular, must be, to use the contemporary term, "demythologized" and interpreted existentially. Kant did not use this vocabulary, but his position is substantially the same: the pictorial language of Scripture must be translated into moral language.

This Kantian view of revelation is one of the main ingredients in what was to become the German "higher criticism" movement. There had already been many Enlightenment thinkers who had dismissed the miraculous elements of Scripture wholesale. Johann Semler (1725–1791) appears to have been the first to advocate the individual consideration, from a critical literary and historical standpoint, of the separate books of the Bible. Kant's contribution to this movement, as we have seen, is the criterion for translating Scripture into a useful contemporary reading and seeking for its moral function. In this operation practical reason remains, of course, the authority.

Kant's influence has clearly extended also to the view of salvation. Since revelation is, at best, an aid to slow and less-developed minds, salvation becomes the dual process of recognition and self-change. For Kant, this recognition is of one's failure to live in true freedom (autonomy) as God intends. For Ogden, and like-minded theologians, this recognition is that we are not maximizing the potential for authentic existence exemplified in Christ. Increasingly, this authenticity is interpreted as freedom. Such has always been true of existential theologians, Bultmann in particular, but in Ogden such an interpretation is now more explicit because of the influence of liberation theology.[63]

Self-change is the other aspect of the process of salvation. This is the deliberate, free, and understanding act of the will. In Kant it is the choice toward purity of maxims. This is simply to say that the possibility of freedom is open when it is recognized. I can change my behavior toward freedom if only I know I can. The identical transition can be found in contemporary followers of Kant. There is no need for redemptive atonement, certainly not for propitiation. There is no just and holy God. Freedom, and thus authenticity, is there for the choosing. Furthermore, this salvation is not only possible but, in some sense, partially present. For Kant, the recognition may need some prodding from revelation. For Ogden, too, it is helpful to have a historical example. But in neither view can revelation be necessary. It is a rational postulate that all men must make in order to make sense of their moral experience. Ogden refers to this recognition as "original revelation" given to all men. Nothing additional could or need be said.[64] For Kant, of course, anything more would be illusory.

The convergence of the characteristics of Kant's position and of those who deny authoritative, inerrant revelation, results from a root identity, namely, in epistemology. I shall simply trace the logic of Kant's position, reversing in the following section the order of the logic of the system and moving toward its starting point.

Kant and Inerrancy

The conclusion of Kant's system is a curious mixture. Kant never denies the possibility of revelation, yet his epistemology precludes its authoritative nature. If the revelation comes in the form of visual or audible data, then it is *known* only by rational judgment. If it is some form of direct intuition or dictation, then it cannot be known—unless judged to be true by an independent reason. In either case, the possibility of an inerrant revelation appears to be precluded. There can be no inspired source that is epistemologically authoritative for man. Revelation can be meaningful only as a sample of moral behavior.

A parallel conclusion is the lack of necessity that pertains to the atonement of Christ. For Kant Christ is an example. For Ogden he is an objectification of human potential. In neither case is there any redemptive value, and even the revelational value is contingent.

All of the conclusions regarding the function of revelation follow from the Kantian principle that a person can do what he ought to do. In other words, man, despite the radical evil in him, is still capable of pure ethical action. While Kant's (and Ogden's) epistemology explains the nonnecessity of the atonement, it is this position of the inherent goodness and ability of man that really implies it.

Again, however, we must ask for the final basis in Kant's system from which his view of revelation and his ethics result. The answer, I think, is found in his doctrine of the autonomy of reason. The first sentence of the preface to the first edition of the *Religion* is this:

> So far as morality is based upon the conception of man as a free agent who, just because he is free, binds himself through his reason to unconditioned laws, it stands in need neither of the idea of another Being over him, for him to apprehend his duty, nor of an incentive other than the law itself, for him to do his duty.[65]

Thus, while religious man recognizes the connection between duty and the will of God, reason itself, whereby he makes that judgment and determines his action, is wholly free. Even knowledge of the sensible universe depends on the operation of that reason. The autonomy of reason is, then, related to the split between reality and appearance, between the noumenal world itself and the phenomenal world that I know.

It is not surprising then that contemporary theologians cannot accept an authoritative, inerrant Scripture. Kantian epistemology still reigns. Ogden, for example, goes so far as to say this:

> Kant's philosophy has come to have unofficially something like the same status among Protestants as Thomas' has long had among Roman Catholics—and this for the very good reason that Kant's distinction between man's theoretical and practical rationality made possible a salvage operation typical of modern Protestantism and comparable in significance to that previously carried out by Thomas in distinguishing between reason and faith.[66]

It is clear, then, that any theology that accepts inerrancy and authority must construct an alternative epistemology to Kant's. To do so will involve destroying two key tenets of his position. The first is the atomic, sensationist theory of empirical data; that is, that there are isolated and purely physical impulses detected by the body without order or meaning apart from the function of reason, and thus that reason and the senses are entirely separable in operation. The second, and closely related, tenet is Kant's principle (the "transcendental deduction") that what is presupposed by our understanding of the data cannot be part of, or included in, the data. Thus time, space, oneness, causality, and so on, are part of the mind's functioning, not of the data.

Traditionally, attempts to refute the Kantian epistemology have involved either some version of realism (that is, that we in some specified sense know the real world), or idealism (that is, that knowledge is of ideas whose source, in some versions of idealism, is God). Kant himself attempted to refute idealism in his first *Critique* by demonstrating the "emptiness" of rational concepts apart from externally derived content. His arguments are, I think, successful. If they are valid, then it may well be that a commitment to the inerrant authority of Scripture rests on a defense and continued refinement of a realist epistemology.

This essay is not the place to attempt any positive construction of an epistemology. It must suffice to point out that neither of Kant's tenets is necessary. The first, that of atomic impressions, he derived from Hume. It is the cornerstone of the Enlightenment model of perception, shared both by rationalists such as Descartes and Leibniz and by empiricists such as Locke and Berkeley. While these philosophers, as well as many subsequent philosophers continuing into the present, disagree as to the value of impressions, they all agree that those impressions are atomic. That is, in their primitive state as apprehended, they are individual sounds, colors, tactile impressions, and so on.

It is not, however, either obvious or clear that we see, hear, and feel impressions rather than reality[67] or individual data rather than a total environment.[68] Choosing the model of atomic data leaves the extremely difficult problem of explaining how and with what authority the mind coordinates these bits and pieces and interprets the results. There is an alternate model, that is, that we apprehend directly a segment of the real world. This model leaves some serious problems as well, but they are not insurmountable. The typical arguments for the atomic model can be countered.[69] We can thus avoid the skepticism about the noumenal world that plagues Humean and Kantian epistemologies.

Kant's second epistemological tenet is similarly susceptible to criticism. A. N. Whitehead has argued that Kant's attempt to base objectivity on subjectivity is "thoroughly topsy-turvy."[70] One does not have to agree with Whitehead's own position to see the cogency of his rejection of Kant's. Because Kant's model of awareness is that of the passive reception of impressions, he must conclude that anything beyond the simple "thereness" of impressions is an active contribution of mind. This necessity falls, however, if we reject Kant's model of atomic impressions and allow for a fully personal interaction with a total environment. But, again, I am not concerned to demonstrate an alternative, only to show that Kant's whole position depends on his epistemology, which itself depends on some debatable assumptions.[71]

The task of constructing an epistemology is extremely crucial. The availability of supernaturalism as a fully rational option, and an inerrant revelation as even viable, let alone factual, hangs in the balance. If Ogden is correct in his assessment of Kant's present influence, and I think he is, it is not surprising that the doctrine of a supernaturally given Scripture, authoritative and inerrant, is held by most of our contemporaries to be not only false, but *incomprehensible.*

TRANSCENDENTALISM: HEGEL

Winfried Corduan

Winfried Corduan is Assistant Professor of Philosophy and Religion, Taylor University, Upland, Indiana. He graduated from the University of Maryland (B.S.), Trinity Evangelical Divinity School (M.A.), and Rice University (Ph.D.). He has written articles on Hegelian philosophy in the Harvard Theological Review *and in the* Journal of the Evangelical Theological Society. *Dr. Corduan is a member of the Evangelical Theological Society, the Evangelical Philosophical Society, and the American Philosophical Association.*

CHAPTER SUMMARY

Hegel's system must be understood as a transcendental philosophy in which shapes of consciousness are successively grounded in each other, the ultimate transcendental category being the Absolute. The transition from the mundane to Spirit is effected in the system on the level of man as he is united to God in Jesus Christ. Thus Spirit overcomes all positivity, including the literal appropriation of the Bible, which must be absorbed into the larger category of speculative thought. Hegel's followers, though divided on details, generally agreed that philosophy provides the tools to go beyond what they considered to be naïve biblical beliefs. Hegel's views can be criticized on several levels: the lack of grounding for his transcendental metaphysics, a misunderstanding of the role of philosophy in biblical interpretation, and the arbitrariness of his conception of truth.

4 *Winfried Corduan*

TRANSCENDENTALISM: HEGEL

THE PHILOSOPHY OF G. W. F. Hegel, (1770–1831), brings to mind the word *system*. Hegel, more than most other philosophers in history, is known for building a system in which each constituent part is intricately related to the whole. Thus, in dealing with one of his philosophical ideas we must realize its position within the entire system. In fact, Hegel asks us to treat his philosophy as a system. All his ideas are intended to be related.

The purpose of this chapter is to analyze Hegel's view of the Bible. But such a task cannot be undertaken without simultaneously referring to his philosophy of religion; and his philosophy of religion stands at the core of his philosophy as a whole. It is therefore legitimate and necessary to evaluate Hegel's view of the Bible in terms of the system that gave rise to that view and to evaluate his system in terms of the view of the Bible that becomes its logical consequence.

The same kind of logical necessity may not be invoked when considering Hegel's legacy among his disciples, of course. There is no reason to assume that any of the later followers of Hegel represent the logical extension of the system, though one or more of them might. This topic will be explored later in this chapter.

Our procedure, then, is to look first of all at Hegel's system, then his philosophy of religion, next his view of the Scriptures, and finally the interpretations his disciples gave him. The chapter concludes with an evaluation and critique of Hegel's influence on biblical errancy.

THE NATURE OF HEGEL'S METHODOLOGY

Critiques of Hegel abound. Most of them, however, are based on erroneous conceptions of Hegel's system. That deficiency makes such critiques practically worthless. A valid critique of Hegel must be faithful to Hegel's own thought. First one must remove the common misconception that Hegel's system consists of the inexorable forward march of reason based on the trichotomy of thesis, antithesis, and synthesis, frequently referred to as "dialectic." But Hegel's understanding of dialectic is different, as we shall see below. Hegel actually mentions this triad only once in his writings, where he derisively ascribes it to Kant and labels it "mindless"![1] How ironic, and what a sad commentary on philosophical scholarship, that this scheme has nonetheless attached itself to the name of Hegel as the epitome of his system! The true nature of Hegel's philosophy is far different.

As is true for any philosopher, Hegel, to be understood correctly, has to be seen within his own historical context. To do this, the most reasonable place to turn is to the philosophies of Kant, the idealists, and the romantics of his day. First and foremost, Hegel must be seen as in dialogue with these thinkers and the issues that animated their world of thought.

Hegel was born in 1770, eleven years before the publication of Kant's *Critique of Pure Reason*. Thus the philosophical climate in which he grew was not that of enlightenment optimism concerning man and his powers of reasoning (an optimism that had always been tempered in Germany anyway) but a climate in which human reason was very much questioned. In this respect Kant had still been moderate. Many romantic scholars after Kant, including Krug and Jacobi, had even less use for reason than Kant did. Thus the discussion current in Hegel's day centered around the question of the very possibility of true human knowledge.

During his early years, when he was struggling to establish himself at the University of Jena, Hegel enjoyed the friendship and support of the younger scholar, F. W. J. Schelling (1775–1854). Together with Schelling, Hegel placed himself against the tide of skepticism. One of the basic contentions of Schelling's philosophy, which Hegel shared, is that true knowledge is not only possible, it is also absolute. Hegel came to make this claim as an outgrowth of the philosophy of Immanuel Kant. Hegel's philosophy, properly understood, is a transcendental philosophy. Very little clarification of Hegel's philosophy is gained by the many popular attempts to see Hegel in terms of other time periods. Whatever links can be discovered between Hegel and Aristotle, Spinoza, or anyone else, they are only indications of how Hegel dealt with his Kantian heritage. Before looking at Hegel's method, then, it will be helpful first to review Kant's transcendental method.

Kant raised the question of what constituent elements of knowledge make knowledge possible and give it certainty. Kant answered in terms of the *forms* of space and time and the pure *concepts* of the understanding. These forms and concepts are synthetic a priori contributions of the mind itself. But these a prioris in themselves are not knowledge; they are builders and guarantors of knowledge that function in conjunction with a certain amount of empirical *content* provided by sensory intuition. Thus, for Kant, knowledge is partially a posteriori and partially transcendental.

Hegel appropriated Kant's transcendental method and pushed it to its limits. In Hegel's hands all knowledge is regarded as transcendental—both in structure and in content. Hegel argued that Kantian philosophy cannot provide absolute knowledge, and only absolute knowledge can be certain knowledge.

Hegel directed an argument against critical philosophy in the introduction to the *Phenomenology*.[2] A common (namely, Kantian) conception of knowledge, he argued, establishes a barrier between the knowing mind and the object of knowledge. In this conception knowledge is pictured either as an instrument that alters its object in the process of assimilating it or as a medium through which the object is perceived in a distorted way. In either case absolute knowledge is not possible. But there is no such thing as nonabsolute knowledge. We cannot have partial knowledge, for either the notion of partiality presupposes that we know what the absolute is, or there is no certainty to our knowledge at all: partial certainty is a contradiction in terms.

Hegel was committed to the idea of absolute knowledge. He

had two options for avoiding the Kantian dilemma. He could simply have ignored Kant and returned to a naïve realism that holds that external objects are known directly. Instead, Hegel chose the other option: he took the Kantian transcendental starting point and extended its application so that in Hegel's philosophy both the content and the structure of knowledge are transcendental.

A Kantian might reply that Hegel cannot ever attain the absolute, since, after all, he is confined to knowledge on the level of experience. Hegel concedes this possible limitation,[3] but then goes on to show that it is on the level of appearance that we first apply the transcendental method: We take knowledge as it appears to us in one of its forms, whether it be in its empirical, rational, intuitive, or commonsensical appearance. ("Forms" here refers only to a *kind* of knowledge, not a technical component of knowledge.) This form of knowledge is evaluated in terms of consistency and self-coherence. The standard for evaluation is the one on which the form of knowledge itself is allegedly based. Our evaluation will reveal, however, that this form of knowledge turns out to be inconsistent and that it cannot persist unless it presupposes another, more refined, form of knowledge. The same process can now be applied to the new form, and we will discover again that this new form also needs support in yet another form of knowledge.[4]

Let me illustrate this method with the opening arguments of Hegel's *Phenomenology of Spirit*.[5] The argument begins with an analysis of the most naïve and, at first glance, most obvious shape of consciousness, sense-certainty. Nothing seems to be surer than the witness of the senses: "Now it is night." "There is a tree." However, the truth of such simple judgments does not persist. Once written down, the sentence "Now it is night" will be false after only a few hours. "There is a tree" can be contradicted merely by changing one's vantage point. But even though each of these individual judgments is only temporary, it is always possible to offer a critique on them and to decide whether they are true or false. Thus we realize that despite particular changes, there are underlying universals that can always be recognized, even if they are not present concretely. But now we have made a transcendental transition: from sense-certainty to the epistemology of perception via universals.

But perception is also insufficient to account for human

knowledge. It is grounded in understanding. Understanding is seen as in need of self-consciousness. Thus the transcendental uncovering goes on.

This transcendental regress continues until we reach the stage of absolute knowledge, where in pure self-conscious self-consciousness no more support is needed. In transcendental terms, each form of knowledge is the "category" facilitating and certifying a previous form of knowledge. Just as in Kant the categories of the pure concepts, as constituents of knowledge, carried out this task of facilitation, so in Hegel it is a kind or form of knowledge as a whole that takes the place of the categories. The absolute is the ultimate category that makes the entire system, and thereby all knowledge, possible. This process is what Hegel calls "dialectical."

Thus the absolute is transcendentally present in all knowledge. But it is not the sole object of all knowledge. Every stage of knowledge retains its significance, although it enjoys the underpinning of the absolute. In this way Hegel protects himself against Schelling's philosophy, which is, for Hegel, "like the night in which all cows are black,"[6] because there only the absolute has epistemological significance.

Hegel's method was a definite response to the discussion of his day on the powers and possibilities of reason. It is indebted to Kant in that it is transcendental, but it is also a radical extension of Kant in that it is all-comprehensive, including both form and content of knowledge.

OVERVIEW OF HEGEL'S SYSTEM

Hegel's method is carried out through all of his writings. His entire system is propelled by transcendental arguments. A sketch of Hegel's system shows how the method works itself out and provides a setting for Hegel's religious views.

Hegel's system is outlined in his *Encyclopedia*.[7] It is divided into three parts: logic, philosophy of nature, and philosophy of spirit. In keeping with the transcendental theme, the system begins with the emptiest of all possible notions—the eternal Idea by itself, devoid of all content. Discovering the implications of the Idea constitutes the study of logic. The Idea is the "representation of God, as He is in His eternal essence before the creation of nature and of finite spirit."[8] But God does create. The second part of the system, the philosophy of nature, deals with creation

essentially apart from God. But creation must stand in relation
to God. How can the two be reconciled?

The third part of the system is the reconciliation of God and
the world. Each of these two poles—God and the world—must
be merged: that is, they must give up their separate identities at
a definite point of contact. This point of contact is first found in
man. Man combines both the materiality of creation and the
spirituality of God. Thus man is the starting point of the total
reconciliation of the universe with itself and with God. Man is
then the transition between nature and Spirit. But this is a complex transition involving many stages.

The first stage—man as an individual—is contained under
the heading, "Subjective Spirit." In overly simplistic terms,
what Hegel accomplishes here is the transcendental overcoming
of the subject-object distinction. Beginning with anthropology,
which for Hegel is the specific study of the human soul, Hegel
develops this topic in three steps—moving from man as a cor-
poreal and sentient being, to man as a conscious being, and
finally to man as an integrated, ethical being. It is in the second
step—the view of man as conscious being—that this abrogation
of the subject-object distinction is actually observed, for the basis
of all consciousness is self-consciousness.

In the next section, "Objective Spirit," the distinction among
all individual subjects is also abolished. This stage is manifested
by the spirit of a particular people as it is expressed in their art,
religion, and philosophy. But these expressions are merely parts
of the greater entity, the human spirit or man seen as a whole.
Thus objective spirit ends in the obliteration of the subject-
subject distinction.

On the way to complete transcendental unity, there is one
further distinction that needs to be overcome—the distinction
between God and man. Hegel undertakes this task in the third
part of the philosophy of spirit titled, "Absolute Spirit."

The first manifestation of Absolute Spirit is in the area of
aesthetics. Art, however, can contain Spirit only in a limited
way. The true freedom of Spirit is discovered only when Spirit
reveals Itself. Then we are in the field of religion. The core of
revealed religion is christology. Jesus Christ is God and man. As
God-man He died on the cross; thus, there both God and man
died.[9] The death was followed by the resurrection. However,
neither man nor God was resurrected again in his original state;

rather, the resurrection brought the ultimate arrival of Absolute Spirit. Thus both man and God have given up their separate identities and merged into Absolute Spirit. The system concludes with the understanding of Absolute Spirit as the epitome of philosophy. We began with the eternal Idea at its emptiest; we end with it at its fullest and completest.

It would be a serious misunderstanding of Hegel to somehow feel that we have now arrived at the final destiny of thought and can rest our philosophizing. The transcendental nature of his philosophy must remind us that we have merely discovered the final *category* of all thought and existence. This final stage must always be seen as the outcome of an arduous transcendental argument. The instant we think that we have *reached* Absolute Spirit, it will vanish from before our eyes, and all that we will be able to see will be the long road of arguments we had to travel in order to get there in the first place.[10]

HEGEL'S VIEW OF THE SCRIPTURES

Now that we are at least cursorily acquainted with the philosophical system, we can look at Hegel's stance toward the Bible and its place in his religious thought. Here we are fortunate in that Hegel has actually given us explicit statements on how he views Scripture.

We have already seen how Hegel's system is propelled: not by the irresistible march of rational deduction, but by the toil of a transcendental uncovering of Spirit. As we saw in the last section, Hegel's philosophy of religion is in itself an integral part of this system; Absolute Spirit could never be realized were it not for the christology in which both man and God died. From some of Hegel's earliest writings to the very last works he wrote, the death of God on the "speculative Good Friday" was of paramount importance because it was a necessary stage to the release of the "highest totality."[11] This highest totality is Absolute Spirit in its work as the most basic transcendental category, and in its more overt manifestations as art, religion, and philosophy. Thus it is Spirit that integrates Hegel's system and that governs the transcendental analysis.

It comes as no surprise then that Hegel claims that Spirit, seen in this way, must also become the final means of understanding all theological and religious issues. Spirit enables us to take religion seriously without becoming stuck in the glue of positivistic religion,[12] that is, mundane religion that takes the facts of revelation all too literally.

There are two religious viewpoints that demonstrate a poverty of Spirit: that of common man who naïvely accepts all religious claims literally without any reflection and that of the rationalist who subjects all beliefs to the skepticism of his own understanding and in the process destroys all possibility of belief. These points of view are alike in that they are both imprisoned in a positivistic world view devoid of Spirit. One whose understanding of religion is based on Spirit will accept the same beliefs as the naïve pietist but will simultaneously be able to interpret them rationally without falling into the skeptic's trap. Thus it is possible to begin with a religious view that is basically orthodox and positive, recognize in it the absolute religion of Spirit, and thereby overcome the positive elements with transcendental philosophy. In other words, naïve, orthodox beliefs are reinterpreted in ways that make them an integrated part of the system. The positive and the spiritual are combined.[13]

There is nothing contradictory in Hegel about this combination of positivity and spirituality. It is necessary, to give an example of Hegel's, outside of religion, that in society a law will begin with the positive, namely, its direct cognizance and application of all relevant facts. But then it will move on to the rational, namely, the expression of human freedom as the goal of all legislation. In the same way there is nothing scandalous about the fact that absolute religion also must begin in positivity. There can be no doubt that it contains historical and factual elements and must therefore reckon with many contingent facts and external appearances, even including miracles.[14]

The positive grounding of the Christian religion is the Bible. In the Bible are found all the necessary doctrines of the Christian faith. Thus Christianity must remain from start to finish biblical.[15]

But that is not to say that the Bible alone is sufficient for doing Christian theology. Hegel claims that it is a fallacy to think that merely citing the Bible makes one a theologian. That method would only be positivity devoid of Spirit and is actually impossible. Take the case of prooftexting a point of doctrine. Hegel argues that even though a Bible verse is being quoted, it is being given a certain extrabiblical context, namely the topic of conversation or the particular point the speaker wants to defend.

Human thinking thus enters the picture, and theology is in fact being done in conjunction with Spirit. Theology is not possible without reflective Spirit. The only question is whether the theologian is being rational or irrational; the incorporation of human thought forms is inevitable.[16]

Hegel contends that the "scientific" theologian will recognize the precedence of Spirit over the Bible. Here as elsewhere Hegel equates Absolute Spirit with the Holy Spirit, who thereby takes on the role of the final category of all knowledge. Thus all literalism must be overcome. Hegel quotes Second Corinthians 3:6: "The letter kills, but the spirit gives life." In the light of Spirit it is then entirely permissible to overcome the historical details that may encumber positivistic religion.[17]

At this point we encounter what has been called Hegel's "conversion of theology into philosophy." A more accurate way of putting this would be to say that at this point we see Hegel's understanding of religion from the standpoint of his transcendental philosophy. Theology is by no means abrogated or given a subordinate position to philosophy; rather, like all human thought forms, it is seen as one expression on the way toward realization of Absolute Spirit.

HEGEL'S FOLLOWERS

After Hegel's death, there was no unanimity among his disciples over what the master had taught. The division arose precisely over this issue of religion and its relationship to philosophy. Hegel's personal example was ambiguous. On the one hand, some strong passages in his writings seem to make theology nothing more than an imperfect approach to philosophy. On the other hand, Hegel attended the Lutheran church regularly and appeared to have identified himself at times with some very conservative views. Further, in many passages he seems to turn philosophy into theology.[18] Thus every faction could make reference to some of Hegel's own words in propagating its party line as the most pure Hegelianism.

Hegel's followers divided approximately into three branches or "wings." At the center stood those who held that for Hegel philosophy is at the core of Absolute Spirit, but there is nonetheless room left in the system for religion. Left-wing Hegelians argued that Hegel had effectively destroyed the need for religion and its place in the world of thought. Finally, right-wing

Hegelians contended that Hegel's system must be understood ultimately in theological terms.

Of these three groups, the left wing became the most influential on the philosophical conception of the Bible. We will consider four representatives: Bruno Bauer, Ludwig Feuerbach, D. F. Strauss, and F. C. Baur.

Bruno Bauer

A fascinating example of a left-wing Hegelian is provided by Bruno Bauer (1809–1882). Beginning his intellectual career as a right-wing Hegelian, he soon switched sides to the left. His most celebrated work is a critical exposé of the atheistic implications of Hegel's philosophy. This book, *The Trumpet of the Last Judgment on Hegel the Atheist and Antichrist*, (1841), was written from the point of view of a devout Christian who denounces Hegel's philosophy as inimical to his beliefs. Actually Bauer is using this parody in order to promote his own anti-Christian viewpoint.

Bauer satirizes those who find Hegel in any way compatible with Christian theology. He acknowledges that the left-wingers were correct in their understanding, though most of them were not sufficiently rigorous in drawing their conclusions. Hegel's philosophy can consistently lead only to an impersonal atheism.[19] All traditional religious notions are utterly demolished by Hegel. Thus a mixture between Hegelian philosophy and theology is self-contradictory. One must either accept Hegel and pursue the route of atheism or accept Christianity and deny Hegel altogether. Hegel's own attempt to synthesize religion and philosophy can only be seen as deliberately deceptive.

On those premises it is clear that Bauer has few kind words to say about the Bible. In contrast to some other left-wing Hegelian critics of the Bible (e.g., D. F. Strauss), he makes no attempt to play down the miraculous and supernatural elements, however. To the contrary, he emphasizes those things in order to support his chief point: that rational philosophy and Christian faith are inherently incompatible and cannot be accommodated to each other. Bauer did not take exception to such doctrines as the Trinity or the deity of Christ. He made no attempt to support the notion that Christ was the first man to understand the divine nature of humanity. He wholly accepted the fact that the Bible teaches that Christ is the Son of God—and then entirely dismissed the Bible as theological rubbish.[20]

Ludwig Feuerbach

Ludwig Feuerbach (1804–1872) began his philosophy at the point of subjective spirit in Hegel's system. In a somewhat simplistic appropriation of the transcendental method, he stated that ultimately all knowledge is not only knowledge *by*, but also knowledge *of*, the knowing subject.[21] In knowing an object, the subject knows himself. This analysis also applies to the knowledge of God by man. In knowing God, man only knows himself, not as a particular man with all his imperfections, but as man in general (objective spirit), an idealized conception of universal man.

All alleged truths about God are then transformed into truths about man. The idea of God is only a projection of man's understanding of his ideal self. Thus "God is love" means "man loves." "God is omniscient" now reads "man's reason has infinite potential."[22]

Since for Feuerbach there is no God, obviously there is also no revelation. Hegel's dichotomy of positive and spiritual truths is useless, since nothing is revealed. The Bible is not only not helpful, it is actually harmful, for it denigrates man, his reason, and his morality. Feuerbach claims that the Bible is full of errors and discrepancies that make the acceptance of the Bible impossible apart from a servile resignation of man's reason.[23]

In a very interesting passage Feuerbach lashes out at those who would hold to some limited view of inspiration.[24] To him such a limited view is the height of sophistry. If the Bible is considered a divine book, the only consistent view is that of complete verbal inspiration and inerrancy. Anything short of such a view, e.g., the idea that the Bible contains spiritual truth that can be discovered after applying historical and literary criticism, really turns the Bible into another human book; for, after all, any book will contain something divine or spiritual. But far more than that is claimed for the Bible. Of course the idea of an inspired revelatory piece of human writing can only be superstition, claims Feuerbach; so our only viable alternative is to reject the Bible altogether.[25]

So far the two left-wing Hegelians we have considered have both arrived at the same conclusion: One can either philosophize with Hegel or theologize with the Bible. It is not possible to do both. Yet the next thinker we will consider attempted to do exactly that. Beginning with the same critical premises, he nonetheless thought he could find some minimal reconciliation between theology and philosophy.

D. F. Strauss

Actually D. F. Strauss (1808–1874) was the initiator of the great post-Hegelian controversy. The lines of debate were drawn according to how people responded to his work, *The Life of Jesus*.[26] In this book Strauss applied the principles of Hegelian philosophy to a critical analysis of the Gospels. The basic premise is that spiritual reality is of a higher order than historical reality. Thus Strauss in effect advanced the very idea that Feuerbach so severely criticized—the dichotomy between factual and spiritual revelation.[27]

Strauss's starting point is philosophical. To him Christianity is essentially a myth; it is an idea or a form of thought, not a historical reality. Singular historical events can never be the conveyors of eternal reality. Thus any literal information derived from the Bible is useless for religious purposes. We cannot know anything about the historical Jesus with certainty, but, even if we did, it would be of no consequence. The only importance of the historical Jesus would be that he may have been the first to recognize the general truth of the unity of God and man, not that he himself was a unique incarnation of God. If Jesus taught this truth, it made him a great teacher; ultimately, however, that truth is expressed far better and more clearly by Hegelian philosophy.[28]

Nonetheless, Strauss concedes that it is possible for the Bible to teach such great spiritual and philosophical truths as the divinity of man. Despite the impossibility of ever penetrating to a historical reality beyond the myth, the myth itself may carry a profound theological truth. This truth is then refined by philosophy.[29]

Strauss is sometimes credited with initiating modern biblical criticism. That is of course not the case at all. His innovation lies in the idea that biblical criticism can remove historical truth and still retain a remnant of spiritual truth.

F. C. Baur

A far more moderate appropriation of Hegel's philosophy is represented by Ferdinand Christian Baur (1792–1860). Becoming acquainted with Hegel's thought relatively late in life,

Baur was first of all a theologian and biblical scholar. His thinking reflects Hegel only indirectly, and he may be thought of as being only on the fringe of left-wing Hegelianism. Perhaps it is precisely because of his moderation that Baur and his new Tübingen school ultimately became far more influential than any other follower of Hegel, with the exception of Karl Marx (and possibly Sören Kierkegaard, if he is considered indirectly related to Hegel).

The elements of Hegel's philosophy are seen in Baur's historiography.[30] Baur maintains that there is no possibility of a purely objective understanding of history that, as it were, merely enumerates the facts. Rather, history must be understood under the categories of philosophy; and there the final category is, of course, Spirit. Thus, very much as Hegel saw history as the uncovering of Spirit, so Baur also sees in history a connected movement, a development of Spirit.[31]

Applied to an understanding of the Bible, Baur's viewpoint is that the Bible is best understood when placed against the background of the disclosure of Spirit. No biblical data are discarded but they are interpreted in such a way as to harmonize with philosophy. In the process, of course, certain details need to be revised. For instance, Baur's understanding of biblical history makes it clear that Paul could not have written the Pastoral Epistles. But such small and (to Baur) insignificant items may easily be sacrificed if the result is a clearer understanding of the development of New Testament history.[32]

Baur's understanding of the New Testament is very briefly this: Original Christianity was basically Judaism with the proviso that Jesus was in fact the Messiah. This theology, represented by Peter among others, was opposed by Paul who advocated a Christianity severed from Judaism and the Jewish law. In John we find a reconciliation of the two points of view. John's theology is considered by Baur to be incipient Catholicism with an emphasis on both faith and works. In order to bring off this contention, Baur is forced to conclude that only Galatians, Romans, and First and Second Corinthians are genuine Pauline epistles.[33]

The Hegelian aspect of this view is to be discerned not primarily in the play of opposites here, but in the fact that Baur allows his philosophical theory to supersede the data of the New Testament. As a scholar in the nineteenth century, he thinks he is in a position to make out the pattern that Spirit must have

used in its first-century manifestation. Details not strictly con-
gruous with this reflection may be written off to inaccurate historical documentation, claims Baur.[34]

Baur's appropriation of Hegel is far more subtle than those of
the other Hegelians we have mentioned so far. For him
philosophy and theology do not merely coexist; they are mutually supportive. In the process, each has to accommodate the
other slightly. When the radical understandings of Hegel became
forgotten, this more conservative understanding persisted.
Baur's followers formed the new Tübingen school, which was
influential until Baur's death in 1860. But even after Baur's
particular theories had been refuted, their principle of formation
was still accepted; namely, that it is permissible to cast biblical
data into the mold of philosophical presuppositions. Thus
Hegel's dictum that the details of positivity must give way before
the ultimacy of Spirit triumphed in Baur and has continued to be
present in the world of biblical scholarship.

Hegel and his followers were certainly not the only foun-
tainhead of the idea that philosophy may determine the veracity
of biblical data. Even in Baur we can discern the influence of
Kant. Baur's understanding of the gospel, for example, reveals a
very Kantian exclusive preoccupation with ethics. But it would
not be inaccurate to say that Hegel and his disciples adopted,
expanded, and popularized Kantian principles.

EVALUATION AND CRITIQUE

Hegel's understanding of the Scriptures and thus of inspiration is of one piece with his entire system. The overcoming of the
positivity of Scripture is only a special case of the entire process
of assimilating finitude within the infinity of Absolute Spirit.
Thus my criticisms will be raised on both levels—the system as a
whole and the system's utilization of the Bible. First we will
reexamine Hegel's view of God and the world by summing up his
position and offering a critique. Next we will look more closely at
Hegel's treatment of Scripture in relation to his view of the nature of truth. Finally, I will offer a critique of the implications of
Hegel's criteria of truth.

Hegel's Understanding of God and the World

Hegel's view can perhaps best be characterized as a panen-
theism, a view of God and the world as contained within each

other. Traditional critiques of Hegel as a pantheist can readily be seen to be inadequate once the transcendental nature of Hegel's thought is understood. Absolute Spirit as the ultimate category is not strictly identical with the world. For Hegel, identity is always identity-in-becoming. The Absolute contains the world, but at the same time it cannot be said that the world is the Absolute or vice versa. The transcendental process establishes a relationship of mutual containment, but it does not infringe on the genuineness of either contributing party, God or the world. But of course Absolute Spirit is not the God of Abraham, Isaac, and Jacob, and here is where our critique must begin in earnest. To be sure, I am not launching into the traditional criticism that Hegel's God is a philosophical God and, therefore, not the God of the Bible. A philosophical analysis ought to yield a philosophical conception of God—a "God of the philosophers." That in itself is no vice, for it is entirely possible that a philosophical God is the God of Christianity. That was true for St. Thomas Aquinas. If some feature of this philosophical God prevents Him, however, from being identified with the God of the Bible, then criticism arises.

The God of the Old Testament is not the God of this age, Hegel claims. The distinction between God and man has been abolished, and both died at Calvary. Thus the ultimate Deity in Hegel's system is not to be identified with the God who disclosed Himself in the history of Israel and who became man in Jesus Christ. This new Deity is Absolute Spirit. The question arises, How could a God somehow be annihilated and replaced by a greater entity? Is not God supposed to be eternal, necessary Being?

The answer comes once again out of the transcendental method. It is not that God literally, physically existed and then suddenly ceased to exist. Hegel would only ridicule such a positivistic understanding. Rather, viewed transcendentally, we see a higher reality, Absolute Spirit, behind God and man. When this category is considered, the reality of both God and man vanishes, and this highest reality appears. This logical, transcendental process is only secondarily expressed in the historical stories of the Crucifixion and the Resurrection. The death of God and man occurs on the *speculative* Good Friday, the *philosophical* Calvary. Thus the death of Christ gives way to the coming of the Spirit, and for Hegel this means the Absolute Spirit of his system.

The last paragraph of Hegel's *Encyclopedia* contains a telling notice on the nature of the Absolute.[35] Heretofore Hegel had stressed the idea of the Absolute as purely self-contained self-conscious self-consciousness. Thereby it serves as the ultimate reality that guarantees absolute knowledge and the world. But it is clear that such a category cannot exist apart from the world. Thus Hegel now says that once we reach this point in our understanding, we must see the Absolute as it once more gives way to multiplicity and a repetition of the entire dialectical road we have traveled previously.

Let me clarify this point by referring back to the transcendental nature of Hegel's philosophical method. The Absolute is the final category. Therefore, the Absolute does not exist by itself. It needs the world; it needs the most elementary form of knowledge—sense certainty. The Absolute is more than the world, but it depends on the world, or it would have nothing to stand behind transcendentally. But a God who is dependent on the world, albeit transcendentally as Guarantor of the world, is not the God of the Bible. I do not mean here to indict every transcendental argument for God's existence. But Hegel does not recognize God's aseity. For him the Absolute has primarily transcendental and not positive metaphysical reality. Such a God is finite; He is dependent on the world.

Furthermore, Hegel's God is dependent on one particular phase of the world. Absolute Spirit is the backbone of finite spirit. Thus it is the transcendental culmination of man's spirit. Traditional critiques have argued that Hegel's God unfolds Himself in the historical development of human spirit. We may with similar effect, turn this around toward a transcendental understanding. Without the provision of the developing human spirit, there could be no Absolute Spirit as ultimate category behind it. Moreover, there is no item of knowledge of which the Absolute is conscious in its pure self-consciousness that is not somehow an aspect of man's knowledge as it is developed through the system. Thus Absolute Spirit is in fact the absolutized spirit of man. It would be a category mistake to identify the two, but the distinction is one of transcendental logic, not of metaphysical content.

The upshot of this first criticism is that for Hegel neither the world nor God is real. The world and finite knowledge are seen only as stages in the transcendental development toward the

Absolute. At the same time the Absolute is only the final transcendental category behind the world and its knowledge. Neither has ultimate reality. We are left with a set of mutually dependent components, God and the world, neither of which has enough metaphysical reality to justify itself. Hence, in the final analysis, Hegel's system lacks all positive grounding. Absolute knowledge is absolute only tentatively, which is to say, it is not absolute at all. The system began with the subjective turn toward a totally transcendental method, where both content and form of knowledge are derived from self-consciousness. And it does not matter with what attributes and absoluteness this self-consciousness is endowed, we can get no closer to the reality and truth of the world. Ultimately God and the world may be only a figment of man's imagination, and Hegel's transcendental analysis may show it to be an absolute figment, but it can do no more.

Hegel's Treatment of Scripture

As we saw before, Hegel emphasizes the priority of Spirit over letter; that is, he argues that Spirit, and not the mundane positive details, ultimately yields truth. Hegel's argument, it will be remembered, is that Bible verses themselves do not yield theological knowledge. A theological statement depends on interpreting the Bible verses, and interpretation incorporates philosophical thinking, whether valid or invalid, into the statement. Thus Spirit overrides the positivity of individual verses.

The problem with this argument is that it fails to observe the proper distinction between revelation and theology. According to the traditional orthodox view, revelation is done by God. God reveals propositional knowledge about Himself and His relationship to man in Scripture. Thus Scripture is inspired in the sense that the very writings are given by the Spirit who is God, and who is very much distinct from the spirit of man. Theology, on the other hand, is the work of man. Taking the scriptural data, man establishes a system for understanding revelation coherently. In doing theology man cannot help but incorporate his own cultural background, historical heritage, and philosophical point of view. The spirit of man, though, of course, illuminated by the Holy Spirit, very definitely determines the interpretation.

Now notice Hegel's confusion. His understanding of the Bible and theology is correct to a certain point. But the traditional understanding is that it is man's finite spirit that determines the interpretation, not infinite Absolute Spirit. Certainly infinite Spirit is present to guide the interpreter, but He is not responsible for the philosophical ideas the theologian brings along. Hegel wants to invoke infinite Spirit without beginning with the Spirit as Revelator. Revealing takes place prior to man's interpretations. Hegel has turned the two separate processes of revelation and interpretation into one process governed by Absolute Spirit.

Actually, Hegel's understanding was predetermined by his methodological starting point. His extreme transcendental method obscured the distinction between human spirit and divine Spirit. If human spirit and divine Spirit are merely different transcendental forms of consciousness, then, ipso facto, there is no distinction between revelation and theology. That is, revelation is not an objective aspect of Scripture but is a process of philosophical appropriation of Scripture by the human subject; for, after all, all knowledge is derived from the self-consciousness of human subjectivity.

Hegel's View of Truth

As we saw in the last section, truth can be truth only insofar as it is carried by the entire transcendental system. There is no guarantee of truth beyond the fact that an idea may be consistent with the outcome of the dialectical process; there is no objective, ontological truth. The pure transcendental method can speak only to the subjective appropriation of truth, not to truth itself.

Because of his view of the nature of truth, Hegel did not, contrary to a popular misconception, regard his system as the last word in the history of philosophy. He assumed it was the *latest* word, that his system was the best philosophy *so far*. Hegel did not claim that his system could not be improved on or advanced further. In fact, Hegel's system is tied to the disclosure of Spirit in history, and as such demands that it be carried further as history progresses. Historicity of truth is an important aspect of Hegel's transcendental dialectic.

The view of the historicity of truth has implications for Hegel's understanding of Scripture. The truth revealed in Scripture is dependent on the vicissitudes of time and the vagaries of philosophical progress, assuming that there is such a thing. It follows that biblical interpretation on those premises can be quite arbitrary. The system demands that, depending on which stage of consciousness has been attained, something may be true at one time and false at another. Such a concept of truth is of course self-stultifying. To be sure, Hegel attributes absolute truth only to the Absolute, but his Absolute is so grand and vague that it presents no solution to the problem of deciding on the truth of any particular theological proposition. In the world of subjectivity something may be true or false simply because an individual wants it to be that way. A system of thought that holds that the mere positive facts are beyond its exalted spiritual position can yield only opinion, not judgments of truth.

Criteria of Truth

This chapter is not the place to establish an epistemology to compete with Hegel's, but a few premises may be laid down with regard to an epistemology of biblical interpretation.

In the first place, once the facts are ignored, the facticity of knowledge can only be accidental. Facts may not be picked up or discarded at an individual's discretion. The moment that one instance recorded in the Bible as historical fact is dismissed as too mundane or "positive," an interpretive principle has been invoked for overriding more facts in the future.

The above statement may seem too crass. The question may be asked, Is it not possible to dismiss one fact and retain all others? Certainly, but in our doing so, facts lose their meaning as the unquestionable bedrock on which knowledge must be based. Speculation, not facts, becomes ultimate. While that is a possible philosophical position, there is then no reason not to dismiss more than one fact, or even all facts.

Second, philosophy that seems to be able to rise above the positive world of facts is not inherently better philosophy than a factual, earthbound philosophy. Hegel fits into the line of succession of modern philosophy that began with Descartes and is based on the Platonic assumption that true philosophy must rise above the world of materiality and history. For Plato, the philosopher who can free himself from the bonds of the cave and can perceive the sunlight of the Forms is the wisest of men. For Hegel, the man who can rise above positivity and can disclose Absolute Spirit is the best philosopher-theologian.

This assumption appears very profound but is not warranted. There are two criticisms that can be directed against this dichotomizing view, one theological and one philosophical. Theologically, it is un-Christian. The crux of Christianity is the fact that Jesus Christ lived, died, and was resurrected within factual human history. To attempt to glorify these historical events by raising them out of the mundane to the realm of the spiritual is actually to rob them of their true significance.

Philosophically, a system totally divorced from the world of facts would be pure subjectivity. A lesser philosophy that accepts some facts, but not all, is merely an arbitrary revision of the same subjectivity. The only consistent philosophy is one that takes all facts into account. Such a view may seem very pedestrian, but it alone yields wisdom.

This is a good point at which to mention Hegel's controversy with Krug. Krug, Kant's successor at Königsberg, challenged transcendental philosophy to deduce something other than abstract and ethereal things, something elementary and simple, such as his pen. Hegel replied in a satirical article[36] that true philosophy must first be concerned with the great universal themes, and as silly a request as to deduce a pen can arise only out of philosophical ignorance. But surely in this instance Krug is correct. A philosophy that can skip the lower levels of reality in order to assert its importance in the spiritual realm has not earned its right to credibility. A wisdom that can ignore the realities of common existence is no wisdom at all.

I began this chapter by emphasizing the transcendental nature of Hegel's philosophy. The transcendental starting point was Hegel's device for avoiding skepticism. However, we saw that it could not fulfill this function adequately. Particularly with regard to the Scriptures, the transcendental method served to undermine the very authority it was intended to conserve; the facts of Scripture became absorbed in the subjectivity of the philosophical system. This vagueness was also reflected in the diversity of the Hegelian schools. Ultimately, because Hegel himself never became specific on particular interpretations, it is possible to make a case for any of the "wings" to be correct.

We see this lack of concreteness persisting into our day, though rarely in Hegelian terminology. Still the notion abounds that philosophical judgments may take precedence over the data of Scripture. Consequently the same subjectivity and vagueness persist as well. Apart from giving biblical facts their proper authority—and this entails accepting them as inerrant—theological propositions can never enjoy certainty. It is not necessary to buy into philosophical presuppositions, Hegelian or otherwise, that prevent this kind of acceptance.

EXISTENTIALISM: KIERKEGAARD

E. Herbert Nygren

E. Herbert Nygren is Professor of Religion and Philosophy at Taylor University, Upland, Indiana. He holds degrees from Taylor University (B.A.), Biblical Seminary in New York (S.T.B.), and New York University (M.A., Ph.D.). He has served in the pastoral ministry in New York, Maryland, and Connecticut and as a member of the faculty at Emory & Henry College, Emory, Virginia. Dr. Nygren *has written articles for* Religion in Life, Christianity Today, Wesleyan Theological Journal, *and* Christian Advocate. *He is a member of the American Society of Church History and the Evangelical Theological Society.*

CHAPTER SUMMARY

Sören Kierkegaard, Danish philosopher of the eighteenth century, adopted the dialectical method of Socrates and emphasized the continuous search for truth as advocated by Gotthold Lessing. Kierkegaard understood Christianity to be faith in the Incarnate God, not dependent on proper creeds or the certainty of past events. He believed it was not possible to ascertain any historical event, not even of those recorded in the Bible. Kierkegaard, nevertheless, had a high personal regard for the Bible, even though he never accepted its inerrant inspiration.

Several contemporary existentially oriented scholars who claim an indebtedness to Kierkegaard have gone beyond him in their denial of the historicity of the events portrayed by biblical writers. Although the modern "dymythologization" of Scripture may have had its roots in Kierkegaardian thought, it has actually gone far afield from Kierkegaard's concept of Scripture and his personal faith in Jesus Christ as the divine Son of God.

EXISTENTIALISM: KIERKEGAARD

SÖREN KIERKEGAARD, frequently considered the first important existentialist, was born on May 15, 1813, and died on November 11, 1855. Nearly all his life was spent in Copenhagen, Denmark. He was born when his mother was forty-four years old and his father was fifty-six. His early childhood was spent in the close company of his father, who inculcated within him an anxiety-ridden pietistic devotion. The melancholy that haunted him throughout his life began in his childhood. Although he was engaged for a period of time, he never married. In fact, the broken engagement is part of the setting in which much of his writing occurs. In addition to his philosophical writings, he also wrote a critical column for the daily newspaper. This column provided him the opportunity to display his sarcasm as he attacked the traditions of his day.[1]

By his own admission, Kierkegaard's main reason for writing was to explain what is involved in being a Christian. Christianity, he believed, had degenerated into "Christendom." He criticized what he considered to be an incompatibility between conforming to the established church and the inward Christian faith.

INFLUENCES ON KIERKEGAARD

Sören Kierkegaard was greatly influenced by Socrates, the classic Greek philosopher. Socrates did not call himself a teacher nor consider himself to be an authority expounding the truth. He believed that truth is a living existential reality that cannot be communicated as a doctrine, but can come to the learner by his own insight. After a series of questions posed in such a manner as to eliminate false assumptions and ill-conceived ideas and to allow corrections, this insight will enable a person to realize the truth.

Inherent in this method is the doctrine of Recollection, which Socrates formulated. This doctrine was based on the idea that the human soul participates in eternal truth; therefore truth lies latent within the soul and needs only to be elicited through questioning.

Although Kierkegaard accepted the Socratic view that truth is within man, he allowed for another view: that it may be that people are strangers to the truth and need to learn the truth from outside, from a teacher. The teacher will then transform a person from one who does not know the truth into one who does. The teacher is God who comes in the form of man, a servant, so that mankind will not be overawed by God as a teacher and thus unable to learn what God has to teach.[2]

Kierkegaard compared the Socratic doctrine of Recollection to what he titled Repetition. He wrote, "Repetition is a decisive expression for what 'recollection' was for the Greeks. Just as they taught that all knowledge is a recollection, so will modern philosophy teach that the whole of life is a repetition. . . . Repetition and recollection are the same movement."[3]

Kierkegaard suggested that "repetition" can be defined as a reintegration of the personality that has become purposeless or at odds with itself. That reintegration can be brought about only through Christianity as one makes the "leap of faith," as in hope he grasps eternity. This very significant concept is developed in a later section of this study.

Kierkegaard used the same indirect means of communication, the dialogue, used by Socrates. Kierkegaard often ascribed his own works to the pen or to the editorship of fictitious persons, often with humorous or high-sounding names (e.g., Johannes the Seducer, Johannes Climacus, The Ladies' Taylor, and Judge William). This use of the pseudonym enabled Kierkegaard to present varied points of view and to relate to the subject of his writings while it safeguarded him from being directly identified with the points of view expressed in them. It has also been suggested that it enabled him under one name ostensibly to attack his own work previously published under another name. His reason for doing this was to avoid the appearance of attempting to construct a consistent system of thought.[4]

While Kierkegaard was a student at the University of Copenhagen, he was confronted with the Hegelian philosophy prevalent at that time. He reacted strongly against it. He accused Hegel of having misused the dialectic in an attempt to present a system of thought. He saw the dialectic of Hegel as passing into a synthesis, moving ever forward in a smooth unbroken continuity until a world view of reality was reached. Kierkegaard believed that Hegel's dialectic was based on abstractions in the realm of concepts and thus it disregarded concrete existence.

Kierkegaard used the dialectic to show absolute distinctions, illustrated by such pairs of words as *holiness* and *love, grace* and *responsibility, eternity* and *time*—each negating, yet resting on its opposite. For example, he insisted that time as ordinarily conceived—as a unitary reality of past, present, and future—is artificial, for time is never standing still. Past time has gone by and can only be grasped in memory; future time does not exist, for we can think of it only in an anticipatory way. Present time is also just a fleeting moment that cannot be grasped and is void of content. Therefore, all of time is a paradox; time cannot become a reality by itself,[5] but can only be experienced dialectically in tension with eternity, which alone gives meaning to time. Eternity, for Kierkegaard, is not infinitely prolonged time, nor is it the time of another world. Both time and eternity are within us but are qualitatively different. The eternal is absolute and timeless: the temporal is relative. Eternity breaks in on time at a point that Kierkegaard calls "The Moment," the point of divine revelation. It is here in the "Moment," as time and eternity meet, that eternal truth comes into being for a man in his temporal existence. This view, it may be noted, was opposed to the then-prevailing theory of revelation as immanent and always present for the believer.

For Kierkegaard, Hegelianism, with its optimistic assumption that human reason is able to solve all problems through dialectic by the successive synthesis of opposites, is guilty of spiritual pride and of deception in making things appear easier than they are. On the contrary, declared Kierkegaard, "Either/Or is the key of heaven. . . . Both/and is the way to hell."[6] That is, in actual life the honest man must discard Hegel's comforting fiction of mediation by both/and, and squarely face the hard facts of incompatibility, of the necessity for radical choice between alternatives and the sacrifice of all but one of them. The true thinker does not try to represent everything about him as clearer than it really is.

Gotthold Ephraim Lessing (1729–1781), German dramatist, critic, and theologian, was cited with much appreciation by Kierkegaard. Lessing was primarily a critic and had no special claim to being ranked as a philosopher of distinction. He was a nonconformist and was never willing to accept, without question, the opinions of society. Although he wrote as one sympathetic to Christian ideals, he did not accept a dogmatic creed. In his play *Nathan der Weise* Lessing expressed a plea for religious indifference on the ground that sincerity, brotherly love, and tolerance are more important than assenting to the affirmations of a creed.[7]

Like Kierkegaard himself, Lessing became a sharp critic of the form of religion. He believed that the Christian religion is not something to be inherited from one's ancestors and that certainly no dogmatic creed is to be considered final. Lessing constantly emphasized the search for truth rather than the results of the search. Kierkegaard said of him: "Lessing has said that, if God held all truth in his right hand, and in his left hand held the lifelong pursuit of it, he would choose the left hand."[8] "Wonderful Lessing, he has no result, none whatever; there is no trace of any result."[9] Kierkegaard expressed his regard for Lessing when he wrote:

> My admiration [of Lessing] has to do with . . . the fact that he religiously shut himself up within the isolation of his own subjectivity; that he did not permit himself to be deceived into becoming world-historic and systematic with respect to the religious, but understood and knew how to hold fast to the understanding that the religious concerned Lessing, and Lessing alone, just as it concerns every other human being in the same manner; understood that he had infinitely to do with God, and nothing . . . to do with any man directly. This is *my* theme, the object of my gratitude (emphasis added).[10]

Lessing made a further differentiation between a generation that is directly contemporaneous with a historical event—the truth of experience—and later generations that have only historical reports. He declared that no later generation can be contemporaneous with past events, for a later generation can know the events only as they are reported to it, and can therefore only *believe* them. Neither historical event nor historical report is *logically* necessary, argued Lessing.[11] Such a position may have caused Kierkegaard to write, "Lessing says that from the historical accounts, i.e. from their admitted reliability, no conclusions can be drawn."[12]

THE STAGES ON LIFE'S WAY

Only when one becomes aware of the significance of "the stages on life's way" in Kierkegaardian thought can one appreciate the significance of *faith* in his understanding of true Christianity. These stages are, in essence, not logical determinations succeeding each other, but kaleidescopic possibilities of life, ranging from existence in immediacy to a spiritual existence by means of faith. The stages are for Kierkegaard the dialectic of existence (as well as the way to faith) and the search of the human soul for God. They have no sharp edges, but overlap each other; the higher does not abrogate the lower, but incorporates it with itself, thus subordinating it. These stages are suggested through the personalities that Kierkegaard created. His creating such characters emphasizes his assertion that one cannot *think* oneself out of one sphere into another by "armchair philosophizing." To make the "leap" out of one stage into another requires the living activity of the entire personality.

The Aesthetic Stage

The aesthetic stage is presented as that sphere of life in which enjoyment is all-important, and whether that enjoyment is of the spirit or the body matters little. The aesthetic man is existentially revealed to be an uncommitted man who shuns all responsibility and declines to take part in society for fear of becoming bored by the routine of life. In Kierkegaard's view, the aesthetic personality is actually that of a libertine, devoid of all interest in social obligations and the establishing of a home through marriage. One who lives in this stage is wandering and roving through life, without fidelity or responsibility. Here is Epicureanism personified, hedonism at its extreme.

Kierkegaard may have been indebted to Kant for his criticism of the life devoted to natural enjoyment. To be truly meritorious, Kant had affirmed, means to act from duty and not inclination. A dutiful action is right in itself and does not derive its worth from its consequences. Strictly moral behavior is founded on a universally applicable maxim: *"Act only on that maxim whereby thou canst at the same time will that it should become a universal law."*[13] Kant constantly attacked the ethics of living merely for happiness. The man, in Kant's opinion, who cares only for the enjoyment of life does not ask whether the ideas are of the understanding or the senses, but only how much and how great pleasure they will give for the longest time.

Kierkegaard wrote a series of essays published as the two volumes, *Either/Or,* the title of which he himself declared "is suggestive," for it "exhibits the existential relationship between the aesthetic and the ethical in existing individualities."[14] In these essays the reader is introduced to two "personalities" who are supposedly the authors of the two volumes. Identified merely as the "Papers of 'A'" and the "Papers of 'B'," the two accounts interpret reflectively two different attitudes to life.

"A" presents various aspects of the aesthetic outlook in which is seen the quest that leads to disintegration and despair. The aesthetic life is presented primarily as a life without responsibility. Although everyone wishes to rule and enjoy himself, no one wishes to bear burdens, assume obligations, or be held morally accountable. The individual living an aesthetic life is restless, seeking always to avoid boredom, which gives rise to weariness and loathing.

"Don Juan" is the epitome of the sensual genius. "Don Juan is . . . flesh incarnate, or the inspiration of the flesh by the spirit of the flesh."[15] He is wholly and completely a seducer, who cannot and will not give himself to life; his only relations are mere enjoyment at the expense of another. His only love is sensual, and sensual love, according to his conception, is faithless.[16]

The ultimate in the aesthetic life is brought out in the "Diary of the Seducer," in which a certain Johannes is described as a diabolically clever and entirely immoral personality. In this "diary" the tale is told of how Johannes wins Cordelia's complete devotion and becomes engaged to her. By his wily charm he is able to excite her to the highest pitch, to the point of sacrificing all for him.[17] Then step-by-step he persuades her that an outward tie such as an engagement is only a hindrance to love and makes her willing to break the engagement to become his paramour. Then he abandons her. Johannes thus represents one who desires variation, freedom, and the satisfaction of having seduced a girl whom he does not intend to marry. To his diary he confides, "I am intoxicated with the thought that she is in my power."[18] And further, "I have never given any girl a marriage promise. . . . Insofar as it might seem that I have done it here, that is only a fictitious move."[19] Johannes is thoroughly aesthetic, feeling that the curse of an engagement is always its ethical side. "Under the heaven of the aesthetic, everything is light, beautiful, transitory; when the ethical comes along, then everything becomes harsh, angular, infinitely boring."[20]

A review of the aesthetic stage is found in "In Vino Veritas," a dramatic presentation of five incarnations of the aesthetic life who are guests at a banquet at which each makes a speech about love. Finally, the banqueters hear from Johannes the Seducer, the character of the "Diary," who calls himself an erotic living on the principle "Enjoy thyself." He expresses the wildest sensuality in the most festive manner. Woman exists only for man's enjoyment, and only a seducer knows how to enjoy a woman without being caught and imprisoned in the trap of marriage and the drudgery of life. In Johannes is presented an existential illustration of a man who is morally dead. With this drama as a living picture of the aesthetic stage of life—the life that cares not for another but only for the enjoyment of one's own miserable self—the banquet comes to a close.[21]

Kierkegaard tended to identify the aesthetic way of life with what the Bible calls the "natural man," a man whose desire is for things of the flesh, who follows his own desires in his search for enjoyment. Ultimately, however, to the aesthetic man who attempts to enjoy himself, even with careful discernment, there comes an increasing weariness and self-disgust, as he finds himself enslaved by passion, no longer able to exercise his own will, almost in despair. At this point Judge William, the pseudonymous "author" of the second volume of *Either/Or*, admonishes the aesthetic individual to choose despair, for despair is not only the bankruptcy of the aesthetic life, it is its only remedy.

The individual looks on his past with its hollowness and futility and, having rejected it in his soul, comprehends the ethical as a possible higher way of life. He is polemical in his attitude toward the aesthetic life and finds it no longer tolerable. It is then that he contemplates the ethical life, which he has not yet entered. Having decided to choose rather than to be led by passion, he finds himself in the ethical stage of life. In the ethical stage there is choice; in the aesthetic stage there is the refusal to choose.

The Ethical Stage

The ethical stage is existentially presented as one of wholesome, concrete interests where one is open to the needs and rights of others and wholly honest. The individual who is living in the ethical stage takes his proper place in society and shares life experiences with others. He is confronted with rules, demands, and tasks. Since the ethical life *is* the life of mutual obligation, Judge William posits marriage as an illustration of the ethical life. He argues that the basic characteristic of a true marriage and of the ethical stage is frankness on the highest possible plane between persons.[22] He seeks to defend marriage against romantic objections, recognizing that although romantic love is the physical basis of marriage, yet the basic characteristic of a true marriage is the relationship of sharing.

The Judge attempts to make clear that not only marriage, but friendship, vocation, and the whole of life must be ethical. The finding of oneself in the act of living requires that one plumb to the depths those experiences that involve personal obligations to others and the social order. Only so can one fathom life. An ethical man cannot stand aloof like a detached spectator, observing the performance on the stage of life, but must give himself to life tasks. All his personal relationships are based on the principle that every man is universal man; therefore he subjects himself to a standard of what is right for all men. He is bound by a responsibility to humanity and thus does not follow his own inclinations in pursuit of enjoyment, with no consideration for others.

Kierkegaard, through Judge William, insisted that the ethical life is the only life that is really aesthetically beautiful, for the morally good alone has true beauty. He stressed *choice* as the heart of the ethical stage, in contrast to the aesthetic stage in which there is no decisive "either/or."

The ethical categories, however, are purely ideal, and Kierkegaard presented them with a mental reservation, for if the realization of the ethical ideal were wholly possible, there would be no need for the religious life. Man in his natural state pursuing aesthetic and sensuous ends is incapable of performing the ethical task that requires absolute devotion to absolute ends. He becomes aware of a contradiction within himself. As St. Paul put it, "What I do is not the good I want to do; no, the evil I do not want to do—this I keep on doing."[23] As the individual recognizes the incommensurability between himself and his task, he realizes that a change must take place within him to enable him to live ethically and that this change can come only from the Divine. In fact, Kierkegaard admitted that the "ethical sphere is a transitional sphere,"[24] the only function of which is to develop a need and a receptivity for religon.

The Religious Stage

Even as the aesthetic stage is one of immediacy and the ethical one of requirement, so Kierkegaard pointed out in *Fear and Trembling* that the religious stage is one of fulfillment. Kierkegaard believed that there is a natural "religiousness" in man that evolves from a sense of wonder at that which is beyond his grasp. As the religious stage unfolded in his mind, Kierkegaard developed his conception of the distinction between Religion *A* and Religion *B*, a characterization made as a result of his personal experience.

Religion *A* is essentially a passive relation to the Divine. It is a simple heart-felt expression of a realization of God that must, however, be present before there can be any possibility of one's awareness of Religion *B*, which is the Christian religion.[25]

Kierkegaard suggested three characteristics of the religious experience called *A*. The first of these is *resignation*. When one determines to change his life, he becomes aware that he has been entirely occupied with such things as personal enjoyment, worldly ambition, and social success—all relative ends. To achieve a relationship with the absolute, he realizes that he must totally renounce and sever the ties that have bound him to the temporal world. "Infinite resignation," Kierkegaard wrote, "is the last stage before faith, so that those who have not made this movement have not got faith, for it is only in infinite resignation that I become conscious of my eternal worth, and it is only then that there can be any question of grasping existence by virtue of faith."[26]

Having been freed from the relative, one experiences *suffering,* the second characteristic of religious experience *A*. This suffering is not to be construed as physical self-torture as was prevalent in many medieval monastic orders even in Kierkegaard's day; it is, instead, "soul-suffering."[27] As a result of his renunciation, the individual undergoes mental distress, anguish, and sorrow at the loss of all the things of the world that he had previously held dear. Inward religious suffering results from the need of a transformation in the personality by which its inadequacy for the task is corrected. Should the question be raised as to why the personality is inadequate, the answer would only intensify the suffering, for the answer would reveal that at the bottom of inadequacy lies *guilt*, the third characteristic of Religion *A*.

Kierkegaard said that guilt is not the memory of one wrong act; it is the consciousness of a quality affecting the whole personality. St. Paul summed this truth in a simple exclamation: "What a wretched man I am!"[28] This consciousness of guilt expresses the relationship of an individual to an eternal blessedness in terms of the very breach in the relationship. Yet the relationship is never completely broken, for the sense of guilt, unlike the sense of sin, is still on the immanent level.

The concept of Religion *A* comprises both paganism and the conventional church-religion of his day, which, in Kierkegaard's opinion, was passive acceptance of creeds and ceremonies. On the other hand, Religion *B* is true Christianity, in which faith alone is the valid determinant. The object of this faith is the paradox, the absurd. Religion *B* is based on the acceptance of the Incarnation as a historical *fact*, the fact that eternity entered time and God became man. Kierkegaard said that the only one to experience Religion *B* is the person who *believes* that the Incarnation is *fact* and who thinks of God as a person and not an idea.[29] Furthermore, Religion *B* insists on a personal relationship to a historic fact; "Christianity is not a *doctrine* but an existence-communication."[30] It is this belief in the Incarnation that makes Christianity a historical religion in a peculiar sense, for God is not to be found in one's own inwardness, but in Bethlehem and on the cross. It is here that the stress of faith becomes prominent, for to think of God become flesh, or eternity entered into time, is absurd and can only be grasped by a faith that transcends all reason. This is the great paradox of Christianity, which will be discussed further in subsequent pages.

A second characteristic of Religion *B*, according to Kierkegaard, is the realization of *sin*. Sin is not merely an isolated act but is a continuous state of the soul. Sin lies in the will, not in the intellect, and is often characterized as disobedience.[31] Kierkegaard did not believe in the historical entrance of sin into the world. He interpreted the biblical story of Adam and Eve as a story of every man in his essential being and not as a story of a historic couple. Adam is originally in a state of innocence in which he does not know the difference between good and evil. The divine prohibition, "Thou shalt not eat," induces a state of dread in man, because it has awakened within him the possibility of freedom to exercise his will. "Dread is the reality of freedom as possibility anterior to possibility."[32] It was Kierkegaard's belief that an individual will understand how sin entered the world only from personal experience, and even then he cannot explain precisely what sin is, because he is in sin.[33]

Moreover, unlike the individual in Religion *A*, who experiences guilt only toward an unknown God, a mere idea, the individual of Religion *B* recognizes sin as the offense against a personal God. With this awakened awareness of sin, the tie that was only partly severed in Religion *A* becomes completely broken, and the individual senses himself to be absolutely different from God. Without this consciousness of sin there is no transition to true Christianity, for this realization leads one to a new passion—faith. It is this consciousness of sin that distinguishes Christianity from the best in paganism.

The final characteristic of Religion *B* is an emphasis on *spiritual living*. Kierkegaard described Religion *A* as a life of the flesh, a religion of time. He said, "The temporal never is and never will be the element of spirit."[34] It is only in Religion *B* that the life of the spirit is attainable. For Kierkegaard, the spirit is equated with the self in the reborn individual. The life of spirit is that of humanity and the world redeemed. Kierkegaard's antithesis is substantially the same as that made by St. Paul in the eighth chapter of his Epistle to the Romans. Like Paul, he believed that if we live after the flesh, we die, but if we live after the Spirit, we will inherit eternal life.

The state church of Denmark, at that time under the leadership of Bishop Primate Mynster, regarded all citizens except Jews as Christians. This view failed to recognize the personal aspect of Christianity and the need of religious or spiritual awakening in the lives of the people. Kierkegaard was keenly aware of the fact that the church lacked even the message for meeting the need. "Christendom has done away with Christianity," he wrote, "without being quite aware of it. The consequence is that, if anything is to be done, one must try again to introduce Christianity into Christendom."[35]

THE BIBLE

It must be noted that Sören Kierkegaard did not regard himself as a Bible scholar. He was quick to assert that regarding study of the Scripture "the present author is far from arrogating to himself an unusual scholarly acquaintance."[36] Yet, Kierkegaard did state that the study he *had* made had "succeeded in proving about the Bible everything that any learned theologian in his happiest moment has ever wished to prove."[37] He also said concerning the Bible, "These books," and "their authors" are "trustworthy . . . as if every letter were inspired."[38]

In addition, Kierkegaard quoted from the Bible in his own works, indicating his own regard for Scripture. Included are: "The opposite of sin is faith" as is *affirmed* in Romans 14:23" (emphasis added).[39] "It is one of the most *decisive* definitions that the opposite of sin is not virtue but faith" (emphasis added)[40]; and: "To be *sure*, Mary bore the child miraculously" (emphasis added).[41]

In addition, Kierkegaard used the account of Lazarus's being raised from the dead, as recorded in John's Gospel, to express his own belief that "death itself is a transition unto life" and that "death is not the last thing."[42] In his *Training in Christianity* several general references are made to indicate Kierkegaard's affirmation of the miraculous as portrayed in Scripture.[43] The implications are legion that Kierkegaard's *personal convictions* were well within the boundaries of orthodox Christian beliefs. "This word of God, very simply, contains God's will for us and his commands."[44]

Moreover, Kierkegaard's lack of enthusiasm about the use of secondary sources in the study of Scripture is a reflection of his regard for the first-hand authority of Scripture. "Above all," he wrote, "read the N.T. without a commentary. Would it ever occur to a lover to read a letter from his beloved with a commentary!"[45] He added, whimsically, "Following the path of the commentators is often like traveling to London; true, the road leads to London, but if one wants to get there, he has to turn around."[46]

It is interesting to note that Kierkegaard's regard for Scripture does not depend on the historicity of all of the Bible. The opponents of Scripture who, he said, "have succeeded in proving what they desire about the scripture" have not "thereby abolished Christianity." Since Scripture is written as history, it must first be recognized that behind Kierkegaard's view of the authenticity of the record lies his view of the writer's ability to record what *actually* happened. He was convinced that "the greatest attainable certainty with respect to anything historical is merely an *approximation.*"[47] In Kierkegaard's *Philosophical Fragments* one finds the suggestion that uncertainty is attached "to the most certain of events."[48] Kierkegaard continued, "Even if the fact we speak of were a simple historical fact, difficulties would not fail to realize an absolute agreement in all petty details." Yet Kierkegaard was to write in the *Postscript:* to "discover that all historical knowledge is only an approximation . . . is no disparagement of historical investigation, but it illuminates precisely the contradiction involved in bringing the utmost passion of subjectivity into relation with something historical."[49]

Kierkegaard insisted that one must not allow faith to be "misdirected upon the merely historical as its object."[50] Only faith that has come to know *uncertainty* can at its own risk grasp the historical. Thompson, in his interpretation of Kierkegaard's position suggested that this means that "if anybody . . . by any so-called objective thinking, imagines he can conquer doubt, he is mistaken."[51]

Walter Lowrie in a comment in his introductory essay to the *Postscript* wrote, "The Christian . . . has to renounce the comfort of calm assurance bolstered upon objective proofs."[52] Kierkegaard wrote, "Suppose that doubt hit upon and came up with a kind of probability that Paul's letters were not by Paul and that Paul never lived at all—what then? Well, scholarly orthodoxy might give up hope."[53] The implication is that he himself would not be concerned. In the *Postscript* one finds this parable that suggests that the documents in themselves are of minimal importance.

If a woman who is in love were to receive at second hand the assurance that the man she loved (who was dead and from whose mouth she had never heard the assurance) had affirmed that he loved her—let the witness or witnesses be the most reliable of men, let the case be so plain that a captious and incredulous lawyer should say it is certain—the lover will at once detect the precariousness of this report. . . . In case a man had to find out from historical documents with absolute certainty whether he was a legitimate or an illegitimate child, and his whole passion was involved in this question . . .—do you suppose he would be able to find the certainty which would satisfy his passion . . . ?[54]

The *Postscript* is concerned primarily with the matter of a person's becoming a Christian. This is not, in Kierkegaard's thinking, an *objective* problem but a *subjective* one. Thus, the concern of historical criticism and speculative philosophy are both summarily dismissed. In fact, there is even the suggestion that one finds a direct correlation between objective uncertainty and subjective truth.

Kierkegaard seems to reject any attempt to prove that Christianity is true only for the purpose of allowing others to become Christians. Such "proofs," it would seem, would actually eradicate the difference between ordinary history, which can be made only probable at best, and the Incarnation, which represents the improbable to be accepted by a "leap of faith." To be sure, "Christianity's fundamental claim is that it is founded on historical fact, but for *all* things historical . . . one can never be completely sure."[55] "The Holy Scriptures," Kierkegaard mused, "are the highway signs: Christ is the way."[56]

Kierkegaard's disregard for both "The System"—current Hegelian philosophy—and the formal Christendom of the state church of his day bears witness to his position on objective certainty in history. To speak of objective faith, he stated, is as if Christianity "had been promulgated as a little system, if not quite so good as the Hegelian; it is as if Christ—aye, I speak without offense—it is as if Christ were a professor, and as if the Apostles had formed a little scientific society."[57] "The teachers in Christendom," he wrote, "commit themselves to conform to the New Testament in their teaching. . . . But . . . Christianity is no 'doctrine.'"[58] "Emphasis on the Bible has brought forth a religiosity of learning and legal chicanery."[59]

His position was expressed even more strongly in the *Postscript* when he declared, "To know a confession of faith by rote is paganism, because Christianity is inwardness."[60] Kierkegaard asserted, "Christianity protests every form of objectivity; it desires that the subject should be infinitely concerned about himself. It is subjectivity that Christianity is concerned with, and it is only in subjectivity that its truth exists."[61] Since Kierkegaard did not speak of the truth of either eternal reason or history, but only of the truth of revelation given by God and accessible to man by *faith,* his understanding of faith must now be examined. On *believing* he said that the Christian believes "by virtue of the absurd." Since God is an eternal being, and Christianity says that God existed in time, there appears to be a logical and ontological contradiction, in which there can only be *belief.* That God became man cannot be verified historically for "immediate sensation or cognition, either for a contemporary or for a successor." Yet, Kierkegaard went on to suggest, it *is* a historical fact, though "only for the apprehension of Faith."[62] Speaking about Christ, he said, "This man is also the God. How do I know? I cannot know."[63]

"The object of faith," Kierkegaard affirmed many times, "is not a doctrine, for then the relationship would be intellectual. . . . The object of faith is not a teacher with a doctrine; for when a teacher has a doctrine, the doctrine is *eo ipso* more important than the teacher, and the relationship is again intellectual. . . . The object of faith is the reality of the teacher. . . ."[64] Kierkegaard continued, "Precisely because Christianity is not a doctrine it exhibits the principle . . . that there is a tremendous difference between knowing what Christianity is and being a Christian."[65] Another statement closely related to this view is found in the collected *Journals:* "Christ did not teach redemption; He redeemed."[66] Further, he noted:

> The Savior of the world, our Lord Jesus Christ, did not come to the world to bring a doctrine; He never lectured. Since He did not bring a doctrine, neither did He seek to prevail upon anyone by reasons to accept the doctrine, nor seek with proofs to substantiate it. His teaching in fact was His life, His presence among men.[67]

Kierkegaard's emphasis on faith led to yet another significant aspect of Christianity: the Theology of Paradox. "The paradox," for Kierkegaard, "emerges when the eternal truth and existence are placed in juxtaposition with one another . . ."[68] When eternity and time, the infinite and the finite, the transrational and the rational meet, the paradox emerges. Paradox becomes a decisive word with ontological importance. "When the eternal truth is related to an existing individual it *becomes* a paradox" (emphasis added).[69] Because of sin man has fallen away from God and now exists as a divided being, belonging to both the temporal and the eternal. For this reason he cannot grasp thought and being as a unity but only in sharp contrast, in a seemingly contradictory form, in the tension of opposites. Man need not apologize for this fact but must seek to grasp more fully that the paradox *is* a paradox. Kierkegaard believed that this paradox will remain as long as finite man exists. This view is unlike Hegel's theory that the paradox will be resolved in an explanatory synthesis when man obtains higher knowledge.

This doctrine of the paradox is an example of the passionate honesty in Kierkegaard, for though he could not discredit either the divine or the human elements in Christianity, he could not accept them both by reason alone. It is also a protest against to interpret Christianity as an intellectual system easily explained or understood. However, that for Kierkegaard the paradox is not a concession but a category that expresses the relation between existing cognitive spirit and eternal truth. Even though it cannot be comprehended fully by human thought, the paradox is the only basis for man's eternal blessedness.

Kierkegaard accepted the Athanasian christology, stressing the implicit paradox contained in it.[70] To him the statement that Christ was fully man and fully God, eternal and temporal, one person in two natures, was not to be dismissed lightly. "The contradiction between being God and being an individual man is the greatest possible, the infinitely qualitative contradiction."[71] Jesus came into the setting of the strictest monotheism ever known and claimed to be God and man, the most absurd claim anyone could possibly make. "That God has existed in human form, has been born, grown up, and so forth, is surely," said Kierkegaard, ". . . the absolute paradox."[72] To appropriate such a revelation, each individual must enter into a personal and existential faith-relation to Christ. The relation is to the very existence and life of the individual and not to his understanding. For there can never be any intellectual or objective certainty concerning this paradox. "To 'know' signifies exactly that the reference is not to [Christ]."[73] As Hugh Ross Mackintosh expressed it:

> The person of Jesus is a logically preposterous entity against which, in Kierkegaard's vivid phrase, "reason beats its brow till

the blood comes." Yet the absurdity is a fact, and with it the Gospel stands or falls.[74]

"The God-Man must require faith and must refuse direct communication,"[75] said Kierkegaard. (Or in H. V. Martin's descriptive phrasing, "Just as colours exist for sight, and sounds for hearing, so the absolute paradox exists only for faith.")[76] Therefore, he argued, when one "does away with faith . . . one does away at the same time with something else—the God-Man. And if one does away with the God-Man, one does away with Christianity."[77]

Kierkegaard said that the paradox as the object of faith began with the introduction of Christianity nineteen centuries ago when God walked on the earth incognito, and men came face-to-face with a man like themselves, one in whom they discerned the mystery and power of the Godhead. To be a Christian, then, is to be "contemporary with Christ," and to be contemporary with Him is to recognize in His humanity the Absolute God. "This contemporaneousness is the condition of faith and, more closely defined it is faith."[78] This definition of faith eliminates the question which might be raised: If God became man once-for-all nineteen centuries ago, can the paradox of the God-man be anything but a thought-paradox for us today? Kierkegaard insists that God is the absolute whom time cannot essentially change. Even though Christ's life on earth was a historical fact, it is also an eternal event, the manifestation of the absolute eternal in relative time. Since Christ as the God-man *is* this eternal manifestation of the absolute, He *is* contemporaneous with every historical age. "For in relation to the absolute there is only one tense: the present. For him who is not contemporary with the absolute—for him it has no existence."[79] The paradox in which Christ presents Himself is equally real to every generation.

This contemporaneousness is not achieved by transposing ourselves to the first century in imagination, nor by transposing Christ to the twentieth century in like manner. True contem-poraneousness is an attitude of our inner life toward Christ. The time at which one can truly become contemporary with Christ is the present moment in one's inner life when the individual comes face-to-face with Christ as the absolute and eternal reality. In being confronted with the claim and challenge of the "Word made flesh," one is faced with the existential decision of faith or offense. This decision is not merely one of relative and temporal importance but is of absolute and eternal significance.

This is not meant to imply that had we only been *there* when the Christ was born, we could *then* know. Even then, we could have reported only what we *believed*, which is in fact what the biblical writers are alleged to have done.

In the *Philosophical Fragments* one finds this observation by Kierkegaard: If the historian "succeeded in bringing to pass a complicated account, consistent to the letter and to the minute, he would beyond all doubt be deceived. He would have obtained a certainty even greater than was possible for a contemporary observer, one who saw and heard; for the latter would quickly discover that he sometimes failed to see what was there, and sometimes saw what was not there, and so with his hearing."[80]

The only thing that the contemporary-with Christ can do for an individual of subsequent generations is "to inform him that he has himself believed."[81] No historical fact, Kierkegaard suggested, could ever be communicated to another as historical fact.[82]

To summarize Kierkegaard's utilization of the Bible, it must be noted that, in dealing with history, if the immediate eyewitness were to record *every* event Jesus did, he would have nothing other than the *what* of history, like a portrait; if he were to hear *every* word spoken, there would still be nothing other than a freedom from error of what Jesus said. Such awareness is not discipleship. In fact, one can never *prove* historically that Jesus existed, for there is never necessity involved in historical becoming. Apart from *faith* one is never sure He existed, much less that He was the God-man.

Scripture, it may be said, serves the same purpose for the reader as sensation did for the eyewitness. It can beguile the inquirer into treating it in such a way that no concern is noted for the actuality of Jesus' existence. Kierkegaard illustrated this by making reference to the birth story of Jesus. There is "only one human being who is fully informed, namely the woman of whom [God] permitted himself to be born." No "eyewitness" or later "reader" can have knowledge.[83] Knowledge cannot have "for its object the absurdity that the Eternal is the historical."[84] "For a person to be able unconditionally to express the unconditioned, he must have an immediate relationship to God, and God must *in concreto* say to him what he *in concreto* is to do. . . . From this we also see that the New Testament cannot absolutely directly and literally be normative for us. . . ."[85]

Kierkegaard claimed that there is a limit beyond which reason cannot go, and beyond this limit dwells *faith*. Faith in the existence of God in human history and in one's own individual experience is accepted as axiomatic and beyond either proof or dispute. This does not imply that faith in God or Christ is meant to be an objective certainty, for faith is of a passionate nature and cannot be a matter of certainty in the same way as logic, mathematics, or science.[86] Faith, to Kierkegaard, needs no proof. In fact, "It must even regard the proof as its enemy . . .; [only] when faith begins to cease to be faith, then a proof becomes necessary so as to command respect from the side of unbelief."[87]

Yet when Kierkegaard said that faith is not interested in the proofs that are the desiderations of the systematic philosophers, he did not mean that Christianity has abolished philosophy. He was attempting only to clarify his assertion that a Christian is not dependent on the artificial security of philosophic reasoning, for if it were true that faith is dependent on some metaphysical system, faith would then be valid only as long as that system is valid.

In the *Postscript* one finds the most concerted argument against any attempt at intellectual proof of Christianity. It is, Kierkegaard contended, a complete misunderstanding to try to establish the objective truth of Christianity and to build one's faith on such proofs. To embrace Christianity one needs no proof of its doctrines but only a subjective faith in the Christ of Christianity. Kierkegaard maintained that if the *how* of faith is rightly grasped and the leap of faith is rightly made, then the *what* of belief is given with it. Reflection on doctrine can never enable a man to become a Christian. A simple unreflective man can make the movement of faith without the agonizing struggle that awaits the intellectual man. Kierkegaard even denounced the use of the Bible as a proof of Christianity. All such efforts, he insisted, cannot ensure the obtaining or the strengthening of faith. In the midst of a lengthy discussion concerning the futility of defending the Bible, he asked rhetorically, "Has anyone who previously did not have faith been brought a single step nearer to its acquisition?" Then he answered, "No, not a single step. Faith does not result simply from a scientific inquiry. . . ."[88]

Kierkegaard did not regard Christianity as a communication of knowledge to be understood, as apparently did Hegel, who had written, "In order to remove [religion] out of the region of caprice and of accidental opinions and views, and to preserve it as absolute truth and as something fixed, it is deposited or stated in creeds."[89] For Kierkegaard, Christianity is a communication of existence beyond comprehension and beyond reason; it is a personal relationship of faith in a person, not in a doctrine.

SUBSEQUENT TO KIERKEGAARD:
EVALUATION AND CRITIQUE

The influence of Kierkegaard has been far-reaching. The "Melancholy Dane" seems to have prophesied this when he wrote three years prior to his death, "Denmark has need of a dead man."[90] "My life will cry out after my death."[91] It was not, however, until the early twentieth century that the "dead man" began to speak. Although Kierkegaard left no system, and, therefore, could not in the strictest sense have any disciples, he can claim a vast posterity who, like him, have a great distrust of reason as a means of approaching God and of history as a means of discovering Jesus Christ. Among these are such theologians as Karl Barth, Rudolf Bultmann, Paul Tillich, and Reinhold Niebuhr.

When Karl Barth published his *Commentary on the Epistle to the Romans,* the world learned that a man called Sören Kierkegaard once lived and wrote, for Barth's writings contain many a Kierkegaardian strain. One salient example: "The gospel requires faith," Barth wrote; "it can therefore be neither directly communicated nor directly apprehended. . . . If Christ be very God, he must be unknown, for to be known directly is the characteristic mark of an idol."[92] Barth borrowed numerous phrases from Kierkegaard, such as "infinite qualitative distinction" between God and man.[93]

When asked for proof of the doctrine he expounded on the validation of faith itself, Barth referred to the words of the life of Christ as found in the Bible. He, like Kierkegaard, insisted that man's faith need not depend on the language of human reason or philosophy, for "no philosophy can deliver the key to us."[94] "The theologian," he asserted, "is under (no) obligation to 'justify' himself in his utterances before philosophy."[95] "We do not demand belief in our faith," he said again, "for . . . it is unbelievable."[96]

Also, filtered through the existential ontology of Martin Heidegger, the Kierkegaardian influence can be seen in the extreme denial of New Testament history found in the writings of Rudolf Bultmann. (Kierkegaard himself, as previously noted, indicated his own willingness to accept the truth of biblical miracles, not on historical grounds but through faith.) Like Kierkegaard, Bultmann despaired of reclaiming the historical events of Jesus' life. Instead, Bultmann consistently maintained that all one could hope to do would be to discover the interpretation of the data by the New Testament writers. His writings utilize the distinction in the German language between *historisch*—the historical, and *geschichtlich*—the interpretation of the historical. One can never know *what* happened; one can only know what the early church *proclaimed* as having happened. In fact, the Bultmannian understanding of the textual material suggests that it is three steps removed. The Gospel writers actually edited earlier oral and written traditions that were, in turn, interpretations of what Jesus said and did, about which we have very little, if any, real knowledge.[97]

Paul Tillich, in his philosophical and biblical writings, also suggested that the techniques of historical criticism have shown that it is impossible to meet the historical Jesus "because the Jesus of whom we have reports was from the very beginning the 'Christ of faith.' "[98] One must prevent "theology from confusing the venerating . . . of a character of the past with the manifestation of the unconditional in the present."[99]

Another modern thinker who was skeptical regarding the certainty of history was Reinhold Niebuhr. Professor Niebuhr wrote, "Christology is not understood by a naturalistic version of the Christian Faith in which the 'Jesus of history' becomes the norm of life."[100]

The New Testament as "apostolic proclamation" or *kerygma* was interpreted by these contemporary writers as having been given in the thought form of that age, a thought form that must be altered into one relevant for our own day. This "demythologization" ostensibly makes it possible to find the kernel of truth in the midst of a hopelessly outmoded language pattern or world view. It would appear, however, that Bultmann read the New Testament through the glasses of twentieth-century Logical Positivism or

Heideggerian subjectivity. To accept Heidegger's ontology is to surrender at the outset one's interpretation of New Testament Scripture as having any uniqueness. Moreover, to accept Positivism is to dismiss the supernatural as quite meaningless. The miracle, then, is relegated to the realm of myth, since it obviously does not coincide with the investigator's predilections.

To the "demythologizers," Christ is to be encountered not in the saving events of Calvary and the empty tomb, but in the proclamation of salvation which, in reality, is understood to be merely one's own "new life." It is this "new life" that comes mythologically portrayed in the classic doctrine of the atonement. ("The idea of the atonement is mythological," wrote Bultmann.) Not only the atonement but also the resurrection and the New Testament teaching about eternal life are relegated to the realm of mythology. Bultmann's words are clear: "The Jesus of history is not kerygma. . . . For in the kerygma Jesus encounters us as the Christ."[101] History does not and cannot give us Jesus as the Christ.

The dehistoricization of the New Testament by Bultmann extended to other doctrines. The New Testament doctrine of the preexistence of Christ and the "legend of the virgin birth . . . are clearly attempts to explain the meaning of the person of Jesus for faith."[102] Furthermore, when Bultmann came to the resurrection narratives in the Gospels, he wrote: "An historical fact which involves a resurrection from the dead is utterly inconceivable."[103] No matter how many witnesses there ostensibly might have been, it is still impossible to establish "the objective historicity of the resurrection."[104] In another passage Bultmann referred to the "legend of the empty tomb and the appearances" to the disciples. These are quite obviously "embellishments of the primitive tradition."[105] The following dogmatic statement depicts clearly the end result in the writings of Bultmann when the historical is relegated to the realm of the dubious:

> The resurrection itself is not an event of past history. All that historical criticism can establish is the fact that the first disciples came to believe in the resurrection. . . . The historical event of the rise of the Easter faith means for us what it meant for the first disciples—namely, the self-attestation of the risen Lord, the act of God in which the redemptive event of the cross is completed.[106]

To be sure, Kierkegaard would not have accepted the radical rejection of the supernatural suggested by Bultmann. The ultimate outcome of Bultmann can be understood only by taking his own methodology even further. Why did he stop with the *fact* that Jesus did live? Why not reject even that kernel of history? Bultmannian thinking soon falls prey to sheer subjectivism or total skepticism.

In an essay, "Modern Theology and Biblical Criticism," found in *Christian Reflections*, C. S. Lewis expresses his thoughts regarding the literary genre of the New Testament. Lewis suggests that an honest examination of the text leads the reader to the conviction that in the New Testament a *real personality*, Jesus Christ, has been met, and not a character of fiction or subjective interpretation. Why should it be supposed that because an account does not fit the interpreter's view of reality or what he thinks *could* have happened, that the written record is so quickly judged on that criterion alone?[107]

It would seem to be "begging the question" to assume that the miraculous was read back into the past by the followers of Christ. It may very well be true that the text does suggest that the disciples did *preach* what was in the New Testament; but they preached it because they were convinced that the events did *in fact* happen. The Christian cannot debunk history. The Christian faith holds that God entered history in His Son; the New Testament, inspired by God's Holy Spirit and written by Christ's devoted followers, is a record of what *did happen* in history and not merely mythological interpretations of totally natural events.

Two such diverse scholars as "traditional evangelical" Harold Lindsell and self-styled "new evangelical" Richard Quebedeaux agree that commitment to the inspiration and authority of the Bible is the *sine qua non* for the evangelical Christian. Lindsell has declared:

> Inspiration extends to all parts of the written Word of God and it includes the guiding hand of the Holy Spirit even in the selection of the words of Scripture. . . . If any part of it is not infallible, then that part cannot be inspired. If inspiration allows for the possibility of error, then inspiration ceases to be inspiration.[108]

In somewhat different terms, Quebedeaux affirms that "the complete reality and final authority of Scriptures in matters of faith and practice" stands first in the premises of contemporary evangelicals.[109]

Such contemporary concern regarding Scripture is a reaction
against the prevailing mood that debunks the conviction that one
can read Scripture and be certain that the sentences recorded are
indeed God's Word. As has already been observed, this posture
on errancy has a clear Kierkegaardian ring, for Kierkegaard
himself minimized all objective truth. His own words are: "Precisely because God wants Holy Scripture to be the object of faith
and an offense to any other point of view, for this reason there
are . . . discrepancies. . . ."[110] And, "The New Testament cannot absolutely . . . be normative for us."[111]

In many of Kierkegaard's writings the emphasis is on the
meeting between God and man, between Christ and disciple, instead of on reading and exegeting the recorded Word of God.
According to Kierkegaard, it is in that *meeting* that truth is conveyed and not in some revelation of God found in Holy Writ for
all time and for all persons. Should this be true, as Kierkegaard
suggested, then the only *essential* is that some two millennia ago a
figure died, a figure, who, his followers believed, was one with
God, and the preserved record of the New Testament is of virtually no importance for the twentieth-century disciple.

Contemporary scholarship continues to distinguish sharply
between what is referred to as "propositional revelation" and
"personal revelation." Although Kierkegaard never denied, personally, that there is an objective dimension of truth, nor that the
Bible is true, he did aver that Christianity can never be a collection of doctrinal propositions. In a moment of reflection, an
evangelical Christian must admit that Christianity *is* more than
the acceptance of a creed and the admission that specified data of
history are correct. Christianity *is* indeed a commitment to
Christ. And yet one must ask the question, Can that commitment to Christ which acknowledges the saving power of God
through the death and resurrection of His Son really be significant
if, concomitantly, the propositions found in the New Testament
affirming that Christ *is* the Savior are not accepted as true?

Kierkegaard was convinced that in "objectivity one tends to
lose that infinite personal interestedness in passion which is the
condition of faith."[112] He formulated a disjunction between personal revelation and propositional revelation. Perhaps this disjunction is not as absolute as Kierkegaard and those influenced
by him would suggest. Is not the proposition a very personal
vehicle for divine revelation? "God so loved . . . that he gave"

(John 3:16); "God was reconciling the world to himself in Christ" (2 Cor. 5:19); "he was raised on the third day" (1 Cor. 15:4). To cite Paul even further: "If there is no resurrection of the dead, then not even Christ has been raised. And if Christ has not been raised, our preaching is useless and so is your faith. More than that, we are then found to be false witnesses about God, for we have testified about God that he raised Christ from the dead. But he did not raise him if in fact the dead are not raised" (1 Cor. 15:13–15).

To be confronted by the resurrected Christ and to confess, "My Lord and my God," is surely the moment of salvation. But is that moment not true because biblical statements so affirm? Salvation in that commitment would surely lose credibility without the simultaneous acceptance of the biblical record with its witness to Christ's saving act. Taking Kierkegaardian influence full-course may lead to a religion so subjective that it can become unintelligible. It may be said that a religious faith without an objective standard will lead to a private faith that one can be sure of only on the basis of one's own feelings.

It is important to recognize that the New Testament is in fact an inspired document bearing witness to the self-revelation of God in Christ. An evangelical Christian is less interested in whether or not the quotations in the New Testament are the *ipsissima verba* of Jesus *in toto* than he is in affirming that the preserved record bears witness to the authoritative truth revealed by God. A Kierkegaardian emphasis may cause one to lose this aspect of divine revelation.

Paul's letter to the Corinthians clearly emphasizes that he depended on the truth of historical events and that his readers were expected to put emphasis on the datum of history and also on the interpretation of what that datum meant as recorded by the apostle himself.

ATHEISM: NIETZSCHE

Terry L. Miethe

*Terry L. Miethe is Associate Minister, First Christian Church, Pomona, California. He holds degrees from Trinity Evangelical Divinity School (M.A.), McCormick Theological Seminary (M.Div.), Saint Louis University (Ph.D. in Philosophy), and the University of Southern California (Ph.D. Cand. in Social Ethics). He is a member of Phi Beta Kappa, Alpha Sigma Nu, Phi Alpha Theta, Eta Sigma Phi, and Psi Chi honor societies and was a finalist and alternate for a Fulbright Fellowship to the United Kingdom in 1976. He has taught at Saint Louis University, Fuller Theological Seminary, Azusa Pacific College, and Regent College and has been a visiting scholar at the School of Theology at Claremont, California. Dr. Miethe has had ministries in Indiana, Illinois, and California. He has written two books—*Thomistic Bibliography: 1940–1978, with Vernon J. Bourke, *and* Augustinian Bibliography: 1970–1980—*and numerous articles in various scholarly periodicals, including* Augustinian Studies, The New Scholasticism, The Modern Schoolman, *and* Journal of the Evangelical Theological Society. *Dr. Miethe is a member of the Evangelical Theological Society, the American Philosophical Association, the Evangelical Philosophical Society, the American Academy of Religion, and the Society of Biblical Literature.*

CHAPTER SUMMARY

Philosophical questions, more than factual ones, are responsible for the drift away from the inspiration and/or inerrancy of Scripture. The thought of Friedrich Nietzsche has contributed to this drift. Therefore this chapter examines: Nietzsche: The Man and His Thought; Major Ideas in Nietzsche's Philosophy; Nietzsche on Absolutes and God; and Nietzsche on Scripture and Christian Values. The critical approach to Scripture, philosophical and cultural relativism, and the death-of-God theology of Nietzsche contribute strongly to the Weltanschauung that denies the reliability of Scripture.

ATHEISM: NIETZSCHE

$\mathbf{M}$ANY PEOPLE NO LONGER recognize the existence of absolutes. Everything is relative. In the discipline of ethics, discussions involving the resolution of conflicting ethical choices are no longer conducted in terms of "right" or "wrong" as if there were objective ethical norms. Rather, an action is based on the *subject* and the *situation* in which one is found. The ends justify the means. In philosophy, truth is no longer talked about as if there were absolute content to truth, i.e., a statement is true in and of itself. Rather, the "truth" is contingent on this system or that condition. In the history of philosophy, and indeed in the English language, there is no proper plural form of the word *logic*. A thing was judged logical or illogical based on an absolute standard of undeniable logical principles. Today, however, many talk, for example, as if "x" may be logical and therefore true in Western thought, but not logical or true in Eastern thought.

What is taking place in philosophy is also happening in theology today. Scripture is talked of as "reliable" or "infallible" but not "inerrant,"[1] of being inspired but not totally trustworthy. Many philosophical principles, or rather denials of historically accepted principles, have crept into modern theologies at the presuppositional level. The result is that a faithful interpretation of Scripture is made next to impossible. The real problem in the drift away from the inspiration and/or inerrancy of Scripture is not so much factual as it is philosophical. Therefore, it is important to trace the influences of the major philosophers that caused this drift. This chapter deals with the influence of Nietzsche.

Friedrich Wilhelm Nietzsche (1844–1900) was a product of his time. Van Riessen calls his time the calm before the storm. Nietzsche stands at the threshold of our time as the prophet of the coming century—the century our grandparents, parents, and we ourselves grew up in. He struggled throughout life to attach some real significance and meaning to his idea that man is self-sufficient. He felt that man is to be his own standard and is his own destiny. Van Riessen feels that it was the pressure to find humanistic answers that caused Nietzsche's mind to crumble.[2]

Nietzsche prophetically envisaged himself as a madman: to have lost God means madness.

> *The Madman.* Have you not heard of that madman who lit a lantern in the bright morning hours, ran to the market place, and cried incessantly, "I seek God! I seek God!" As many of those who do not believe in God were standing around just then, he provoked much laughter. Why, did he get lost? said one. Did he lose his way like a child? said another. Or is he hiding? Is he afraid of us? Has he gone on a voyage? or emigrated? Thus they yelled and laughed. The madman jumped into their midst and pierced them with his glances. "Whither is God" he cried. "I shall tell you. We *have killed him*—you and I. All of us are his murderers. . . . Is not night and more night coming on all the while? . . . God is dead. God remains dead. And we have killed him. . . ."[3]

When mankind discovers that it has lost God, universal madness will break out. This apocalyptic sense of dreadful things to come hangs over Nietzsche's thinking like a thundercloud. Much of Nietzsche's philosophy is a forceful denial of what philosophy had for thousands of years considered truth. Nietzsche said all truth is relative; man must make his own truth. He announced the death of God to mankind. This "death of God" was really a denial of absolutes in general and a denial of God, the supreme absolute, in particular.

There has been great disagreement about Nietzsche's philosophy, due largely to the Nietzsche legend that arose even before his death. Most of the legend can be traced to Nietzsche's sister, Elisabeth Förster-Nietzsche. For soon after her brother had become insane, she realized that his fame had begun its upward move. Elisabeth's interpretations of her brother's thought were immediately accepted almost everywhere. She was the guardian of yet unpublished material, so nobody could challenge her interpretations with any authority. She laid the groundwork for the two most common forms of the legend. By putting Friedrich's notes together in various forms and continually republishing the material with change after change, she helped foster the idea that her brother's thought was hopelessly incoherent. By bringing to her interpretations the heritage of her late husband's anti-semitic philosophy, she prepared the way for Nietzsche to be interpreted as a forerunner of the Nazis.

Only relatively recently has the true Nietzsche been presented to the public, and this largely through the efforts and great studies of Karl Jaspers and Walter Kaufmann.[4] But some points of Nietzsche's philosophy still remain unclear. Among these unclear points is the question of the death of God. Did Nietzsche only pronounce the death of God "culturally"? Did he in fact leave room for the existence of a transcendent Being—the Christian concept of God? Or does his philosophy (based on an examination of its consistency and its logic) do away with any possibility for Supreme Being? And what effect does his view have on Scripture?

NIETZSCHE: THE MAN AND HIS THOUGHT

Nietzsche's Early Life

Both of Nietzsche's grandfathers had been Lutheran clergymen, as had his father. One of the grandfathers had written a book on the eternal survival of Christianity. The Christianity of Nietzsche's pious home was distinctly patriotic, and he was named Friedrich Wilhelm Nietzsche after the reigning King of Prussia.

Although it is surprising, we learn from Nietzsche's writings that as a young man (1856–1868) he expressed impulses and thoughts belonging to his later philosophy. Even then Christianity had been an object of question and not just a form that provides assurance of profound truths. Jaspers substantiates this in the following quote:

> As early as this, Christianity has ceased to be just a form that provides assurance of profound depths and has become the object of a question: "Great revolutions are in the offing, once the masses

understand that all Christianity is based on assumptions; the existence of God, the authority of the Bible, immortality, and inspiration will remain problems forever. I have tried to deny everything: Oh, it is easy to tear down, but to build up!" He speaks of the *"break with everything that exists,"* of the "doubt whether humanity has not been misled for two thousand years by a phantom picture."[5]

In later years a gradually increasing activity replaced mere questioning and helped his determination to undermine Christianity, morality, and traditional philosophy.

Nietzsche was sent to Schulpforta at the age of fourteen and was given a *freistelle*—a scholarship covering room, board, and tuition. Schulpforta was a boarding school that was celebrated for its uncommonly outstanding humanistic teachers. Even though Nietzsche was greatly questioning Christianity already at this age, he had ideas of becoming a minister and he began the study of theology at the University of Bonn in 1864. At the university he was allured by Greek culture and he soon decided to go into classical philology as his main field of study.

At the age of twenty-four Nietzsche was called to the University of Basel. This surprised Nietzsche, as he had not yet received his doctorate. Soon after he got his professorship he served as a volunteer nurse in the Franco-Prussian war. He caught dysentery and diphtheria during this service and, after delivering his charges to a field hospital, required medical attention himself. He returned to Basel in October 1870, his health shattered. The possibility of an incomplete recovery from the dysentery and diphtheria has never been clarified conclusively, but after this sickness he had spells of migraine headaches and painful vomiting, which made him miserable repeatedly during the next ten years.

There is no indication of Nietzsche's madness prior to December 27, 1888. The day before, Nietzsche had fallen down in the street when he tried to stop a man from beating his horse. Overbeck, a former teacher and friend, went to his home the next day. Nietzsche rushed toward him, embraced him violently, and then sank, in twitches, back onto the sofa. Overbeck described his behavior:

> He launched forth in loud songs, ragings on the piano, scurrilous dances and leaps, and then uttered, "in an indescribably soft tone, sublime, wonderfully clairvoyant, and inexpressibly awesome things about himself as the successor to the dead God."

Nietzsche became increasingly demented until his death in 1900 in Weimar. Jaspers thinks that Nietzsche's madness was due to an organic brain disease that derived from an external cause.[6]

Nietzsche and Other Great Thinkers

Nothing in the world was as significant to Nietzsche as the great men whom he "devilized" or deified. He saw in Goethe, Napoleon, and Heraclitus unequivocal and indubitable greatness. Nietzsche thought others were so highly ambiguous that they must be evaluated in opposite ways, depending on the circumstances in which they appear. These great men were Socrates, Plato, and Pascal. Nietzsche always rejected the apostle Paul and Rousseau and almost always rejected Luther. He admired Thucydides and Machiavelli for their pellucid truthfulness and realistic incorruptibility. He declared that men like Kant and Hegel were merely his "servants" and "laborers," but his task was greater far than theirs. His was the task of value-legislation. Nietzsche thought of the model philosopher as a physician who applies the knife of his thought "vivisectionally to the very virtues of the time." He said, "They will have the attitude expressed in 'Plato's *Theages*': 'Each one of us would like to be lord over all men if possible or, even better, be God.'"[7]

Nietzsche's most famous friend was Richard Wagner. As a student, Nietzsche had been enamored by *Tristan;* he loved much of Wagner's music and considered the composer Germany's greatest living creative genius. Wagner's influence was what convinced him that greatness and real creation were still possible. Wagner inspired Nietzsche, first with a longing to equal Wagner, then with a desire to outdo him.

Nietzsche later broke his friendship with Wagner and viewed this event as the focal point that helped crystallize his basic intentions. Legend has it that Nietzsche, the pagan, broke with Wagner because in *Parsifal* Wagner turned Christian. This is plainly false. Nietzsche even made the comment: "If Wagner was a Christian, well, then Liszt was perhaps a Church father!" "What I never forgave Wagner? . . . that he became *reichs-deutsch.*"[8] Nietzsche, the champion of the ideals of Voltaire and the Enlightenment, advocated intermarriage between races and propagated the vision of the "Good European"—views that he never repudiated. Nietzsche had realized how dangerous Wagner was.

The Three Periods of Nietzsche's Thought

The course of Nietzsche's thought is usually divided into three periods: (1) 1872–1876, a time of veneration, resting on faith in culture and great geniuses; (2) 1876–1880, a period of faith in science combined with dissecting criticism; (3) 1880–1888, the era of the new philosophy. This three-part division rests on Nietzsche's own view of himself and coincides with his decisive transformations.

Period one: By the publication of the fourth of the *Untimely Meditations: Richard Wagner in Bayreuth,* Nietzsche and Wagner had already begun to drift apart. This break with the composer represented the end of the first period in his development. The best way to understand the first period is to compare and contrast it to the second. In the first period Nietzsche decried Socrates, the rationalist; in the second he tended to exalt him. In the first period culture, and human life in general, was depicted as finding its justification in the production of the genius, the creative artist, poet, and musician. In the second period Nietzsche preferred science to poetry, questioned all accepted beliefs, and pretty well played the part of a rationalistic philosopher of the French Enlightenment.

Period two: Characteristic of this second period is *Human, All-Too-Human.* In a sense this work is positivistic in outlook. Nietzsche attacked metaphysics in an indirect manner. He tried to show that the features of human experience and knowledge are capable of explanation on materialistic lines. He thought the moral distinction between good and bad had its origin in the experience of some actions as beneficial to society and of others as detrimental to it. Through the course of time the utilitarian origin of the distinction was lost and the result was the present distinction between good and bad.

Period three: In 1881 Nietzsche published *The Dawn of Day* in which he opened his campaign against the morality of self-renunciation. Also in 1881 the idea of eternal recurrence came to Nietzsche. In infinite time there are periodic cycles in which all that has been is repeated, and repeated again and again. This is similar to a Greek cyclical view of history. *Thus Spake Zarathustra,* with its ideas of Overman (or Superman) and the transvaluation of values, expresses the third period of Nietzsche's thought. Its poetic and prophetic style gives it the appearance of being the work of a visionary. In the third period Nietzsche explicitly stated his relativistic and pragmatist view of truth.

Looking back from the third phase, Nietzsche could see his entire path as a meaningful whole. To him the three phases appeared as an overpowering necessity, the dialectic of which had required precisely these three phases. In 1888 he finally gained a euphoria unprecedented in his long experience of illness and recovery. And within six months he wrote *The Birth of Tragedy: The Case of Wagner, Antichrist, Ecce Homo*, and *Nietzsche Contra Wagner*.

MAJOR IDEAS IN NIETZSCHE'S PHILOSOPHY

Eternal Recurrence

For Nietzsche's philosophy the idea of eternal recurrence is essential. It is the idea that in an infinite amount of time there are periodic cycles in which all that is past is repeated. To Nietzsche it was the most over-powering idea. This idea was not new; it had occurred in many ancient philosophies. Nietzsche set it over against the modern idea of linear, continual progress, and against Christianity.

Nietzsche had three presuppositions that he stated as supporting arguments: (1) He said things are always becoming and being transformed. The present situation is by no means final, but everything is in flux. Nietzsche thought Heraclitus, the philosopher of becoming, to be the philosopher who showed his philosophy most clearly. Heraclitus saw in the strife of opposites the basic principle of life. (2) Nietzsche presupposed the absoluteness of time. He thought change is part of being, and consequently temporality likewise. Space is a subjective form, but time is not. (3) He asserted the finiteness of space and the limitation of energy.

Nietzsche placed such importance on this idea of eternal recurrence because for him it finalized the "death of God" and, in addition, amounted to an overcoming of nihilism. He felt that eternal recurrence is not a surrogate to the loss of God but is superior to it. He declared that eternal recurrence is the "religion of religions." Thus the question is: God or cycle? Eternal recurrence is a physico-cosmological hypothesis.

A person is only himself when he lives in relation to transcendence. It seems that this necessity is inescapable. When he rejects one form of transcendence, some surrogate is bound to appear.

140

BIBLICAL ERRANCY

Nietzsche chose to live without God since his honesty (he thought) required him to believe that life with God involves self-deception. Just as his actual loss of communication with men gave rise to the association with his invented friend Zarathustra, so his denial of God had to give rise to a surrogate "god." In his middle period, when he was indirectly attacking metaphysics, he thought mankind was the power that provided a surrogate.

Nietzsche had the idea that the ability to create takes the place of freedom, or, in other words, is freedom. In the sense employed by the philosophy of *Existenz*, freedom exists in relation to transcendence. Freedom is the potentiality of a finite being. The decision as to what has eternal significance is made through freedom. That is, freedom exists historically as the union of the temporal and the eternal and as the decision that it itself is merely an appearance of eternal being. Nietzsche rejected this freedom. He professed to follow Spinoza because the latter denied the freedom of the will, the moral order in the world, and genuine evil. Creation without transcendence, or self-being without God, must lead to the two conclusions to which Nietzsche actually came. When human finiteness ceases to be evident as finiteness (it is no longer enclosed by any infinite; i.e., when creative freedom faces nothingness instead of transcendence in the classical sense), then either creation is absolutized as a temporal actuality to which no valid standard applies, or it is deified. Neither of these relates to classical transcendence. Nietzsche tried to express both consequences in a singularly daring language in which all logical thinking reverses itself. In assuming a position outside of morality, Nietzsche believed that he was in agreement with Jesus. Creation, which Nietzsche substituted for existential freedom as the sole immanent actualization of his kind of freedom, ends itself or is lost, since it has only itself to depend on.

But in Nietzsche's third period he became disillusioned with man's being able to "raise himself up by his own bootstraps." His last attempt to find a kind of transcendence, as we have seen, was in the form of eternal recurrence. He felt that this was in fact superior to the concept of a "god" that had been absolutized and made into a "God." It is evident that, if Nietzsche left any room for a "god," it is not the Christian concept of God. He clearly rejected the Christian concept of "God" as Spirit who transcends reality and breaks into it. The only "god" that he left room for is the "god" that comes into existence from the absolutizing of the idea of eternal recurrence. But it should be pointed out here that according to Nietzsche's own methodology the act of giving eternal recurrence the status of a transcendent absolute should be greatly questioned. Nietzsche's analysis that there is no absolute truth calls into question the giving of the status of transcendent absolute to anything, even eternal recurrence.

Nietzsche did not deny the idea of transcendence, and this (in the form of eternal return) was his "god." When Nietzsche became disillusioned with man as the possibility of creativity, he did not go to some form of "divine" transcendent Being. He turned to a circular view of history and the future in his doctrine of eternal recurrence. He said that he found no "God" in or behind nature.

Thus the question is not: Did Nietzsche believe in God? It is evident that he did not. The question becomes: What kind of transcendence did Nietzsche leave room for in his philosophy? This question is best answered by looking at a typology of transcendence.[9] The seven types of religious transcendence are: (1) *The retrospective dimension of transcendence.* Retrospective transcendence means that the direction in which the religious man transcends toward the Transcendent is a "backward" one. He tries to go back to a point of origin to find religious "reality." This is the characteristic feature of the primitive religious experience. (2) *The vertical dimension of transcendence.* Plato is an example of an "upward" transcendence. One leaves the world of shadows and ascends to the world of pure Forms above. Vertical transcendence is more explicit and more clearly religious in Plotinus. (3) *The eschatological dimension of transcendence.* This form of transcendence is possible only in the view that history is going somewhere. Hegel was the first to attempt to spell out an eschatological transcendence by the unfolding of Absolute Spirit in history. "Hegel wrote that God is dead and Nietzsche took it seriously."[10] Altizer saw the implications for the "death of God" in a kind of eschatological transcendence. Altizer said, "One must speak of God as a dialectical process rather than as an existent Being. . . ." This is why Altizer says Nietzsche was the first radical Christian.[11] (4) *The introspective dimension of transcendence.* This is the idea that a man can transcend in an "inward" direction or in "depth." This kind of transcendence is seen in the mystics. There seems to be a connection between a modern trend to transcend in "depth" and the rejection of some other directions of transcendence. Bishop Robinson is the classic modern example of "introspective" transcendence. (5) *The circumferential dimension of transcendence.* This is an outward transcendence toward the circumference of all things. According to Meister Eckhart, God is an infinite sphere whose center is everywhere and whose circumference is nowhere. That is, God is the boundaryless outer limit to man's transcendent quest. (6) *The foundational transcendence.* In reaction to the God "up there" or "out there," some modern "death of God" theologians, such as Bishop John Robinson, called for a downward transcendence of the "Depth" of our being. Paul Tillich's "Ground of Being" could be placed in the same classification. (7) Finally, *cyclical transcendence.* It is in this category that Nietzsche's willing of eternal recurrence best fits, although the cycles move ever onward and in this sense partake of a kind of eschatological transcendence too. The point is simply this: in denying the Christian God, Nietzsche did not avoid transcendence. He too tried to "go beyond" in a quest for the "eternal."

Nihilism

Nietzsche turned to nihilism, for nihilism is the negation of all values. It is the affirmation of the meaninglessness of all existence. Nietzsche was never able to break away from nihilism. For him reality was characterized by the eternal return to nothingness. He calls Brahmanism, Buddhism, and Christianity nihilistic religions because they have all glorified nothing—the very opposite of life—as the goal, the *summum bonum,* or as "God." [12]

The Superman Symbol

Nietzsche finally turned away from human actuality. He saw in the symbol of the superman a creed that expresses in an indefinite way what man will become when he conquers himself. The superman is a Caesar with the soul of Christ. He did not coin the word for superman, *Übermensch.* The *hyperanthropos* is to be found in the writings of Lucian, in the second century A.D. Nietzsche had studied Lucian. In German, the word had been used by Heinrich Muller, by Herder, by Sartre, and by Goethe (in a poem [*Zueignung*] and in *Faust* [Part I, line 490]).

Nietzsche later gave the term a new meaning. The English translation "superman" is misleading. Nietzsche's conception depends on the associations of the word *über* (over). Thus a better translation of the German word *Übermensch* would be "overman," not "superman." What was really present here is a substitute for the Godhead, like the doctrine of eternal recurrence, which plays that role at a later date: "God has died, our desire is now that the superman live."[13]

The Will to Power

The Will to Power was not Nietzsche's last work as is sometimes supposed. That work was abandoned by him before *The Antichrist* was written. Nietzsche's sister later uncritically took some of his notes that he did not intend to use or had already used and she posthumously brought them out in an edition called *The Will to Power*. The world, the universe, is a unity, a process of becoming. For Nietzsche the will to power is the inner reality of the universe. The will to power is an interpretation of the universe, a way of looking at it and of describing it, rather than a metaphysical doctrine about a reality that lies behind the visible world and transcends it. Subsequently Nietzsche reduced all drives to that single "will to power." Thus he offered not only an account of a variety of drives but also a doctrine of one single basic force.

NIETZSCHE ON ABSOLUTES AND GOD

Nietzsche thought he could proceed to the authentic truth by demolishing all that was established as eternal truth. Authentic truth was one with the source and illumined the path of living *Existenz* itself. A cognizing living being calls truth the way in which he conceives of his world. This life is the *sine qua non* of the mode of being of everything that has authentic value. Nietzsche believed that the concept of truth was nonsensical. "True-false" has to do only with relations between living beings. Thus truth for Nietzsche is something that has to be created.

Traditional absolutes such as truth, reason, justice, morality, Christianity, and Christ were not absolutes at all to Nietzsche. He believed that these were concepts created by man out of his human experience to help to explain that experience. But these concepts, or absolutes, lost their value for man (because man allowed these ideas to be absolutized) and thereby negate life. Nietzsche tried to make all these human "absolutes" relative. His method destroys every kind of absolute knowledge in order to replace it by the unchallenged possession of a determinate knowledge of particulars with which it can accomplish something within the world. Knowledge is valuable in that it impugns so-called absolute knowledge.

The Idea of God

In the time of the kings, Israel stood in the right—that is, the natural—relationship to all things. Their Yahweh was the expression of a consciousness of power, of joy in oneself, of hope for oneself. Through him victory and welfare were expected. The Israelites, through Yahweh, trusted nature to give what the people needed above all—rain. In the festival cult, sides of the self-affirmation of a people find expression. They are grateful for the great destinies that raised them to the top; they are grateful in relation to the annual cycle of the seasons and to all good fortune in farming and planting.[14] This was the view Nietzsche had of Israel's Yahweh. God is really nothing more than the Israelites affirming life, a response that is natural to mankind.

Yahweh changes at the hands of the priests of Israel. He is no longer an expression of the self-confidence of the people. All unhappiness is now a punishment for disobeying God, i.e., sin: "that most mendacious device of interpretation, the alleged 'moral world order,' with which the natural concepts of cause and effect are turned upside down once and for all."[15] Nietzsche uses "god" with a lowercase g when he is talking about how Israel stood in the right, natural relationship to all things. But when he talks about the concept god changing in the hands of the priests, he uses "God" with a capital G. Thus Nietzsche is saying that "god" was not a personal being to the Israelites during the time of the kings, but an idea of every people that is in power and has a good conscience. At the hands of the priests "god" became "God."
Nietzsche said:

> How can anyone today still submit to the simplicity of Christian theologians to the point of insisting with them that the development of the conception of God from the "god of Israel," the god of a people, to the Christian God, the quintessence of everything good, represents progress?[16]

So the priests changed the concept of God, and they were then helped by the apostle Paul. Nietzsche said that Paul invented "God" as a "God" who ruins the wisdom of the world. "God" is in truth merely Paul's own resolute determination to give the name "God" to one's own will.

Christianity then took up doctrines and rites from all the cults of the Roman Empire, the nonsense of all kinds of sick minds. This is how the final concept of "God" and Christianity came into being. Christianity had to become as sick, mean, and vulgar as the sick, mean, and vulgar needs it was intended to satisfy. Jesus, who brought blessings and victory to the poor, the sick, and the sinners, was but temptation in its most sinister and irresistible form. He was bringing men, in a roundabout way, to precisely those Jewish values and renovations of the ideal. This was all invented by the apostle Paul. Nietzsche said the whole realm of morality and religion belonged under the conception of imaginary causes. It is "the explanation of disagreeable general feelings." [17] This explanation of disagreeable general feelings was produced by trust in God. They are produced by the consciousness of good deeds.

Nietzsche declared that Christian doctrine, using absolute standards, relegates all art (creativity) to the realm of falsehood and in so doing condemns it. An example of these absolute standards is "God's absolute truth." Christianity, and its doctrine of God, had a furious, vindictive hatred of life implicit in its system of ideas and values. In order to be consistent with its premise, a system of this sort was forced to abominate art, which was for Nietzsche the ultimate in human expression of life. This the concept of God negated.

The "God is dead" insight dominated all the later writings of Nietzsche and was proclaimed even before 1872: "Either we die of this religion, or the religion dies of us. I believe in the primitive Germanic saying: All gods must die." Toward the end of the seventies he wrote: "The loss of faith is notorious, . . . and now follows the cessation of fear, of authority, and of trust." [18] Nothing remains but living according to the moment. The idea of God's death recurs in one new version after another.

The Rejection of God

Nietzsche rejected God because he thought God was a conjecture. He wanted man's conjecture limited to what was realistic. He said:

> Could you *think* a god? But this is what the will to truth should mean to you: that everything be changed into what is thinkable for man, visible for man, feelable by man. You should think through your own senses to their consequences. [19]

But what caused man to come up with this delusion? The degeneration of rulers and the ruling classes has made part of this possible. Nietzsche clearly attributed the "concept of God" to psychological causes without ever trying to explore the possibility of transcendence breaking into human history.

The basis for Nietzsche's rejection of God is fourfold: (1) God is a manmade conjecture. (2) Then Christianity took up doctrines and rites from the Roman Empire and compounded the error. (3) Christianity takes a basic need and absolutizes it and makes it transcend man. (4) The concept of God and religion are of great danger to mankind, in fact, so dangerous that they destroy any possibility for creativity in man.

Metaphysical thought from Plato and Christianity to Kant accepted and built on the theory of two worlds. Behind our world of the finite and perishable, of becoming, and of the temporal and illusory is a world of being in itself. That world is timeless, unending, eternal, and true. This concept expressed in religious terms is this: There is a God. Nietzsche was decidedly against this two-world theory.

Nietzsche's inquiry whether values could be maintained without supernatural sanctions was based on his "existential" questioning of God's existence. And because he really questioned it, he lacked Lessing's and Kant's easy conviction that our ancient values could be salvaged after the ancient God had been banished from the realm of philosophic thought. It is foolish to seek outside of mankind an absolute source of the values we hold.[20]

Nietzsche believed that the idea of God as truth, and truth as divine, is the same as the faith of Plato. Therefore he blamed Plato for the Christian concept of God just as he had blamed the Jewish priests, Paul, and the weak. God Himself turns out to be our longest lie. Here we must pause and take thought, said Nietzsche.[21]

In the past the fact that the ascetic ideal has so far governed all philosophy, and that truth was premised as Being, as God, or as supreme sanction was not allowed to be called into question. But now we have withheld our faith from the God of the ascetic ideal and we have to question even truth. This is so because the concept of truth was based, as was shown by Descartes, on the Christian concept of God. With this concept of God going by the board, so does our concept of truth. The only truth and the only

God man can have is that produced by him to enable him to enjoy life and to create.

In *Zarathustra*, Nietzsche declared that Zarathustra too cast his delusion beyond man at one time. The world was the work of a suffering and tortured god. The world, god, and himself all seemed a dream. It all seemed like "colored smoke before the eyes of a dissatisfied deity." [22] This probably refers to what happened to Nietzsche himself. As a young boy he believed in "god," and as a boy blamed the problem of evil on "god," but this all was as smoke before the eyes until he overcame himself.

In Christianity neither morality nor religion has even a single point of contact with reality. Nietzsche declared that Christianity is nothing but imaginary causes: "God," "soul," "ego," "spirit," etc. And on the other side of Christianity we have nothing but imaginary effects: "sin," "redemption," "grace," "punishment," etc. Christianity is intercourse between imaginary beings, imaginary natural science, and imaginary psychology. It is nothing but misunderstandings about the nature of man. [23]

God is the enemy of life. He is a concept that is totally against the instincts of life. He is the condemnation of these "natural" instincts. Life has come to an end, according to Nietzsche, where the "kingdom of God" begins. "Perhaps the day will come when the concepts 'God' and 'sin' will seem no more important to us than a child's toy and a child's pain seems to an old man." "And wouldn't this be—*circulus vitiosus deus?*" [24] (a vicious circle made god? or: God is a vicious circle?).

Kaufmann says that if Nietzsche proclaimed the death of God, it may be said he did not question all that is questionable. Beyond question the major premise of Nietzsche's philosophy is atheism. This is often the interpretation of Nietzsche by thinkers. It has even been said that Nietzsche's atheism was a reaction to the narrow-minded Christians of his provincial hometown (Figgis in particular). Kaufmann thinks that Nietzsche may appear to accept as an absolute presupposition the claim that there is no God. But in that case we would have laid our hands on a questionable assumption that he failed to doubt. But, according to Kaufmann, this is not a tenable position. Nietzsche was an atheist by instinct. [25] This I reject.

Nietzsche said the metaphysicians made the error of mistaking the spirit as the cause for reality. They made the spirit the very measure of reality, and called it God! Also in *Twilight of the Idols*, he talked about the "four great errors." The first of these is the error of confusing cause and effect. There is no more dangerous error than this. He called it the real corruption of reason. This error is hallowed among us and goes by the name of "religion" or "morality." Nietzsche plainly meant the concept of God. He was talking about the error of saying that the cause of mankind is "God." "The effect God" was caused by mankind, not the other way around.

Zarathustra says that God is thoroughly dead. He declares that a god became God.

> For the old gods, after all, things came to an end long ago; and verily, they had a good gay godlike end. They did not end in a "twilight," though this lie is told. Instead: one day they *laughed* themselves to death. That happened when the most godless word issued from one of the gods themselves—the word: "There is one god. Thou shalt have no other god before me!" An old grimbeard of a god, a jealous one, thus forgot himself. And then all the gods laughed and rocked on their chairs and cried, "Is not just this godlike that there are gods but no God?" He that has ears to hear, let him hear![26]

This is a plain denial of the metaphysical existence of God. Zarathustra was saying that God is a conjecture. Nietzsche plainly denied the Christian concept of God. He said so over and over again. The second period of Nietzsche's thought attacked metaphysics and the third attacked and denied the supreme absolute—God.

The extent of the rejection of God in Nietzsche, according to Jaspers and Kaufmann, is only cultural. Nietzsche did not deny the existence of God, they say. And it is true that in places Nietzsche's rejection was based on an analysis of culture. But even so, the "god" Nietzsche left room for is not a metaphysical transcendent Being. It must be remembered that Nietzsche totally denied the Christian concept of God in his writings. So even if Nietzsche was "only" pronouncing the cultural death of "God," his denial of the Christian God certainly indicates that he did not believe in any transcendent Being, as Spirit.

The Results of the Rejection

To escape nihilism (escaping seems involved both in asserting the existence of God and thus robbing this world of ultimate

significance and also in denying God and thus robbing everything of meaning and value) was Nietzsche's greatest and most
persistent problem. When Nietzsche made his great claim on a
deeper unattained source, he believed that it can be reached only
without God. "To rule and no longer be God's vassal—this is
the means left to us for ennobling man."[27]
    If what Nietzsche said is true, then his philosophy attempts to
initiate a new and higher human reality conceived as a way of
thinking that impels man upward. The question still remains as
to whether Nietzsche worked out the "how" of this view of man
that would indeed impel him upward. For, though God be dead,
His shadow still lives. Nietzsche suggested that man's nature
being what it is, there will probably be caves for thousands of
years to come in which His shadow will be shown. Yes, we still
have to vanquish even His shadow. But this is no easy task that
can be accomplished as a matter of course. In Nietzsche's view
man can place no trust in any power beyond himself. Thus he
must take his entire destiny in hand. The necessary purpose of
this intentionally nontranscendent thinking is to make man conscious of this very task.
    The absence of classical transcendence in his philosophy of life
places in man's hand all the possibilities of being as though he
were entirely subject to his control and capable of being realized
through his creative efforts. Thus we have the secret of human
nobility, a possibility of magnificent independence. In man must
be the heroic something that amounts to the reality of the world.
In opposition to classical transcendence, to God and morality,
Nietzsche demanded the "reinstatement of nature," the "recognition of a nature-morality," and "purely naturalistic values in
the place of moral values." Only insofar as Nietzsche involun-
tarily created for himself a substitute for God can the totality,
even momentarily, assume validity within a harmonious world
vision, and then only as the myth of a mon-atheism, so to speak.
    Many people make the inference that one could not stand life
if there were no God. As they say in the circles of the Idealists,
one could not stand life if it lacked the ethical significance of its
ground. Thus there must be a God (or an ethical significance of
existence). This Nietzsche forceably denied. Faith in God is dead
as a matter of fact. Now it is up to man to give his life meaning by
raising himself above the animals. We must make something of
ourselves. Our so-called human nature is precisely what we

would do well to overcome. The man who has overcome it Zarathustra called the overman. Once the sin against God was the greatest sin; but God died, and those sinners died with Him. To sin against the earth is now the most dreadful thing, and to esteem the unknowable higher than the meaning of the earth.

The results of the rejection of God for Nietzsche and the world are very great. Nietzsche said universal madness would break out when news of the death of God reached the ears of man. Nietzsche himself said he lived in a solitude that really did not exist for even Dante or Spinoza because Nietzsche did not have a "God" for company. He said his life (after 1885) consisted of a wish that somebody might make his truths appear incredible to him. Nietzsche felt that without "God" man had a solitude that was very hard to bear. He became insane during the time he was trying to find ways to bear it.

NIETZSCHE ON SCRIPTURE AND CHRISTIAN VALUES

On Christianity in General

Nietzsche believed that Christianity, far from being the fulfillment of Judaism, was the destruction of all that was good in Judaism. To him Judaism represented everything natural, every natural value, and these Christianity opposed. Christianity grew up as a form of mortal enmity against reality that has never yet been surpassed. He definitely thought that Christianity did come from Judaism. Some Jews produced an ultimate formula for its "instinct" that was logical to the point of self-negation. Nietzsche indicated that originally the Jews had distinguished all other powers on earth from themselves as "unholy," as "worldly," as "sin"; and they fell because they negated this insight, which was a form of reality. Part of the Jewish reality was that the Jews were "holy people," the "chosen people," and Christianity by universalizing this destroyed the reality with which the Jews were in touch.

Christianity was and is mortal enmity against the "lords of the earth." It is against the "noble" of the earth. It negates the body and wants only the "soul." Nietzsche said that Christianity is the hatred of the *spirit* (human spirit), of pride, courage, freedom, and liberty of the spirit. Christianity is the negation of everything human and good, of everything that is joyous.

Nietzsche said that when we hear the ancient bells ringing on a Sunday morning, we ask ourselves if it is really possible that a

Jew crucified two thousand years ago can command this recognition just because He said He was God's Son. He thought Christianity was an antiquity projected into our times from remote prehistory. He believed that the fact that the claim was believed was perhaps the most ancient piece of this heritage. Nietzsche said:

> A god who begets children with a mortal woman; a sage who bids men work no more, have no more courts, but look for the signs of the impending end of the world; a justice that accepts the innocent as a vicarious sacrifice; someone who orders his disciples to drink his blood; prayers for miraculous interventions; sins perpetrated against a god; atoned for by a god; fear of a beyond to which death is the portal; the form of the cross as a symbol in a time that no longer knows the function and the ignominy of the cross—how ghoulishly all this touches us, as if from the tomb of a primeval past! Can one believe that such things are still believed?[28]

Nietzsche thought that his account of the origin of Christianity was a historical insight that was now acceptable to the people of his time. Man had advanced far enough that the errors of Christianity could now be exposed, because people no longer believed them anyway.

Much of Nietzsche's attack on Christianity was similarly based on what he took to be the Christian repudiation of reason and the glorification of the "poor in spirit." He ever insisted that "the first Church fought against the intelligent ones." Nietzsche thought that the people to whom the Church addressed itself simply lacked the power to control, sublimate, and spiritualize their passions. They were "poor in spirit."

Christianity was in Nietzsche's eyes a necessary evil. Christianity as a substantive faith and dogma was alien to Nietzsche even from his youth. He affirmed it only as symbolic human truth. "The main doctrines of Christianity merely express the basic truths of the human heart," he wrote in 1862.

Nietzsche thought that Christianity rested on exceptions. The existence of God, immortality, biblical authority, inspiration were nonexistence for him. In *Beyond Good and Evil* he said that "Christianity has been the most calamitous kind of arrogance yet." He declared that men who were not good enough to be artists, not strong, not noble enough to see the difference in rank, were the men who as Christians held sway over the fate of Europe. One of the worst Christian errors was the "equal before

God" concept. The idea that men were equal and on a par with each other under God to Nietzsche was most annoying.[29] He felt that Christianity was inspired by the hatred of the weak against the strong. It has carried on a war to the death against the higher type of man. And it has been successful.

If all this is true about Christianity being successful over the higher type of man, why did Nietzsche not at least explore the possibility that it was Christianity that in fact produced the higher type of man? When one looks at world history and sees the genius in all forms, art, philosophy, law, that Christianity has inspired, one has to wonder why Nietzsche could not conceive that maybe true Christianity has the answers to man's nature and not "primitive nature" as he thought. Why did he not realize that the very spirit of gloom he accused Christianity of having really hung like a leaden cloud over himself? Nietzsche could not believe in God, and that, to a large extent, explains his interpretation of Christianity, of Paul, and of Jesus. According to him, everything found in Christianity and in Paul that deals with God, heaven, immortality, and judgment, is based on lies and is due to the power-lust of the "herd" and the priests. These lies stood in the way of Nietzsche's ideal of culture, and hence Christianity was his great enemy. He rejected it because he thought he could discern the exposure of these lies in his times.

On Jesus Christ

Nietzsche rejected the premise that Spirit came into the world in a supernatural way and that a Christian God or even a devil was responsible for its "intrusion" into nature. He thought Jesus did not presume anything special about His nature for Himself; this was the responsibility of Paul. Nietzsche, says Kaufmann, was "aware of the discrepancies between his picture and that which he found in the Gospels; but he thought that any differences could be explained in terms of the psychology of the disciples and first followers."[30]

Nietzsche respected the man Jesus to some degree but he did not believe He was anything but a man. Most famous among his pronouncements about Jesus is this statement: "In truth there was only one Christian, and he died on the cross."[31] Nietzsche's attitude depends on his conception of Jesus, and this conception is not only heretical theologically but it also does not recommend itself on purely historical grounds. He thought Jesus died too early. If He had not died at such an early age, Jesus would have recanted His teaching. Nietzsche meant that He would not have allowed anyone to make claims of deity for Him.

In one place Nietzsche would call Jesus the worst of men and in another the noblest. He scoffed at the cross, that most evil of trees, the most corrupting power; despite this he called it the most elevating of symbols. When he came to the root of the question, he knew he must choose between Jesus and the claims that center around Jesus on the one hand, and his own humanism, on the other. At this point he became the prophet of the Antichrist in his later writings. He thought it was a fundamental mistake to link Jesus with historical Christianity, or even the Christianity that (he thought) Paul created.

On Pauline Interpretation

Nietzsche said that without Paul there would be no Christendom. Paul, unable to live the Jewish law, not to speak of Jesus' so-much-more-demanding way of life, conceived of faith in Christ as a substitute. This was his "escape" and his revenge against the law and those who were able to follow it. Paul had the same experience that Luther had centuries later. He realized his inability to become the perfect man of the clerical ideal and one day he began to hate, as Luther had, the clerical ideal, the saints, and the whole clergy. Faith that is really an escape and revenge, a way to screen one's fanatical hatred, is the essence of the Christianity of Paul, Augustine, and Luther. Nietzsche thought that Paul alone made it possible for these later resentful people to consider themselves Christians. Paul substituted faith in Christ for the Christlike life.[32]

Nietzsche really thought that Paul, whose home was in the main seat of Stoic enlightenment, intentionally lied and made up the story that he had had a vision of Jesus (on the road to Damascus). Paul dressed up a hallucination as *proof* that the Redeemer still lives. He even said that Paul did not believe the hallucination himself:

> Paul wanted the end, *consequently* he also wanted the means. What he himself did not believe, the idiots among whom he threw his doctrine believed. His need was for power; in Paul the priest wanted power once again—he could use only concepts, doctrines, symbols with which one tyrannizes masses and forms herds. What is the one thing that Mohammed later borrowed from Chris-

tianity? Paul's invention, his means to priestly tyranny, to herd
formation: the faith in immortality—*that is, the doctrine of the
"judgment."*[33]

Nietzsche called Paul one of the most ambitious and obtrusive of
souls. Paul, to him, was as superstitious as he was crafty.
Nietzsche believed that without Paul we would scarcely have
heard of this small Jewish sect whose master died on the cross.
Paul was the originator of the idea that some good thing must die
for sins, whether it be the world, or history, or reason, or joy, or
the peaceful contentment of other men.

How did Nietzsche get such a perverted idea of Christianity
and of Paul? It must be remembered that the religion with which
Nietzsche came in contact had little to do with Christianity, at
least in most of its followers. It had become nothing more than a
meek moralism. The Christian ideals had given way to amiabil-
ity and a reasonable disposition. In Nietzsche's time Christianity
was honored only as tradition. It, for the most part, was empty of
any biblical content.

On Christian Morality

Religion and morality were viewed by Nietzsche largely,
though not entirely, as modes of appearance of the will to power
of the powerless. Morality in the guise of slave-morality is the
means to dominance by the poorly endowed. The emperor's
misuse of power, Nietzsche thought, brought about the victory of
the morality of the powerless throughout Europe. The moral
concepts of Christianity are the means of allowing weakness to
gain the mastery over misused power, the result being that
neither the vanquished power of Rome nor the newly constituted
power of Christianity could, as power, represent the higher
values. Nietzsche said that Roman power was too crude, while
Christian power was wielded by inferiors.

Moral claims in Christianity are unconditional and are taken
to be universally binding. Christianity bases its morality on the
law of God. Christianity, according to Nietzsche, assumes from
the outset that man does not and cannot know what is good and
what is bad for him. Man believes in God who alone knows these
things. Christian morality is a command issuing from a transcendent source. Nietzsche was totally against this. He said that
this view is beyond all criticism; it has truth only if God is the

truth. It stands or falls with the belief in God. And for Nietzsche it fell there because God had died.

Much of Nietzsche's stand against Christianity grew from his opinion that Christianity has tended to consider sexuality as necessarily base. Nietzsche thought this because of his misunderstanding of Paul, Augustine, and early church history. Instead of seeing that the sex drive might be sublimated, Christianity repudiated it. He thought that a good example of this attitude was Jesus' statement that if a part of your body offends you, you should cut it off.

To Nietzsche there is strictly speaking neither unselfish behavior nor completely disinterested contemplation. These are only sublimations in which the essential element would appear to be so flighty that it is discoverable only through the most refined observation. In all ethical matters, Nietzsche declared there were no ethical phenomena. There are only ethical interpretations of phenomena. And this interpretation, for Nietzsche, was of nonethical origin.

On the Old and New Testaments

Nietzsche liked the Jewish Old Testament. He said that in it were men, things, and speeches in so grand a style that Greek and Indian literature have nothing to compare with it. He thought that the Old Testament told a story of man close to that of the "natural man" he sought. He believed that to have put the Old Testament together with the New Testament to form one book was perhaps the greatest "sin against the spirit" that literary Europe had on its conscience. For the Old Testament was "the most powerful book," and for it he had only the highest admiration.

Nietzsche said he did not love the New Testament. Yet he felt ill at ease in his judgment about the New Testament because, at least in tradition, the people of his day had respect for it. Over and over again Nietzsche would dismiss the New Testament with a simple statement and then go on to make a good statement about the Old Testament. In the Old Testament he found great men and, to him, one of the rarest things on earth, the naïvete of a strong heart.[34] Of the New Testament Nietzsche said that it was subtle of God to learn Greek when He wished to become an author, and not to learn it better. This statement is a rather plain indication that Nietzsche thought that the New Tes-

tament claimed, through Paul, to have been written by God, but
that he did not put the same claim to the Old Testament text.[35]

EVALUATION AND CRITIQUE

In Regard to Nietzsche and Contradiction

There are many examples of contradiction in Nietzsche. Any
attempt to understand him calls for understanding his inconsis-
tencies. Inner contradiction was not accidental for Nietzsche. To
arrive at a meaningful interpretation of his contradictory relationship with Christianity, one must put all the statements in
their context and try to interpret them accordingly.[36]

In Nietzsche's view such contradiction expresses the only
procedure that is absolutely necessary after "God is dead." He
called ideals "idols" when they are past, but they signified truth
to him when they belonged to the future. "He who no longer
finds greatness in God does not find it at all—he must deny it or
create it." Nietzsche intended to create it: "You call it the self-
destruction of God; but He is only shedding His outer covering. . . . You shall see Him again soon, beyond good and evil."[37]

In Regard to Nietzsche's Metaphysics

It is not Nietzsche's insight into the limits of science, but
rather his account of truth as illusion, the annulment of all truth
within a constantly recurring circle of ever-changing aspects,
that led him to a skeptical questioning of reason in general.
Whether he dealt with morality, truth, or the death of God, he
seemed always to become lost in nothingness. But what
Nietzsche intended was to pass by means of those extremes to a
being that cannot be rationally apprehended. He sought to reach
this being by dissolving or breaking through reason. His attitude
toward his own method of world-exegesis was self-contradictory.
At times he saw in it the possibility of soaring above life and
discovering true inner strength capable of mastering the antinomy, but at other times he was ready to repudiate this destruc-
tive knowledge of the cognitive process as a logical impossibility.

There are basically three ways to criticize Nietzsche's
philosophy. (1) *Logical criticism:* To proceed logically is to show
that Nietzsche's pronouncements are self-contradictory. But it is
difficult to separate purely verbal contradictions from real ones.
(2) *Criticism of content:* Criticism can deal with what is asserted

and point out errors in fact; this is the best approach. One could probably point out by Hebrew exegesis many errors in what Nietzsche thought was the Israelite concept of "god" and Paul's part in inventing the Christian concept of "God." (3) *Existential criticism:* Finally, criticism may undertake to interpret Nietzsche's *Existenz* as this is disclosed in his books, his letters, and the course of his life. To be sure, *Existenz* is not an object that can be known, and existential interpretation (interpretation being one kind of criticism) is not an expression of knowledge about another person. The most valid types of criticism for any philosopher are logical criticism and criticism of contents.

Reasons Nietzsche's Eternal Recurrence Is Inadequate

It seems that Nietzsche's form of transcendence is inadequate for several reasons:

1. It has no object. Nietzsche denied that there is any metaphysical transcendent Being behind nature. He thought that eternal recurrence might give man time to improve. He thought that eternal recurrence is superior to the very concept of "God." But nowhere did he explain how this change is to take place if what we have is only a cyclical process. Nietzsche's form of transcendence is inadequate because it does not have the power to cause change. There is no object to break into the cyclical process.

2. Nietzsche's form of transcendence is inadequate because it cannot be attained. It seems that Nietzsche posited eternal recurrence mainly to escape nihilism. Nowhere does one find any discussion of how it is to be attained. About all that is said is it will happen over a great period of time. It seems that there are two ways to interpret the possibility of eternal recurrence. First, in the course of recorded history over a period of several thousand years at the very least there will be a return at least culturally to what was before so that the future can be changed. This is not true eternal recurrence because it is not really "recurrence" in the cyclical meaning of the term. Or, second, over vast periods of time there is a complete return of the eons past. Either way it does not seem that eternal recurrence is attainable; nor does there seem to be any phenomenological or historical proof for a cyclical view of history.

3. Eternal recurrence is also inadequate because it does not fulfill Nietzsche's own aspirations for it. Even if it were attain-

able, eternal recurrence does not seem to escape nihilism. Nietzsche's "god" is inadequate because it glorifies nothing. Eternal recurrence understood properly—i.e., as a cyclical view of history—ends up in nihilism, as do religions without a "transcendent object." Eternal recurrence is inadequate because there is no indication that it can fulfill Nietzsche's ideas.

4. It is inadequate because it is inconsistent with other elements of Nietzsche's philosophy. It is inconsistent with Nietzsche's methodology. According to his own view of truth, it is not right to give the status of an "absolute" to eternal recurrence or anything else. It would seem that to absolutize even eternal recurrence would be to do the very thing to "life" that Nietzsche was fighting against in denying the traditional absolutes. Eternal recurrence is inconsistent with Nietzsche's view of truth and with his own methodology.

Thus Nietzsche's philosophy of rejecting traditional absolutes is entirely inadequate because the substitute that it proposes in place of God to escape nihilism is totally inadequate. And it goes without saying that if Nietzsche's foundations for atheism crumble, then so does the heart of his argument against absolute truth and an inerrant revelation from God.

In Regard to Nietzsche's Rejection of Absolutes

Nietzsche rejected all standard "absolutes": truth, reason, the state, justice, morality, and Christ. He felt that nothing was to be considered "absolute" in the sense that philosophy and religion had considered things so in the past. Human beings had believed reason, morality, and God to be objectively valid. But Nietzsche said that none of these are objectively valid. In fact nothing can be "objectively valid" for Nietzsche. These concepts were created by man out of his human experience to help explain that experience. These "absolutes" lost their value for man because man allowed these ideas to be absolutized and thereby to negate life.

Nietzsche had to replace the absolutes he rejected with absolutes of his own in order to escape nihilism. (The question is, of course, Did he ever escape nihilism?) In his philosophy these absolutes were developed during his third period. To escape nihilism he tried to develop the concepts of the superman symbol, the will to power, and eternal recurrence, and these became his attempts at absolutes. In the end he had rejected all but eternal recurrence, which he felt was much superior to all the religious concepts of the world. Eternal recurrence was the religion of religions for Nietzsche. But he never worked out his absolute's place in reality in relation to how it was to provide the force to lift man to the place where he could say yes to life. Many scholars who have studied Nietzsche, e.g., Kaufmann, think this caused Nietzsche untold problems in his attempt to work out his philosophy.

In Regard to Nietzsche's Rejection of Scripture

Nietzsche's view of Scripture is obvious from his view of absolutes in general and God in particular. Although he liked the Old Testament as literature, he laughed at the idea that any part of the Bible, either the Old or the New Testament was the verbally inspired word of God. He said that Christianity was based on assumptions, e.g., the existence of God, the authority of the Bible, and inspiration. One could certainly make a good case for believing that Nietzsche did not at all understand the Old Testament or the New. He did at least indicate in his writings that he understood the New Testament to have claimed divine authorship.

Nietzsche's philosophy, like much of the thought of his day, had profound effects historically on the current question of inerrancy or the trustworthiness of Scripture. Three tenets of his philosophy laid much of the ground for dismissing Scripture: (1) God is dead, (2) truth is relative, and (3) there are no absolutes, at least in the classical sense. If there is no God, then the whole question of inerrancy is superfluous. Obviously, without God Scripture is not inspired by anything but mortal man and is certainly not inerrant. If truth is relative, even if there were a God or some validity to scriptural teaching, there is no way we can say it speaks absolute truth to us today. And if there are no absolutes, knowledge itself is called into question, so even if there were "truths" of value to modern man in Scripture, there would be no way we could know this objectively.

Many theologians of the late nineteenth century and the early twentieth century were greatly affected by the undermining effects of Nietzsche's philosophy. If there is reason to doubt the validity of reason, truth, and even knowledge, and if there are no absolutes, then the Bible cannot possibly be what Christianity has claimed it to be for hundreds of years. Thus it follows that we must be honest with ourselves as theologians and philosophers and speak the truth about Scripture: it cannot possibly be inerrant!

Influence of Nietzsche on the Errancy Position

Few if any modern errantists would claim Nietzsche as a mentor. However, there are several ways in which Nietzsche made important contributions to the "air" errantists breathe. First, Nietzsche added to the critical approach to Scripture that informs the errancy position. Second, Nietzsche contributed significantly to the philosophical and cultural relativism that leads to a denial that any book (including the Bible) can transcend cultural relativity and convey absolute and eternal truths. Third, Nietzsche's logic that declares, "When God died, all absolute values died with him" should cause an errantist to rethink his position. If an absolute God is needed for absolute truth, then what does the denial of the absolute truth of Scripture imply about one's view of God? To deny that "the Bible cannot err" the errantist must either (1) grant that the Bible is not the Word of God or (2) by logical implication he must hold that God can err. The root problem for the errantist may be more theological than bibliological. By *logical implication* the errantist must deny the traditional God (who cannot err) and replace Him with some other form of transcendence, whether Nietzsche's variety or not. But like Nietzsche, the errantist who believes the Bible is the Word of God and yet claims it affirms error has *logically* (if not actually) denied the traditional Christian view of an absolutely truthful God.

NONCOGNITIVISM: WITTGENSTEIN

John S. Feinberg

John S. Feinberg is Assistant Professor of Systematic Theology at Western Conservative Baptist Seminary. He is a graduate of the University of California, Los Angeles (B.A.); Talbot Theological Seminary (M. Div.); Trinity Evangelical Divinity School (Th.M.); and the University of Chicago (M.A., Ph.D.). He has written Theologies and Evil *and has articles pending publication and is in the process of writing several books. A second-generation Hebrew-Christian, he has served in Jewish Missions and held a pastorate before taking up his present position. He is a speaker at prophetic conferences in the United States and Canada. Dr. Feinberg is a member of Phi Beta Kappa, (U.C.L.A.), the American Philosophical Association, the Evangelical Philosophical Society, and the Evangelical Theological Society.*

CHAPTER SUMMARY

The philosophy of Ludwig Wittgenstein divides itself into two basic periods. The philosophy of his earlier period is reflected primarily in his *Tractatus Logico—Philosophicus*, while the essence of his later thought is contained in *Philosophical Investigations*. Though Wittgenstein never discussed the matter of biblical inerrancy, there are many notions in both periods of his thought that, if adopted, would necessitate a rejection of inerrancy. While such notions could be used to deny inerrancy, the basic conclusion from a study of Wittgenstein's philosophy (earlier and later) is that he would have considered the whole debate over inerrancy nonsensical.

7 *John S. Feinberg*

NONCOGNITIVISM: WITTGENSTEIN

FEW PEOPLE WRITE serious philosophy. Even fewer produce a whole system of philosophy. Consequently, the genius of Ludwig Wittgenstein is truly remarkable, for during his lifetime he wrote two different systems of philosophy. Moreover, the second system is a corrective to the errors Wittgenstein himself perceived he had made in his earlier philosophical reflections.

Ludwig Wittgenstein led a most intriguing and unusual life. He was born in Vienna on April 26, 1889, to parents of mixed Jewish descent. Though they were partially of Jewish descent, they considered themselves Christians. Wittgenstein's mother was a Roman Catholic, and Wittgenstein was baptized and brought up in Roman Catholicism. He had various interests, such as music, aeronautics, engineering, and pure mathematics. At various stages in his life he was a soldier, a village schoolmaster in Lower Austria, a gardener in a monastery, a porter at a hospital during World War II, and a professor of philosophy at Cambridge University. It was Wittgenstein's interest in the philosophy of mathematics that led him to visit Frege and to study under Bertrand Russell at Cambridge. At Cambridge he also studied under G. E. Moore, and both Russell and Moore agreed that Wittgenstein was a brilliant student. Before long, they found themselves discussing philosophical issues with him on equal terms.

Wittgenstein left Cambridge to serve in the Austrian army when World War I broke out. While he was on leave from the army in 1918, he wrote his first book, which became known as *Tractatus Logico-Philosophicus*. Years later he submitted the work for his Doctor of Philosophy degree at Cambridge. The *Tractatus* had a considerable influence during Wittgenstein's lifetime as well as after. For example, the Vienna Circle claimed to be greatly influenced by it. Interestingly, Wittgenstein never thought himself a logical positivist. In fact, he claimed that the Vienna Circle never really understood his work in spite of their avowal of its influence on them.

Most of Wittgenstein's writings were published after his death in 1951. His later philosophy, contained in its essential dimensions in the *Philosophical Investigations*, has had a considerable influence on contemporary philosophy. Not only the brilliance of his solutions to philosophical problems but also his very method of approaching such problems has been greatly influential in shaping much of the work in philosophy in the British Isles and America during the 1960s and 70s.

Wittgenstein made a distinct impression not only through his writings but also through his personal lifestyle and his devotion to philosophy. Of his passion for philosophy W. Donald Hudson says:

> "We have never *seen* a man thinking before!" some Swansea students are reported to have said after they first heard Wittgenstein discussing philosophy. The price of genius is often that its possessor must live on the brink of mental illness and some of those who knew him best say that Wittgenstein did so throughout his life. His passion for philosophy was the kind of passion which more frequently induces despair than elation. He worked at the subject with a kind of anguish, feeling each intellectual difficulty as an intolerable burden. Neurotically, he worried lest he would die before he had solved the problem. He appears to have been completely without desire for public acclaim. Only the problems interested him, not the honours which sometimes accrue to distinguished academics. His intellectual integrity made a profound impression on his pupils.[1]

While Wittgenstein's life and work have greatly influenced philosophy, they have also had much significance for religion. Though Wittgenstein never considered himself a religious believer, he came to have a great appreciation for Christianity and respect for believers. His views are enormously important for theological issues in view of their profound influence in shaping the philosophical milieu of our times and in view of his ideas on religious issues. Having acknowledged his importance for theology, however, one should not assume that Wittgenstein spoke to all theological issues. He certainly never spoke of the inerrancy issue, for example, though his views on such matters as philosophy of language have vast implications for an issue such as inerrancy. In particular, there are many notions within his philosophy that, if adopted, could lead one to reject inerrancy. My purpose is to present those notions and show their relation to inerrancy. Given this general purpose, I shall be arguing the following theses: (1) in Wittgenstein's philosophy there are concepts that could, but need not, lead one to claim that the Bible is errant, but (2) the overriding conclusion to be reached from both the earlier and later periods of his thought is that Wittgenstein would claim that it is nonsensical[2] (though a different kind of nonsense in each period) and mistaken even to raise and discuss the issue. Such a method of denying inerrancy is a more radical way to reject it than merely to claim that Scripture has errors. In fact, it is a far more radical denial than most contemporary evangelical errantists would be willing to make.

In order to demonstrate the truth of these two theses, after presenting some preliminary matters, I shall turn to the thought of the earlier Wittgenstein, and my focus will be on the *Tractatus Logico-Philosophicus* with its picture theory of language and its implications. I shall then turn to the philosophy of the later Wittgenstein, and my discussion will center on the notions of the *Philosophical Investigations*. The main notion expounded will be his concept of a language-game and the theory of language that stems from it. Following the presentation of Wittgenstein's views, there will be an evaluation of Wittgenstein's position.

At the outset, it would be helpful to mention several items that will set the framework for discussion. First, in holding that Wittgenstein's philosophy is important to biblical inerrancy, I am not claiming that Wittgenstein personally rejected or accepted the doctrine. In fact, it seems rather clear that he did not make any direct statements in his writings about the issue, though I think it is possible to tell what he would have said about the issue if he had addressed it.

Second, I want to clarify what I am *not* attempting to demonstrate in this study. I am not trying to draw a causal relation

between Wittgenstein's views and a rejection of biblical inerrancy by contemporary evangelicals or nonevangelicals. I do not
know, nor could I *prove* in regard to any specific person, that his
rejection of inerrancy stems from an acceptance of Wittgenstein's
philosophy as a whole or in part. That Wittgenstein's philosophy
has been important for twentieth-century thought is undeniable.
That those who reject inerrancy do not come to such a conclusion in an intellectual vacuum also seems obvious. Nonetheless, I
am not interested in accusing anyone of denying biblical inerrancy as a result of an acceptance of Wittgenstein's notions.
Instead, it is my purpose to show that there are many concepts in
Wittgenstein's thought that, when applied to Scripture and
taken to their logical conclusion, *could* lead one to reject biblical
inerrancy.

Finally, it seems absolutely crucial initially to delineate the
concept of inerrancy that is presupposed for this discussion.
Otherwise, the relevance of Wittgenstein's views to inerrancy
may be at best hard to discern. In this study I am assuming a
notion of inerrancy that rests ultimately on truth and falsity.
Simply put, any true statement is inerrant, and any false claim is
errant, whether it is a biblical or nonbiblical proposition under
discussion.[3]

Philosophy of the *Tractatus*

According to Donald Hudson, there are two important features of Wittgenstein's philosophy (earlier and later). Throughout his life Wittgenstein was concerned with the problem of the
meaning of language and with an understanding of the nature of
reality. Obviously, the two are connected, for language in some
way is supposed to relate to the world.[4] Hudson's point, then, is
that Wittgenstein was always concerned with philosophy of language and ontology. Nowhere are these emphases so evident as
they are in the *Tractatus*. The theory of language of the *Tractatus*
is the picture theory of language. Wittgenstein states, "The
proposition is a picture of reality. The proposition is a model of
the reality as we think it is."[5] A simple enough statement, one
might think, but in order to understand it, one has to explain not
only how Wittgenstein thought propositions picture reality, but
also how he conceived the nature of reality (philosophy of language plus ontology). In fact, an explanation of the latter must
precede the former.

Ontology of the Tractatus

According to Wittgenstein, "The world is the totality of facts, not of things,"[6] or conversely, "The world divides into facts."[7] What is a "fact"? Wittgenstein answers that a fact is a state of affairs *(Sachverhalt).*[8] Initially, one might think it strange for Wittgenstein to make such claims, for it would seem that the world is the totality of things (objects), not the totality of facts. Wittgenstein does say that "objects form the substance of the world";[9] i.e., they are the "stuff" out of which the world is made. But then why does he persist in claiming that the world is the totality of states of affairs, not the totality of things? Pitcher clearly explains the answer as follows:

> Whatever the world is the totality of, it might be argued, a complete list of them ought to tell us what the world is like, ought to provide a complete description of the world. But this is not the case if the world is the totality of things. From a list of all the objects that there are, one can derive only a very inadequate idea of what the world is like. If you are asked to describe a room, and in reply simply list the articles contained in it plus the walls, windows, doors, and so on, you would have performed your job very poorly. What was wanted was not just a list of objects, *but also an account of what they are like and how they are arranged in the room*[10] (emphasis added).

The italicized portion above precisely hits the point. Wittgenstein wants to know not only what objects are in the world, but also what sorts of things they are and how they are related and arranged in regard to one another. Of course, once one begins to speak of such matters, his concern is states of affairs (facts), not merely the *objects* from which the states of affairs that make up the world are constructed.

If the world is the totality of states of affairs, then it becomes important to know what sorts of things states of affairs are. In response, states of affairs have four basic characteristics. First and fundamentally, Wittgenstein claims that a state of affairs (fact) is a combination of objects or things.[11] "In the state of affairs objects hang one in another, like the links of a chain."[12]

Second, Wittgenstein held that states of affairs are either complex (molecular) or simple (atomic), though he certainly spoke most often of atomic facts. Complex facts are reducible to atomic facts, but atomic facts are irreducible. Wittgenstein does not particularly help us understand the distinction, since he gives no examples of an atomic fact. Let me suggest a possible example: The proposition "the cat on the mat is drinking milk from a bowl" presents a complex state of affairs. That state of affairs can be analyzed into *at least* the following simpler states of affairs: (1) there is a cat on a mat; (2) there is a bowl on or next to that mat; (3) there is milk in the bowl; and (4) the cat is drinking the milk. Wittgenstein argues emphatically that all simple or atomic states of affairs "are independent of one another."[13] By this he means that the existence of one elementary state of affairs neither entails nor excludes any other elementary fact. For example, the cat's being on the mat entails neither that there must be nor that there cannot be a bowl of milk also present on or next to the mat, nor does either state of affairs entail the cat's drinking or not drinking milk from the bowl. Moreover, though atomic facts cannot be further reduced to simpler *facts,* they are not absolutely simple, for they are composed of components, but those components are not further atomic facts. They are objects (things). As Wittgenstein states, "The object is simple."[14] Objects "form the substance of the world. Therefore they cannot be compound."[15] As mentioned, though, objects can be configured into atomic states of affairs.[16] Since objects can be configured into *different states of affairs,* Wittgenstein claims that "the object is the fixed, the existent; the configuration is the changing, the variable."[17]

Third, for Wittgenstein a state of affairs may be either possible or impossible, i.e., logically possible or impossible. He claims that "objects contain the possibility of all states of affairs."[18] Moreover, in regard to an object, "the possibility of its occurrence in atomic facts is the form of the object."[19] Thus, for Wittgenstein certain *combinations* would be possible and others impossible for each object. As Hudson explains:

> Wittgenstein offered no examples of objects but *if* a note of music were an object, a possible state of affairs would be for it to be loud; an impossible, for it to be red. "Possible" and "impossible" in this connexion are used in a logical sense. The "form" of an object is a matter of what it is logically possible for the object to be or do in conjunction with other objects.[20]

Finally, any possible state of affairs may be true or false of any possible world, including the world that is *actual.* In regard to the actual world, Wittgenstein distinguishes what he calls positive and negative facts. As he claims, "The existence of atomic facts we also call a positive fact, their non-existence a negative fact."[21] Both kinds of facts relate to us the nature of the world, and the "totality of facts determines both what is the case, and also all that is not the case."[22] If one knows what is and what is not the case, i.e., the totality of facts, then one knows everything there is to know about the world, given that Wittgenstein claims that the world is the totality of facts.

The Picture Theory of Language

In the preceding discussion, I have set forth the ontology of the *Tractatus*, but how does language relate to such a world in which simple objects are configured into simple states of affairs that are then configured into complex states of affairs? The answer is Wittgenstein's picture theory of language. Wittgenstein claims that propositions picture reality. But how do they do that? One would expect to find that just as there are complex states of affairs, there must be propositions that are complex. One would further expect that just as Wittgenstein claims that complex states of affairs can be analyzed into simple or elementary states of affairs, so complex propositions can be analyzed into elementary propositions. Moreover, just as those elementary states of affairs are composed of objects configured together, so one would expect that within elementary propositions there are unanalyzable constituents from which the propositions are "configured." One would expect all of this if Wittgenstein literally means that there must be something about the very nature and structure of propositions that pictures (or even mirrors, one might say) reality as Wittgenstein has described it, and one does find precisely such an account of language.

First, corresponding to the simplest element of reality, Wittgenstein claims there is a simplest element of a proposition. These simple elements are what he calls "simple signs," and he claims that "the simple signs employed in propositions are called names."[23] One should not think that only proper nouns such as "John," "Mary," and "Jim" are names. Such signs as "John," "Mary," and "Jim" do qualify as simple signs, but the key point is that for Wittgenstein names stand for objects. There is a one-to-one correspondence between objects, the simples of reality, and names, the simples of propositions. As Wittgenstein states, "The name means the object. The object is its meaning."[24]

When a name appears in a proposition, it represents the object.[25] Moreover, just as objects cannot be further analyzed, Wittgenstein claims that "the name cannot be analyzed further by any definition. It is a primitive sign."[26]

Second, corresponding to elementary states of affairs are elementary propositions. Just as elementary states of affairs result from a connection and configuration of objects, so the linguistic means for picturing such states of affairs results from a connection of names. "The elementary proposition consists of names. It is a connexion, a concatenation, of names."[27] The relation between elementary propositions and reality is such that "to the configuration of the simple signs in the propositional sign corresponds the configuration of the objects in the state of affairs."[28] Consequently, "the simplest proposition, the elementary proposition, asserts the existence of an atomic fact."[29] Moreover, just as an object that is unrelated to other objects is one about which we have little to say, because we do not fully understand what kind of a thing it is, since it is unrelated to other things, so Wittgenstein claims that names do not have meaning or sense until they are combined in a proposition. They do *refer* specifically to some object in the world, but "only the proposition has sense; only in the context of a proposition has a name meaning."[30]

Third, corresponding to complex states of affairs are complex propositions. Just as elementary propositions picture reality, so do complex ones. Moreover, just as complex states of affairs can be analyzed into atomic facts, so the propositions that picture such complex facts can be analyzed. As Wittgenstein claims, "It is obvious that in the analysis of propositions we must come to elementary propositions, which consist of names in immediate combination."[31] In fact, this is true no matter how complex the world is. As Wittgenstein explains, "Even if the world is infinitely complex, so that every fact consists of an infinite number of atomic facts and every atomic fact is composed of an infinite number of objects, even then there must be objects and atomic facts."[32] Proper analysis of propositions will get one to their irreducible constituents, just as proper analysis of states of affairs will get one to the irreducible simples of reality.

The preceding explanation indicates that the constituents of Wittgenstein's ontology correlate with the elements of propositions, but nothing so far explains *how* propositions picture reality. The explanation of the "how" is the final link of the picture theory. A helpful way to begin is to consider how a literal picture relates to reality. As one looks at a picture, he sees various objects in it that are supposed to correspond to and represent objects in reality. Moreover, the objects in the picture stand together in various relations (e.g., one object is to the right of another) that *represent* the way objects relate to one another in reality.[33] The *connection* of the various elements of the picture is what Wittgenstein calls its structure, and the possibility that such elements can be so structured is called the form of representation of the picture.[34] Initially, a proposition does not seem to bear this kind of relation to the world. Nonetheless, Wittgenstein claims that because a "proposition communicates to us a state of affairs, therefore it must be *essentially* connected with the state of affairs."[35] The connection, however, is not that the proposition is a *spatial* picture of the state of affairs it describes, but rather a *logical* picture of the state of affairs it describes.[36] Pitcher is helpful in explaining what is necessary for a thing to be a logical picture of something else. He writes:

> In order for one thing, A, to be a logical picture of another, B, three conditions must be met: (1) there must be a one-to-one correspondence between the components of A and those of B; (2) to every feature of the structure or form of A there must correspond a feature of the structure or form of B; and (3) there must be rules of projection connecting the components of A and those of B. Rules of projection are rules whereby given A (or B), B (or A) can be reconstructed from it. A good example is the rules connecting a musical score and an actual performance of it; given either the score or the performance, the other can be reconstructed from it.[37]

In other words, the fact that names are configured in a certain way in a proposition to assert the existence of a state of affairs *represents* that in reality the objects to which the names refer are structured together in the way the proposition indicates. Wittgenstein offers the sigh '*aRb*' as an example of a possible proposition, and then explains the sign's relation to the world. He writes:

> We must not say, "The complex sign '*aRb*' says '*a* stands in relation R to b'"; but we must say, "That '*a*' stands in a certain relation to '*b*' says that '*aRb*.'"[38]

Thus, the fact that in the *expression* or *symbol* '*aRb*' '*a*' stands in a certain relation to '*b*' indicates to us that *in the world* whatever '*a*' represents stands in the relation '*R*' to whatever '*b*' represents in the world. That is the kind of relation that shows itself plainly in at least elementary propositions. For Wittgenstein, then, propositions picture reality, because they share the same logical form ("the form of reality") as does reality, and the logical form that is the form of representation is defined as "the possibility that the things are combined with one another as are the elements of the picture."[39]

As one reflects on Wittgenstein's picture theory of language, he recognizes a very important implication of the theory. Given the picture theory of meaning, certain propositions are nonsense (in Wittgenstein's conception of nonsense). If someone said, "Despair orange cup cloudy," indeed, he would have uttered nonsense, but that is not Wittgenstein's concept of nonsense. In order to understand what he means, one must remember his claims about what gives propositions meaning. The point is that propositions picture states of affairs. Elementary propositions are configurations of names, and such propositions and names directly picture objects and states of affairs in the world. In fact, as Wittgenstein argues, what the picture represents is its sense. Thus, if a proposition does not picture any state of affairs in the world, it is without sense, i.e., it is *non*-sense. Given this definition of nonsense, what sort of propositions fall into this category? Wittgenstein is quite clear about that matter. First, propositions of metaphysics are nonsense. For example, Wittgenstein claims that if one were to write a book entitled "The world as I found it," the metaphysical subject "I" would not be in the world. Thus, any talk of it would be nonsense, and as a result, one should remain silent about such metaphysical items.[40] Second, propositions of ethics fall within the category of nonsense. He claims that "the sense of the world must lie outside the world. In the world everything is as it is and happens as it does happen. *In* it there is no value—and if there were, it would be of no value."[41] In other words, as one looks at the world, he sees states of affairs, but he does not see value or lack of value of states of affairs *as objects* also in the world. Thus, whatever value judgments one makes about the world, he makes apart from the objects that are in the world. However, Wittgenstein has told us that propositions have sense only if they picture states of affairs *in the world.* The propositions of ethics are value judgments about the world, but do not picture value in the world. Therefore, they are nonsense. As Wittgenstein states, "It is clear that ethics cannot be expressed. Ethics is transcendental."[42] Third, propositions of religion and theology are also nonsense. Wittgenstein states that 'God does not reveal himself *in* the world."[43] Of course, if propositions are pictures of states of affairs *in* the world, and God is not to be found in the world, then any proposition about God must be nonsense in Wittgenstein's sense of the term. Finally, Wittgenstein also claims that propositions of philosophy are nonsense in that they picture nothing about the world. Wittgenstein writes of his own philosophizing in the *Tractatus:*

> My propositions are elucidatory in this way: he who understands me finally recognizes them as senseless, when he has climbed out through them, on them, over them. (He must so to speak throw away the ladder, after he has climbed up on it.)
>   He must surmount these propositions; then he sees the world rightly.[44]

As one considers the notion that certain kinds of propositions are nonsense, one cannot avoid the conclusion that they ought not to be uttered, and that is Wittgenstein's further point. For Wittgenstein, all that can be said relates to the world; everything else is unsayable. He clearly asserts, "Empirical reality is limited by the totality of objects. The boundary appears again in the totality of elementary propositions."[45] While this is a statement about the limits of reality, it is also a statement about the limits of language. Wittgenstein also writes, *"The limits of my language* mean the limits of my world."[46] What should be equally clear from Wittgenstein's views on the relation of reality to language is that the converse is also true, viz., the limits of the world (even, of *my* world) mean the limits of my language. But Wittgenstein has already set the boundaries of the world, and they leave metaphysics, ethics, and theology out of this world.[47] Of course, if such items are out of this world, then one should not speak about them, since the world's limits set the boundaries for language. "Whereof one cannot speak, thereof one must be silent,"[48] and Wittgenstein has already shown why one cannot speak of such things. It should be noted, however, that Wittgenstein does not claim that unsayable things are nonexistent, only that they cannot be spoken of, because they are not *within* the world. Such things are called the mystical. As he claims, "There is indeed the inexpressible. This *shows* itself; it is the mystical."[49]

Before showing the implications of the picture theory for inerrancy, we need to note three more key items in relation to this theory. First, Wittgenstein argues that while it is necessary for a proposition to share a logical form in common with reality in order to picture reality, a proposition cannot *represent by means of a proposition* that logical form. A proposition can show logical form; i.e., by looking at the way words are configured in the proposition one can see that objects in the world are so configured, but what no proposition can *assert* is logical form itself; it can only *show* that form, and one can see it by looking at the proposition.[50]

Second, of crucial import is Wittgenstein's contention that every proposition is a truth-function on elementary propositions.[51] Wittgenstein claims that all propositions result from truth-operations on elementary propositions, and that a truth-operation is the way that a truth-function is produced out of elementary propositions.[52] Pitcher helps in understanding this when he writes:

> But what are truth-functional connectives and truth-functions? A compound proposition, compounded of the propositions $p_1, p_2,$ $\ldots p_n$, is a truth-functional compound (truth-function) of $p_1, \ldots$ p_n if and only if its truth or falsity (its truth-value) is uniquely determined by the truth-values of $p_1, \ldots p_n$. A connective is a truth-functional one if it compounds propositions into truth-functional compounds. On these definitions, 'and' is a truth-functional connective; for if we know the truth-values of each of the propositions "Smith is in town" and "Jones is in town," then we know the truth-value of the complex proposition "Smith is in town and Jones is in town."[53]

All propositions, then, result from truth-functional connectives being applied to elementary propositions. Moreover, Wittgenstein says there are three types of truth-conditions. There are tautologies, contradictions, and propositions that are neither always true nor always false. It is the last kind which is the genuine proposition which truly pictures reality. In regard to the first two kinds, Wittgenstein writes that "in the one case the proposition is true for all the truth-possibilities of the elementary propositions. We say that the truth-conditions are *tautological*. In the second case the proposition is false for all the truth-possibilities.

The truth-conditions are *self-contradictory*."[54] How do such propositions relate to reality? Wittgenstein replies that "tautology leaves to reality the whole infinite logical space; contradiction fills the whole logical space and leaves no point to reality. Neither of them, therefore, can in any way determine reality."[55]

How does one know whether any given nontautologous or noncontradictory proposition is true or false? One must not assume that all such propositions are automatically true just by being formed. After all, names can be put together experimentally to form a proposition about a possible state of affairs. As Wittgenstein says, "In the proposition a state of affairs is, as it were, put together for the sake of experiment."[56] But just as not every possible state of affairs is actual, so not every possibly true proposition pictures reality as it actually is. How then does one know which ones do picture reality as it is? Wittgenstein answers that the way to tell whether any given proposition is true or false is to go and see whether the picture agrees with reality or not.[57] "What the picture represents is its *sense*" (emphasis added),[58] but "in the *agreement* or *disagreement* of its sense with reality, its *truth* or *falsity* consists" (emphasis added).[59] "In order to discover whether the picture is true or false we must compare it with reality."[60] Not only does Wittgenstein explain how to know whether a given proposition is true, but he also indicates how one can know the truth about all of reality. He writes:

> The specification of all true elementary propositions describes the world completely. The world is completely described by the specification of all elementary propositions plus the specification, which of them are true and which false.[61]

One final item follows from Wittgenstein's conception of truth and falsity and his claim that propositions are truth-functions on elementary propositions. If all propositions are supposed to be truth-functions on elementary propositions, then all genuine propositions must be true or false. If this is true, however, it would seem that one must be able to take a proposition that is true, negate it, and wind up with a different proposition that also has sense. For example, if it makes sense to say "the box is green," it should also make sense to say "the box is not green." The reason for this is that in order for a proposition to have sense, it must picture reality, and if a given proposition does picture reality and is true, then one would expect its negation to picture a *possible* state of affairs, one that does not pertain in the actual world but one about which one can sensibly speak. Wittgenstein clearly states, "The positive *proposition* must presuppose the existence of the negative *proposition* and conversely."[62] Pitcher calls this the principle of significant negation. In the *Notebooks 1914–1916,* Wittgenstein put the same point thus: "In order for a proposition to be capable of being true it must also be capable of being false."[63] In other words, if a sentence is not capable of significant negation, it cannot be factually significant, i.e., the sentence can be neither true nor false, but is meaningless.

Implications for Inerrancy

In the preceding pages I have outlined Wittgenstein's ontology and the theory of language that goes with it as they are presented in the *Tractatus.* How does all of this relate to inerrancy? I should like to point out some crucial implications of Wittgenstein's views for biblical inerrancy. First, given the picture theory of meaning, the sense of a proposition (its meaning) is what it represents, and what it represents is a specific state of affairs via names that have a one-to-one correspondence to *specific* objects in the world. If this is how language relates to the world, then any meaningful proposition must be determinate in meaning. As Wittgenstein says, "Everything that can be thought at all can be thought clearly. Everything that can be said can be said clearly."[64] There can be no genuine propositions that are ultimately unclear in meaning. I see in this notion an idea that fits with the contemporary errantist position. Many errantists claim that inerrancy is not a useful concept in discussions about the Bible. The concept is said to be too unclear to be given a precise definition, and the claim is made that since one cannot precisely define inerrancy, the term *inerrancy* should be eliminated from discussions about Scripture. Notice how Wittgenstein's notion fits with this view and could lead one to it. Wittgenstein says that every genuine, meaningful proposition is determinate in meaning. If "the Bible is inerrant" or "the Bible is errant" is unclear in meaning because "inerrant" and "errant" cannot be clearly defined (as errantists maintain), then, on Wittgenstein's theory of meaning, one would have to say that such propositions are not even genuine propositions and have no sense. Continued talk using such language will get us nowhere, because it does not picture anything about the way the world really is.

We should drop such talk. Such a conclusion is obviously detrimental to inerrancy, for one cannot meaningfully assert or deny inerrancy, if neither the concept nor the word is usable. Second, according to the ontology of the *Tractatus*, simple states of affairs (atomic facts) are independent of one another. As mentioned earlier, that means that the existence of one atomic fact neither entails nor excludes any other elementary state of affairs. I see here a notion that could be used against the inerrantist's position in the following way: inerrantists often argue that *if* the Bible is inspired, *then* it must also be inerrant. If the Bible is the product of God's creative breath and if God cannot lie (both facts taught by Scripture), then the Bible resultant from the inspiration of the Holy Spirit must be inerrant. Inspiration, it is said, entails inerrancy. However, if Wittgenstein's claims are applied to this issue, then the inerrantist's argument about inspiration entailing inerrancy falls flat. While I doubt that either the Bible's being inspired or the Bible's being inerrant would qualify as atomic facts, nonetheless, if complex, they are analyzable into elementary facts, and certainly the atomic facts represented by the statement "the Bible is inspired" would be independent of the atomic facts represented by "the Bible is inerrant." The upshot of this is twofold: (1) inerrantists cannot argue for inerrancy on the grounds of entailment from inspiration, and (2) inerrancy will have to be proved not by looking at verses about inspiration but by proving the inerrancy of each verse in Scripture; i.e., one will have to look at the historical, scientific, and other phenomena to determine whether the Bible is inerrant. Of course, that is just the procedure urged by errantists, for they believe that if one proceeds in such a way, he will ultimately conclude that the Bible has errors. Thus, Wittgenstein's doctrine that one state of affairs does not entail another very clearly could lead to the errantist position.[65]

Third, Wittgenstein's concept of nonsense has significant implications for inerrancy. Wittgenstein said that only propositions that picture reality have sense. He also said that only what has sense can be true or false. What is nonsense can be neither true nor false. Since inerrancy was defined in terms of truth, the implications of Wittgenstein's doctrine are obvious. Scripture is loaded with metaphysical, ethical, religious, and theological propositions, but on Wittgenstein's views, all of them are nonsense, and if they are nonsense, then they can be neither true nor false. But if they can be neither true nor false, any possibility of proving or disproving the inerrancy *or* errancy of a vast number of statements in Scripture is eliminated. The inerrantist must simply drop the notion of the inerrancy of such parts of Scripture. Likewise, the errantist must remove any talk about the errancy of such propositions, but not because he has to admit their inerrancy. Clearly, the inerrantist loses more when Wittgenstein's views are applied to this whole matter of biblical inerrancy.[66]

In response to the preceding one might reply, "At least this leaves all scientific and historical statements as having sense, and thus, one can talk about their errancy or inerrancy." However, such a claim evidences some serious misunderstandings. The claim rests on the mistaken notion that no historical proposition of Scripture is also theological in nature. Obviously, some rather important historical propositions are theological as well. For example, "The Word became flesh and lived for a while among us"; "Jesus of Nazareth is the Son of God"; "The Son of God died on the cross for our sins"; "God raised Christ from the dead"; and even "In the beginning God created the heavens and the earth" are all statements about historical events (some also have scientific implications), but they all are also theological. However, given the claim that God is not *in* the world, one must then state that each of these *historical* statements about God's activities in the world must be nonsense, and if nonsense, then neither true nor false, neither errant nor inerrant. Inerrancy is again dealt a telling blow.

While such implications are devastating, the matter becomes even more severe when one considers Wittgenstein's views about what can be said. His basic point about nonsense allows statements of Scripture about ethics, metaphysics, and theology to be stated (though they would all be considered nonsense), but his position on what is sayable necessitates that much of the Bible should not have even been written (or said). It is extremely difficult, if not impossible, to talk about the errancy or inerrancy of that which cannot even be said, and of course, since on this view much of the Bible contains things that cannot really be said, it is clearly a mistake to discuss the errancy or inerrancy of Scripture. The topic ought to be dropped from serious discussions about Scripture. Thus, inerrancy suffers substantially.

Finally, Wittgenstein's notions of truth, falsity, and meaning are of importance to the inerrancy issue. One can find in his views something very much akin to what one finds in the writings of later philosophers. Whereas the Logical Positivists had claimed that verifiability is crucial for meaningfulness, later philosophers have urged that falsifiability is equally important as verifiability. For example, Antony Flew, following the lead of John Wisdom, argues that a proposition must not only be capable of verification, but, even more important, one must be able to specify what would falsify it. His complaint with the propositions of theology such as "God loves us" is that one cannot specify under what conditions such a statement would be false. In fact, he complains that believers would be unwilling to allow that such a statement could be false under any circumstances. However, if that is the case, argues Flew, then such propositions must be vacuous and must "die the death of a thousand qualifications."[67] The point of all this for inerrancy should be obvious. If one rejects the statements of theology, metaphysics, ethics, as meaningless because they cannot be significantly falsified, then one must reject much of the Bible as meaningless. Of course, it must then be irrelevant to speak of the Bible's errancy or inerrancy, for such notions presuppose one's ability to verify or falsify statements, but on Wittgenstein's views, much of the Bible is neither verifiable nor falsifiable. Thus, it can be neither errant nor inerrant.

PHILOSOPHY OF THE LATER WITTGENSTEIN

Since Wittgenstein's later philosophy essentially involves a rejection of his earlier views, one might think that biblical inerrancy would fare much better in conjunction with it. Though some of Wittgenstein's later views are helpful to the inerrantist, the overwhelming conclusion again is that if one were to apply Wittgenstein's later philosophy to the issue of inerrancy, one would find ample cause for a resounding rejection of inerrancy. I should like to sketch some of the major themes of the later Wittgenstein and show why they could lead to a rejection of inerrancy. The first is the most involved and, it seems to me, the most significant.

Language-games and the Use Theory of Meaning

It would seem virtually impossible to grasp Wittgenstein's later philosophy without an understanding of his central notion of a language-game. In the *Tractatus* Wittgenstein claimed that propositions picture objects in logical space. Consequently, if one knows what simple objects there are as well as the names that name them, one could anticipate what propositions could be constructed from them, and one could know what they mean. A new proposition would simply involve rearrangement of the names one already had. In his later philosophy Wittgenstein was still interested in discovering the meaning of propositions, but no such theory about the nature of language as the picture theory is presented. Instead, language is referred to as a complex of language-games that are distinct one from another, and yet interdependent. If this is so, one will not be able to make predictions about what sorts of new propositions might be constructed nor about what they might mean.

In speaking about the nature of a language-game, Wittgenstein gives perhaps his fullest definition of the concept when he writes, "I shall also call the whole, consisting of language and the actions into which it is woven, the 'language-game.'"[68] In other words, language is more than mere words. Language is always used in a context, a context that includes behavior. Wittgenstein writes that "the term 'language-*game*' is meant to bring into prominence the fact that the *speaking* of language is part of an activity, or of a form of life."[69] A form of life is a complete way of doing a certain activity, whether the activity is playing a game, teaching a skill, exhibiting one's religious devotion, or expressing pain. As such, a form of life includes both verbal and nonverbal behavior. Wittgenstein writes that "it is easy to imagine a language consisting only of questions and expressions for answering yes and no. And innumerable others. . . . And to imagine a language means to imagine a form of life."[70] To the question, How many forms of life (language-games) are there? Wittgenstein would respond that one should try to think of the different contexts in which language can be used, and, of course, a good place to begin would be to consider how many kinds of sentences there are. What one comes to see is that there is a vast complex of language-games and that the multiplicity is not something fixed. Wittgenstein writes:

> But how many kinds of sentence are there? Say assertion, question, and command?—There are *countless* kinds: countless different kinds of use of what we call "symbols," "words," "sentences." And this multiplicity is not something fixed, given once for all; but

new types of language, new language-games, as we may say, come into existence, and others become obsolete and get forgotten. . . . Review the multiplicity of language-games in the following examples, and in others:

> Giving orders, and obeying them—
> Describing the appearance of an object, or giving its measurements—
> Constructing an object from a description (a drawing)—
> Reporting an event—
> Speculating about an event—
> Forming and testing a hypothesis—
> Presenting the results of an experiment in tables and diagrams—
> Making up a story; and reading it—
> Play-acting—
> Singing catches—
> Guessing riddles—
> Making a joke; telling it—
> Solving a problem in practical arithmetic—
> Translating from one language into another—
> Asking, thanking, cursing, greeting, praying.[71]

If the appropriate way to look at language is as a complex of language-games, and the appropriate way to think of a language-game is as a form of life constituted by both verbal and nonverbal behavior, then how does one explain the meaning of the verbal part of language? Does one see what it pictures? Wittgenstein's answer is a resounding rejection of the picture theory of language. What flows very naturally from the concept of a language-game is a use theory of meaning, and that is exactly what is to be found in the later Wittgenstein's philosophy.

There were various reasons why Wittgenstein came to reject the picture theory of meaning,[72] but a common notion underlying his rejection is that sentences have meaning, not because they picture objects or states of affairs, but because of their use. Wittgenstein says that "for a *large* class of cases—though not for all—in which we employ the word 'meaning' it can be defined thus: the meaning of a word is its use in the language."[73] What is true of a word is also true of a sentence, for Wittgenstein claims, "Look at the sentence as an instrument, and at its sense as its employment."[74] How many different ways can a sentence be used? "Well, how many language-games are there?" Wittgenstein would reply. Obviously, there are countless kinds of language-games, and thus there are countless kinds of sentences and uses of a given sentence. The connection between Wittgenstein's notion of a language-game and his use theory of meaning should be evident. Wittgenstein viewed sentences and words as tools with which one can make particular moves in a language-game. He writes:

> Think of the tools in a tool-box: there is a hammer, pliers, a saw, a screw-driver, a rule, a glue-pot, glue, nails and screws.—The functions of words are as diverse as the functions of these objects. (And in both cases there are similarities.)
> Of course, what confuses us is the uniform appearance of words when we hear them spoken or meet them in script and print. For their *application* is not presented to us so clearly.[75]

A third point of significance about language-games is their relation to one another. Specifically, is there any overlap between language-games? For example, just because the language-game of religion is not that of science, can one not legitimately apply notions of empirical truth or falsity to statements used in the religious language-game? In response, it must be recognized that for Wittgenstein, while various words or sentences may appear in several language-games, this does not mean that what one is doing with them in one language-game is the same thing he is doing with them in another. Each language-game is logically distinct from every other. Consequently, to speak of propositions of religious belief as though they were scientific propositions to be verified or falsified is to make a major blunder. It is not the kind of blunder one makes when he presents poor evidence for some scientific hypothesis he claims is true. It is a more serious blunder, for it shows that the person presenting evidence for the truth of the religious belief does not even understand that such propositions are not the sorts of things for which one presents evidence as though they were propositions of science.[76] Suppose, for example, someone uses a dream as evidence that he knows what the Last Judgment will be like. If another person were to respond that the dream is poor evidence, he would be making a bad mistake. Compared with evidence for a claim that it will rain tomorrow, the claim about the Last Judgment on the basis of a dream is no evidence at all, Wittgenstein argues.[77] Wittgenstein's point is that belief in a Last Judgment is not the same sort of thing as belief that it will rain tomorrow. They are in two logically distinct language-games, and thus, one does not use such beliefs in the same way, nor should one treat them the same way; i.e., one should not try to verify a religious belief by some kind of presentation of evidence as he might if he were verifying his belief about the weather. Wittgenstein helps to clarify this matter when he writes about the Last Judgment:

> Those who said: "Well, possibly it may happen and possibly not" would be on an entirely different plane.
> This is partly why one would be reluctant to say: "These people rigorously hold the opinion (or view) that there is a Last Judgment." "Opinion" sounds queer.
> It is for this reason that different words are used: "dogma," "faith."
> We don't talk about hypothesis, or about high probability. Nor about knowing.
> In a religious discourse we use such expressions as: "I believe that so and so will happen," and use them differently to the way in which we use them in science.
> Although, there is a great temptation to think we do. Because we do talk of evidence, and do talk of evidence by experience.[78]

The language-games of religion and science are logically distinct. If one tries to make religious belief a matter of evidence in the way that scientific belief involves evidence, then "this would in fact destroy the whole business."[79]

A fourth key concept about language-games is Wittgenstein's claim that one must accept a form of life (a language-game) as given and not try to justify it. According to Wittgenstein, there are certain things which are so fundamental that they can neither be sensibly doubted or proved. Such matters are the forms of life, our language-games, and as Wittgenstein says in *On Certainty* (as well as in *Investigations*), forms of life, as the given, are to be accepted, not doubted *or* proved, for they do not rest on any ground; they are simply there.[80] Wittgenstein writes:

> But more correctly: The fact that I use the word "hand" and all the other words in my sentence without a second thought, indeed that I should stand before the abyss if I wanted so much as to try doubting their meanings—shews that absence of doubt belongs to the essence of the language-game, that the question "How do I know. . . ." drags out the language-game, or else does away with it.[81]

Wittgenstein also makes the further point that unless these basic language-games are beyond doubt, doubting of anything would be impossible. Such things as the existence of one's body, the earth's existence, and one's consciousness are the presuppositions for doubting or knowing anything else. As Wittgenstein says, "Doubt itself rests only on what is beyond doubt."[82] "If you tried to doubt everything you would not get as far as doubting anything. The game of doubting itself presupposes certainty."[83] Certain things are so fundamental they cannot be sensibly doubted or proved. In fact, one cannot even imagine sensibly how he would go about proving such things to be true, nor if he convinced someone of the truth of such things would he be able to say why. Wittgenstein writes:

> If someone said to me that he doubted whether he had a body I should take him to be a half-wit. But I shouldn't know what it would mean to try to convince him that he had one. And if I had said something, and that had removed his doubt, I should not know how or why.[84]

If forms of life are given and not to be doubted or justified, then what about religion and propositions of religious beliefs? Evidently, this form of life too must be just accepted as neither true nor false, doubtable or justifiable, but just there. Religious propositions as a whole, including all the propositions of Scripture, are not to be doubted or justified as a whole; they are just to be accepted.

A final and corollary point about language-games follows. Having read the preceding, one might think the propositions of Scripture must be *much less certain* than those of science, i.e., that one cannot be anywhere near as sure that he has the "right" propositions of religion as he can that scientific propositions are the "right" ones. Wittgenstein would reply that such a notion is again mistaken. Both kinds of propositions are equally certain, but "the kind of certainty is the kind of language-game."[85] Notice that Wittgenstein did not say the *degree* of certainty, but the *kind* of certainty. What is the point? The point is that one may claim to know propositions from two separate language-games with an equal *degree* of certainty, but the *kind* of certainty is not thereby the same. In the language-game of science the *kind* of certainty one has depends on the marshaling of empirical evidence. In religious matters, whatever the basis of certainty, it is definitely *not the same kind of basis* (the kind that I have been using that is relevant to the meaning of "inerrant" and "errant") as for science. The degree of certainty in religion can be the same as the degree in science and history, but it cannot be the same *kind* because of the difference in language-games.

Depsychologizing

A second broad emphasis in the philosophy of the later Wittgenstein is what can be called his depsychologizing theme. Traditionally, when philosophers have talked of thoughts, sensations, pains, etc., they have wanted to analyze what was going on "within" a person. This has led to many problems in philosophy of mind, not the least of which are the legitimacy of claiming to know whether someone else has a mind and claiming to know what is happening within another's mind. In typical fashion, Wittgenstein argues that the problem in these areas is that philosophers have been approaching them from the wrong perspective. They have tried to analyze such issues by discussing private sensations and thoughts, but such an approach is a dead end. Progress on these issues will come only as the focus of the discussion is that which is public. In a word, philosophers must depsychologize their talk and their thought of such matters. Several examples of the application of this principle illustrate how Wittgenstein used the notion to answer longstanding philosophical dilemmas.

First, Wittgenstein argues at great length that much of the fog that surrounds inner sensations such as pains can be removed, if philosophers would just stop trying to get at the inner mental states of a person who is in pain. In a given case, how would one know whether a person is experiencing the internal sensation of pain? Wittgenstein replies that one certainly would not know it by means of anything other than what is public. Suppose someone claims to be in pain and exhibits various kinds of pain behavior. He may be simulating pain, unless the circumstances that surround the behavior demand that he is not acting. If someone is hit by a car, has huge gashes on his body, and screams that he is in pain, there is simply no room for wondering if he is simulating pain. Both his pain behavior and the circumstances that surround the behavior require that observers believe he is in pain. As Wittgenstein says, "If I see someone writhing in pain with evident cause I do not think: all the same his feelings are hidden from me."[86] "Just try—in a real case—to doubt someone else's fear or pain."[87] What really matters here is not what is going on internally, but that which is public. Wittgenstein likens private sensations, such as pains, to having a beetle in a box:

> Now someone tells me that *he* knows what pain is only from his own case!—Suppose everyone had a box with something in it: we call it a "beetle." No one can look into anyone else's box, and everyone says he knows what a beetle is only by looking at *his* beetle.—Here it would be quite possible for everyone to have something different in his box. One might even imagine such a thing constantly changing.—But suppose the word "beetle" had a use in these people's language?—If so it would not be used as the name of a thing. The thing in the box has no place in the language-game at all; not even as a *something*: for the box might even be empty.—No, one can "divide through" by the thing in the box; it cancels out, whatever it is.[88]

One must be careful here not to think that Wittgenstein is claiming that there really are no such things as private mental states or sensations. His point is that such things, though they exist, do not make any real difference to discussions about pains, sensations, etc. What truly matters is totally public. In response to an imagined objector who would claim that Wittgenstein is saying there is no internal sensation, he replies:

> Not at all. It is not a *something*, but not a *nothing* either! The conclusion was only that a nothing would serve just as well as a something about which nothing could be said. We have only rejected the grammar which tries to force itself on us here.[89]

The "grammar" referred to is the surface grammar. It seems that because the propositions "I describe my state of mind" and "I describe my room," for example, have the same surface grammar (subject, predicate, direct object—syntactical sameness), that means one must do the same sort of thing in describing the one as he does in describing the other. However, it must be remembered that different language-games are involved.[90] Describing a state of mind and describing a room fall within different language-games.

Probably the most famous example of depsychologizing in Wittgenstein is his argument against the possibility of anyone constructing a language private to himself in order to name his own internal sensations. Wittgenstein imagines someone trying to name his sensations with a private language. The individual associates one sensation with the sign 'S', and he keeps a written record of every time 'S' appears before his consciousness. How does he know which sensation is 'S'? He has a private "ceremony" whereby he concentrates on the sensation the first time it appears, "inwardly points" to it, and says to himself, "That's 'S'. Wittgenstein claims that this person has not named or given any meaning to anything private. Since he cannot actually observe the sensation, he has no justification for using the sign 'S' each time he thinks the sensation appears. The second time he thinks 'S' occurs, another sensation, 'E', might actually be there. He has no criterion for telling whether the sensation is 'E', 'S', or anything else, and thus, he has no basis for saying he uses 'S' correctly in his private language. Someone might reply, "But his memory of the sensation 'S' is his criterion for the right use of the sign 'S'!" Wittgenstein replies that there is no criterion whatsoever (including memory) for the right usage of 'S'. In such a case, it is senseless to discuss whether 'S' has been used correctly or not.[91] Wittgenstein concludes that only public language is language at all.

A final area of particular importance to this chapter in regard to this emphasis on the public deals with Wittgenstein's analysis of intending, and especially with his position on intending a meaning. Wittgenstein argues that the key to intending a meaning when someone utters a sentence has nothing to do with what goes on within his mind. He writes:

> But didn't I already intend the whole construction of the sentence (for example) at its beginning? So surely it already existed in my mind before I said it out loud!—If it was in my mind, still it would not normally be there in some different word order. But here we are constructing a misleading picture of "intending," that is, of the use of this word. An intention is embedded in its situation, in human customs and institutions. If the technique of the game of chess did not exist, I could not intend to play a game of chess. In so far as I do intend the construction of a sentence in advance, that is made possible by the fact that I can speak the language in question.[92]

What Wittgenstein is asserting is that if one wants to know a writer's or speaker's intention, one must simply look at what has been written or said, i.e., that which is public, the text itself. One

must not try to go "behind" the public into the author's mind to
find his intention. "But, suppose someone told us his intention.
Wouldn't that indicate what was going on 'inside' his mind?"
Wittgenstein flatly rejects such a notion. He explains the difficulty with such an idea when he writes:

> But if you had said the words, would you necessarily have meant
> them quite seriously? (Thus the most explicit expression of inten-
> tion is by itself insufficient evidence of intention).[93]

Even if someone tells us about his mental state of intending, he
could be lying. Thus, even if an author states his intention, the
reader still does not know *by that alone* what he intends. It is not
that Wittgenstein would deny that there are such things as intentions, but only that "a nothing would serve as well as a something about which one could not speak."

In all of these examples, what is the problem? That is, why is it
that one must remove talk of what goes on within the mind and
focus on that which is public? Wittgenstein states the point quite
succinctly when he writes, "An 'inner process' stands in need of
outward criteria."[94] Until there are public criteria, one has no
bases for judging whether or not anything is going on internally,
and, on the other hand, if such criteria are available and then
someone sees public behavior that meets the criteria, he has a
right to assume that the internal process did occur.

Concept of Criterion

Wittgenstein claimed that a criterion is something by which
one is justified in saying that a thing is so or is not so.[95] What he
was speaking of is a set of standards that must be met for some
specific thing to be an instance of something. In *The Blue Book*
Wittgenstein explains this principle and relates it to evidence as
follows:

> When I said that if we moved our hand upward a little, we touch
> our eye, I was referring to tactile evidence only. That is, the
> criterion for my finger touching my eye was to be only that I had
> the particular feeling which would have made me say that I was
> touching my eye, even if I had no visual evidence for it, and even
> if, on looking into a mirror, I saw my finger not touching my eye,
> but, say, my forehead.[96]

Thus, if one is going to be justified in claiming on a *particular*
occasion that something is the case, he must initially know what

criteria must be met for that thing to be the case on *any* occasion. Criteria must not be confused with evidence. For example, one can speak about criteria (standards) to be met in order for some state of affairs to exist, even if it were impossible ever to produce any *evidence* that such criteria had been met. Criteria and evidence are not the same. One can better understand Wittgenstein's concept of a criterion by seeing how he uses it in the following portion from the *Investigations*:

> It is as if I were to say: "You surely know what 'It's 5 o'clock on the sun' means. It means simply that it is just the same time there as it is here when it is 5 o'clock."—The explanation by means of *identity* does not work here. For I know well enough that one can call 5 o'clock here and 5 o'clock there "the same time," but what I do not know is in what cases one is to speak of its being the same time here and there.[97]

Wittgenstein's point is that one can *say* it is the same time on the sun as on earth, but one has no justification whatsoever for that statement, because he cannot point to any criteria for asserting identity. The sun is not divided into time zones as is the world. Moreover, it is 5 o'clock in Portland, for example, because the earth has rotated on its axis to a certain point so that Portland's position in relation to the sun justifies our saying that it is 5 o'clock there; i.e., one of the criteria for telling time on earth is the earth's location in relation to the sun. Of course, that immediately leaves out the possibility of identity of the statements "It is 5 o'clock in Portland" and "It is 5 o'clock on the sun." There are simply no criteria for claiming that 5 o'clock is the same time in both places.

Anti-essentialism and Its Implications

In the *Tractatus* Wittgenstein set forth what he thought to be the essence of language and reality, i.e., what he thought to be common to all languages and all of reality. In his later thought, he thoroughly rejected the idea that one could speak about what is common to all languages or to any other phenomena such as games, pains, etc. The *Investigations* is full of such comments. Here is one in regard to the notion of a language-game:

> Here we come up against the great question that lies behind all these considerations.—For someone might object against me: "You take the easy way out! You talk about all sorts of language-

games, but have nowhere said what the essence of a language-game, and hence of language, is: what is common to all these activities, and what makes them into language or parts of language. So you let yourself off the very part of the investigation that once gave you yourself most headache, the part about the *general form of propositions* and of language."

And this is true.—Instead of producing something common to all that we call language, I am saying that these phenomena have no one thing in common which makes us use the same word for all,—but that they are *related* to one another in many different ways. And it is because of this relationship, or these relationships, that we call them all "language."[98]

A further concept naturally stems from Wittgenstein's anti-essentialism. Wittgenstein claimed in the *Tractatus* that meaning is determinate. One could plot the boundaries between one word's meaning and another word's meaning, because there were supposed to be such sharp boundaries. However, once Wittgenstein rejected the notion that one could talk of the essence of things, it naturally followed that no longer could clear boundaries be drawn to set one concept off from another. Wittgenstein claimed that on occasion one can draw and does draw boundaries between games, concepts, and languages for a purpose, but that does not mean there truly exist such boundaries.[99] "I said that the application of a word is not everywhere bounded by rules. But what does a game look like that is everywhere bounded by rules? whose rules never let a doubt creep in, but stops up all the cracks where it might?—"[100]

Implications for Inerrancy

In the preceding pages I have outlined the major themes of Wittgenstein's later philosophy. In the following pages I suggest the relation of these various themes to the inerrancy issue. Though inerrancy fares somewhat better in relation to Wittgenstein's later philosophy, one recognizes that the philosophy of *Investigations* contains much that is negative for inerrancy.

Implications of Language-games and Use Theory of Meaning. As one reflects on Wittgenstein's concept of language as a complex of language-games and on his use theory of meaning, one realizes that they have many important implications for the inerrancy issue. First, Wittgenstein argued that if one is to understand what a word or sentence means, he must look for its use. Sentences are instruments (tools), and their use determines their sense. It seems that this notion can have both a positive and a negative relation to the issue of inerrancy, depending on how one would choose to *use it.* On the positive side, one could use it to answer critics in regard to specific alleged errors. For example, in cases where the claim is made that a biblical statement is historically or scientifically false, one may respond that the critic fails to understand that the statement is not being *used* to teach history or science. Instead, it is being used to teach some moral or religious truth. Thus, to require exact factual accuracy as if the statement were being used to teach history or science would be to mistake its use. However, given its use, it *accurately* accomplishes its purpose, and thus biblical inerrancy is upheld. In fact, it seems to me that some evangelicals do respond to certain claims of alleged errors in just this way.[101]

On the negative side, if one attempts to answer claims of alleged errors by this means, he may be making what some would consider to be some damaging concessions to errancy. The point is that using this line of argument commits the inerrantist to saying that at certain places the Bible *does* contain factual errors, but nonetheless, since the sentences involved are not being used to state facts but to teach a moral or religious lesson, the Bible is still to be considered inerrant. Since in the case of many alleged errors, inerrantists do not admit factual error and then plead for inerrancy on the grounds that the sentence accurately does whatever it is supposed to do, but instead try to show that the statement is factually correct without any attempt to escape the dilemma by appealing to use, the errantist could charge the inerrantist with inconsistency and special pleading. The errantist might say, "You inerrantists want to have things both ways. On the one hand, you say there are no historical and scientific errors, and on occasions you try to remove such alleged errors by showing that the propositions are *historically* and *scientifically* correct, but on the other hand, sometimes you want to be allowed to remove alleged errors not by producing facts to show *historical* and *scientific* accuracy but by telling us that in spite of such factual errors, there is really no error, since the sentences are being used to assert moral truths. You ignore the 'use strategy' on occasions when you have facts to prove your case, but you demand that you be allowed to use it on occasions when you find no way to remove the *factual* error. The whole project sounds very subjective." Let me state at this point that I am not claiming that there is no response to such an attack. In fact, I think there is a very appropriate one.[102] My whole point, though, is that there may be some inerrantists who feel a bit uncomfortable with such a way of resolving alleged discrepancies, and there may be many more errantists who feel that such a method of answering alleged contradictions is subjective and special pleading, and would, therefore, tell inerrantists that if the "use strategy" is the best that can be done to remove the alleged error, then it is not good enough. The "use approach" is not an altogether unmixed blessing (or perhaps, some would say, "unmixed curse").

Second, there seems to be a much more devastating application of the use theory of meaning. Suppose the proposition under consideration is "the Bible is inerrant" (one could substitute, if he so chose, the biblical "your word is truth" from John 17:17). What does this proposition mean, and is it true or false? Wittgenstein would reply, "Look at its use in its language-game and you will have your answers." But what is its language-game and, whatever the language-game, in *that* language-game does one speak of truth or falsity of propositions? The answer that could be given is, " 'The Bible is inerrant' is a proposition in the language-game of religion. In that language-game propositions are not assertions of empirical facts about the world in the way that propositions in the language-game of science are. Consequently, whereas it does make sense to ask whether the propositions of science are empirically true or false, it does not make sense to ask whether propositions of religious belief are true or false, nor does it matter if they are empirically false. They are not being *used* in the way the propositions of science are, and thus, one is not to expect of any of them, including 'the Bible is inerrant,' that it be factually, empirically true." Indeed, there are modern philosophers who have argued that statements of religious belief are not empirically significant (let alone true), for they are not being used in that way.[103] If these notions are applied to "the Bible is inerrant," one could arrive at the following conclusions: (1) If one insists on treating the proposition as empirically significant, it is false because of the supposed errors in Scripture, but (2) given its language-game, "the Bible is inerrant" is not being used as a statement of empirical fact, so one should not really ask whether it is true or false, and

(3) therefore, talk of biblical inerrancy or errancy is mistaken (the notions should be dropped), because such talk mistakes the use of such a proposition *in its own language-game,* a language-game that is different from that of science, in which one does make statements about the empirical world that are true or false.

Third, Wittgenstein's claims about the independence of each language-game could be applied to the inerrancy issue in the following ways: the notions of errancy and inerrancy that are built on truth and falsity seem to presuppose that we are dealing with matters that are to be verified or falsified as though they were matters of science. However, when one realizes that the Bible is filled with religious beliefs, he recognizes that they are not the same kinds of things as the propositions of science. To think that they involve evidence in the way that science does is to "destroy the whole business." Thus, it does not even make sense to speak of the errancy and inerrancy of such propositions. To do so is to make a big blunder. Moreover, one could claim that the same comments could be made in regard to statements of Scripture that appear to be purely historical or scientific. One could say, using Wittgenstein's notions, that since such statements appear in a religious book, we must see them as part of the language-game of religion, not as part of the language-games of science and history. However, if such statements are to be treated as part of the religious language-game, and if that language-game is logically independent of the language-games of science and history, then it no longer makes any sense to speak about errancy or inerrancy of *any* of Scripture. The notions should be dropped and debate about the Bible's inerrancy stopped.

Finally, Wittgenstein claimed that language-games are not to be justified but merely accepted. Consequently, religious propositions as a whole are not to be doubted or justified as a whole; they are just to be accepted. Of course, if this is true, I then cannot speak of the inerrancy or errancy of such propositions, because I am defining those concepts in terms of truth and falsity, but truth and falsity are not said to apply to the language-game as a whole.

Someone may respond, "But even if one does not justify the language-game as a whole, can there not be justification of specific items *within* the language-game? For example, granted that one does not justify the language-game of religion as a whole, can he not justify certain things within the language-game such as specific propositions of Scripture?" The answer is that there is obviously justification within a language-game according to the rules for justification specified by the language-game itself. While one does not justify the whole language-game of science, one may indeed justify or disprove a *specific* hypothesis that falls within the broad domain of science. However, the cause of inerrancy is still not helped when one remembers what Wittgenstein said about the logical independence of language-games and the *kind* of language-game we have with religious belief. One can speak about justification of religious beliefs, *but not as though they are to be proved or disproved by evidence as if they were scientific propositions.* In fact, religious propositions even turn out to be just as certain as scientific propositions, but their equal degree of certainty does not indicate the same kind of certainty, since the language-games differ. Consequently, religious propositions have meaning, use, certainty, and justification *within their language-game,* but since Wittgenstein holds that in *that* language-game there is not proof or disproof as in science or history, there is still no validity in applying the terms *inerrant* or *errant* to propositions of religious belief, for such words are defined in terms of a notion of truth and falsity that is relevant to verification of *scientific* propositions, not to the nonempirically testable propositions of religion. Thus, the inerrantist is not helped even when justification within a form of life is admitted.

Implications of Depsychologizing. The relation of Wittgenstein's depsychologizing theme to inerrancy actually turns out to be positive, though initially one might fear that it will harm the inerrantist's case. In particular, there are those who might fear that this theme would be used against inerrancy in the following way: In response to an alleged error in the text of Scripture an inerrantist might respond that one must go behind the words of the text to the writer's intended meaning, for once it is known, it becomes clear as to how he is using the sentence and, as a result, it becomes obvious that there is no error at all. Of course, someone might respond at this point that on the basis of Wittgenstein's views it must be denied that any such appeal to a writer's intentions is legitimate. Since Wittgenstein's position entails that all that can be known of a writer's intentions is what is written, the public document, and since the public document appears to be in error, one must conclude that what the writer must have intended to write is something that turns out to be in error. There are those who have taken this matter even further than Wittgenstein did. Wittgenstein speaks of knowing the writer's intention by looking at that which is public, but there are many modern literary critics who claim that one can *never* know the intention of the writer on any grounds (public or private). One must totally detach the writer from what he has written. One must not ask what the *writer* says, but rather what the piece of literature says. Any attempt to discern the meaning of a sentence or of a whole work of literature by appealing to the author's intended meaning is thoroughly illegitimate. Appealing to the author's intention is what Wimsatt and Beardsley have condemned as the Intentional Fallacy.[104] Wittgenstein was at least willing to talk of a writer's intentions, though in a way that some might suspect undermines inerrancy, but this more radical approach totally eliminates any appeal whatsoever to a writer's intentions to uphold inerrancy of a statement or to do anything else in regard to a piece of literature.

In spite of the initial fear that Wittgenstein's views undermine inerrancy at this point, what needs to be recognized is that his emphasis really is supportive of inerrancy. As a matter of fact, if one had to determine the truth or falsity (or even the meaning) of any statement by leaving the text and investigating the author's private mental states in search of his intention, one would have to withhold judgment about the truth or falsity of any and every statement in all of literature. How would anyone ever be able to do a "psychological history" on any writer (living or dead) to determine the origin, development, and meaning of any of his ideas? None of us has such direct access to his private mental states. Even if the author states his intention, as Wittgenstein says, that would still be insufficient evidence about the writer's intention. He could always be lying, or perhaps he could even have forgotten what he intended when he wrote. Thus, if the reader had to depend *solely* on entering the author's mind to determine either the meaning or truthfulness of any of his statements, the reader would have to withhold judgment on such matters, for he could not know. An intentionalist theory of meaning and truth will not help in this matter. On the other hand, Wittgenstein's emphasis on determining the author's intention through the public document is just the corrective needed. In fact, it fits precisely what the inerrantist holds, viz., that if there is a proper understanding of the text through literal, grammatical, historical hermeneutics, it will become clear that the text is not in error. The author's intended meaning is available in the text, and through a proper awareness of the historical and cultural setting (publicly available) in which the words were written as well as an understanding of the linguistic and grammatical considerations involved (also publicly accessible), one can determine the meaning of the passage and see that it is not in error. In fact, if one could not discern the apostle Paul's meaning (for example) from the text, how would one ever decide what he meant to say? Thus, contrary to what inerrantists might fear, Wittgenstein's depsychologizing theme is tremendously helpful to inerrancy. The Wimsatt and Beardsley thesis carries matters too far—in fact unnecessarily far—because it is built on the presupposition that one either ignores intention altogether or he winds up trying to reconstruct the author's private mental states, which would obviously be objectionable for the reasons mentioned. Wittgenstein's emphasis on the intention being embedded within the text is just the corrective needed for both of the other extremes, and when properly applied, it aids the inerrantist's case.

Implications for the Meaning of "Inerrancy." A final set of implications stemming from Wittgenstein's later philosophy focuses around the meaning of the word *inerrancy*. While there are views in the *Tractatus* that could be used to argue against the possibility of defining the word and using the concept, there seem to be even more notions in the later Wittgenstein that lead to that conclusion. In particular, Wittgenstein's concept of a criterion, his anti-essentialism, his views on the unboundedness of concepts, and his use theory of meaning have application to the meaning of "inerrancy."

In relation to the concept of a criterion, it must be remembered that there are errantists who claim that the word *inerrancy* cannot be defined and the concept cannot be used, because it is impossible to come to any agreement as to the criteria for a proposition to be inerrant. It may be possible to produce seemingly endless evidence for the inerrancy of given statements, but until there are clearly defined criteria for the inerrancy of *any* proposition, no one can know whether or not any of the evidence marshaled is even relevant to establishing the inerrancy of any proposition. Wittgenstein's notions fit quite well with the views of errantists on this matter. Moreover, his concept of a criterion has even further possible applications. On the one hand, it can be claimed that there are no set criteria for inerrancy, especially since it seems that standards of truth and error, accuracy and inaccuracy have varied at different times in history, and thus any attempt to define "inerrancy" or use the concept of inerrancy is destined to futility, for not only is there lack of clarity about what inerrancy is, but it is impossible to attain such clarity. On the other hand, it could also be claimed that it is *possible* to specify criteria for inerrancy, but no one has yet done so successfully. Consequently, until such criteria are delineated in a way agreeable to all sides in the debate, usage of the term and the notion must be dropped.

Second, Wittgenstein's anti-essentialism can be applied to the issue of the meaning of "inerrancy." For example, suppose it is applied to the language-game of inerrancy. Can one specify the essence of inerrancy? Given Wittgenstein's anti-essentialism, one cannot define the essence of what it means for a proposition to be inerrant. In other words, neither the sufficient nor the necessary conditions of inerrancy can be defined. The reason has nothing to do with human intelligence or knowledge, but rather is a consequence of there not being (on Wittgenstein's views) essences of objects or concepts. Of course, if all of this is true, then it must not be possible to define the term *inerrancy* or use the concept, and that is exactly what many an errantist wants to impress on the mind of the inerrantist.

Third, Wittgenstein's claims about concepts not having clear boundaries sounds much like what many errantists say about using the term *inerrancy* and the concept of inerrancy. Errantists claim that the concept of inerrancy cannot be defined in a way that shows exactly what it means. Since it has no sharp and clear boundaries that indicate what it is and is not, the notion ought to be dropped altogether. What needs to be understood at this point is that applying Wittgenstein's views in this way takes him further than he went, and it actually goes contrary to his own views. Wittgenstein admitted that one cannot draw sharp boundaries, but he claimed that he did not know what a totally bounded concept is, anyway, so he saw no problem with being unable to draw sharp boundaries. As he argued, even an indistinct picture is still a picture, is it not?[105] It is crucial not to miss Wittgenstein's statement when he writes:

If I tell someone "Stand roughly here"—may not this explanation work perfectly? And cannot every other one fail too?
    But isn't it an inexact explanation?—Yes; why shouldn't we
call it "inexact"? Only let us understand what "inexact" means.
For it does not mean "unusable"[106] (emphasis added).

The italicized words are of crucial importance. Wittgenstein
would agree that the concept of inerrancy, as any other concept,
is inexact, but he would add that inexact does not mean unusable. Many contemporary errantists, it would seem, deny such a
claim. Inerrantists are told that the concept must be exact for it
to be usable, that inerrancy is inexact, and thus, it ought to be
recognized that talk employing such an inexact concept must be
dropped.

    Finally, from Wittgenstein's use theory of meaning there are
grounds for rejecting the concept of inerrancy as having fixed
meaning. Given Wittgenstein's use theory, if one were to ask for
the meaning of the word *inerrancy*, he would be told that there is
no absolute meaning of the word. Its use in one language-game
will not necessarily be the same as its use in another. From what
has been seen about Wittgenstein's comparison of the
language-games of religion and science, one can be certain that
the word *inerrancy* cannot be used in the same way in those two
language-games. The result of all of this for inerrancy should
again be obvious. If the word has different uses in different
language-games, and if meaning of a word is determined by its
use, as Wittgenstein has said, then it is impossible to give *the*
meaning of inerrancy. Of course, the errantist will say that because no one can produce *the* meaning of inerrancy, it must be
dropped from discussions about the Bible. It should be noted,
however, that while one could use Wittgenstein's notions in this
way, the result for the errantist would be devastating, too, if
he applied these notions across the board. Many evangelical errantists want to reject talk of inerrancy, because they claim the
word can't be precisely defined, but, given Wittgenstein's views,
what happens to talk of infallibility, authority, and inspiration,
all terms and concepts quite acceptable to errantists? Obviously,
if the errantist is consistent in his views, he must recognize that
these concepts, *on Wittgenstein's use theory* (or even without it), are
also inexact, and if the errantist insists that inexact means unusable, then he had better drop such words from *his* vocabulary.
Clearly, if the errantist were to use Wittgenstein's views to reject

inerrancy as a meaningful and usable concept, he would not only
have undermined the inerrantist's position, but also would have
come to conclusions that would destroy his position as well, if he
were to be consistent in his usage of these notions.

EVALUATION AND CRITIQUE

The picture that has been painted thus far is indeed negative
for inerrancy. However, must one be led to adopt Wittgenstein's
notions and accordingly use them in the ways mentioned to
reject inerrancy? I see no reason for that to be the inevitable
result of a study of Wittgenstein, and I should like to point out
why. Since Wittgenstein's later philosophy embodies a critique
of his earlier thought, I shall not focus on the earlier Wittgenstein, but instead center my thoughts around his later philosophy.
Moreover, in confining my remarks to his later philosophy, I
recognize that not all of it need be perceived as harmful to inerrancy. In fact, as already noted, his depsychologizing theme,
when properly applied, is an enormous help to the cause of
inerrancy. However, there are some items in regard to Wittgenstein's concept of a language-game that are worthy of comment.

Wittgenstein's concept of language-games seems essentially
correct, and I think that one's theory of meaning is going to have
to adopt in some way the notion of "use." My problems, however, center around some of the items involved in Wittgenstein's
development of the language-game concept, items that I believe
lead to negative consequences for inerrancy, but need not be
accepted. First, Wittgenstein emphasizes very heavily that the
language-games are logically independent. There may be sentences that have use in several language-games, but nonetheless,
the language-games are logically independent. Thus, the
language-games of religion and science are totally logically independent. Science is a game of empirical verification and falsification; it is the realm of objective certainty. Religion is not that sort
of game. It does not rest on evidence. One can have the same
degree of certainty in religion as in science, but the kind of
certainty (shall we say, subjective, based on personal conviction
rather than evidence) differs. It is at this point that I must
object. While I agree that science, history, and religion are distinct language-games, I do not agree that they are absolutely
logically distinct. It just seems that the only kind of religion
worthy of commitment is the kind that ultimately rests on state-

ments that are *factually* significant. More to the point, though, it seems obvious that Christianity, for example, is a religion that rests on many factual statements that are empirically testable, and in that respect it is like science and history. For example, the following statements all express religious convictions, but they also make empirically testable claims: "Jesus of Nazareth is the Son of God," "Jesus rose from the dead," "The Word became flesh and dwelt among us," and even "The Bible speaks truth in all areas of knowledge that it addresses." The truth or falsity of such claims is accessible to empirical testing as are the claims of history and science. Anyone who would present evidence for or against the truth of any of these statements cannot justly be accused of making the kind of major blunder Wittgenstein mentioned. It is just not true that none of the propositions of religion have any affinity with the kinds of propositions used in the language-games of science and history.

In addition to the problem already mentioned in regard to this independence of language-games notion, I see a further reason within Wittgenstein's own system for rejecting the idea. As we have seen, Wittgenstein held to anti-essentialism. However, it would appear that his anti-essentialism contradicts his claim about the logical independence of language-games. If one holds that each language-game is logically distinct from all others, it seems possible to define the essential nature of each language-game as opposed to each other language-game. If not, then how does one know that all language-games are logically independent? However, this seems to contradict Wittgenstein's claim that one can never define the essence of a thing, since there is much interdependence between things. Something seems to be amiss, and I suggest that in view of the problem mentioned in the preceding paragraph, the difficulty rests with the independence claim. Of course, if one rejects the independence claim on the grounds presented, then he admits that it does make sense to talk about the verifiability/falsifiability of Scripture's statements. The inerrancy debate does not rest on a mistake; one can meaningfully talk of the truth or falsity of Scripture's statements.

A second major problem that stems from Wittgenstein's concept of a language-game is his *implicit definition* of the language-game of religion. Not only does Wittgenstein claim that religion is an independent language-game, but it would seem obvious that he would define it as a language-game in which statements are not factually significant. There are, of course, various ways that philosophers have analyzed statements of religious beliefs. Some see them as expressions of emotion, and others as statements of intention of the speaker to act in a certain way (conative).[107] However, the main point is that these philosophers claim that while statements of religious belief are meaningful, they are not to be taken as assertions of empirical fact. Certainly, I would not want to claim that all the propositions of religion are empirically testable, but on the grounds already presented, I do not see that one needs to accept the notion that no religious proposition is empirically testable. Consequently, I think that Wittgenstein's implicit definition of the language-game of religion is to be rejected in favor of one that includes the concept that at least many of its propositions are empirically testable. Of course, once such a definition is adopted, it again becomes obvious that the inerrancy debate is about matters that can be empirically shown to be true or false; it is not a debate that is mistaken.

The conclusion to be drawn from a study of Wittgenstein would seem to be that even the parts of his later philosophy that are philosophically acceptable need not be taken as negative to inerrancy. Certainly, a modification of his concept of language-games as suggested offers a notion that is not harmful to inerrancy. The depsychologizing theme can be used in favor of inerrancy. Even the items used to attack the meaningfulness of "inerrancy" can be used in inerrancy's favor. For example, the attempts to show that "inerrancy" is not an exact, bounded concept (even if accepted) need not eliminate the usage of the notion, for as Wittgenstein argues, inexact does not mean unusable.

In spite of the fact that Wittgenstein's philosophy can be used to support inerrancy, the bases for denial of inerrancy are certainly available in both periods of his philosophy. From both periods there are grounds for claiming that the Bible is errant, but the main implication from Wittgenstein's philosophy as he presents it seems to be that one should simply reject all talk of both inerrancy and errancy. Those notions are meaningless when applied to Scripture, though the kind of nonsense involved in Wittgenstein's earlier views is not the same as the kind necessitated by his later philosophy. The overriding conclusion for anyone who would accept the philosophy of either period is the same, though; the whole debate about biblical inerrancy is mistaken—much ado about nothing!

MYSTICISM: HEIDEGGER

Howard M. Ducharme, Jr.

Howard M. Ducharme, Jr., is a doctoral student at the University of Oxford, Oxford, England. He graduated from Hope College, Holland, Michigan (B.A.), and Trinity Evangelical Divinity School, Deerfield (M.A.). He is a past member of Campus Crusade for Christ (1972–1978) and was a part-time instructor at College of Lake County, Grayslake, Illinois, and Chapman College (1978–1980) during his studies for his master's degree at Trinity. He is a member of the Christian Reformed Church.

CHAPTER SUMMARY

The philosphy of Martin Heidegger is intricate in structure and often perplexing in meaning. Yet its influence on contemporary theologians like Bultmann, Tillich, and those of the New Hermeneutic is pervasive. In order to understand Heidegger's work (and subsequent theologies) a detailed discussion of its central core, a mystical way of knowing, is developed. This is seen as impending in his early work and unleashed in his later works. The concluding evaluation bears on the clash that ensues with such an epistemology—the clash with hermeneutics in general and biblical inerrancy in particular.

MYSTICISM: HEIDEGGER

O NE CANNOT ADVANCE very far in the understanding of contemporary hermeneutics without finding repeated indebtedness given to the German philosopher Martin Heidegger (1889–1976). As John Macquarrie writes, "His influence seems to appear everywhere—in demythologizing and the problem of hermeneutics; in the doctrine of man; in theories of revelation; in the debate about God."[1] Even though Heidegger considered himself to be "nontheological," it can be said that "he is a maker of theology, in the same way in which Plato and Aristotle and Kant have been makers of theology."[2]

Inerrancy is intimately related with hermeneutics because it is the original autographs, *"properly interpreted,"* that are held to be "wholly true."[3] How is a text to be "properly interpreted"? Does the "meaning" reside in the intention of the author, or in the time frame of the reader? Heidegger has much to say on these and related questions. An analysis of his work shows that he exhorts us to abandon "calculative" thinking, a thinking that breaks reality into subject and object, and to embrace "primordial" or "essential" thinking, a thinking that is held to be prior to objectification. This mode of thinking is called "releasement" *(Gelassenheit).*[4] It is explicitly discussed in Heidegger's later works but is dependent on the existential, analytic writings of his early work found in *Being and Time.* In order to understand this thinker who is almost legendary in his complexity, brief comments will be made about a general categorization of his thought, which will then be divided into the early and later Heidegger for easier access.

CATEGORIZING HEIDEGGER'S THOUGHT

There are at least four different directions from which Heidegger's thought may be approached. First, he may be classified with Jaspers as a cofounder of German existentialism by stressing heavy indebtedness to Nietzsche and Kierkegaard. The difficulty with this approach is that after 1946 Heidegger himself repudiated the "existentialist" label. Also, the principal concern of Heidegger is the meaning of Being (rather than "existence"), which marks him off as an ontologist. His ambition was to restore Being to its original, pristine position in thinking.

A second approach is to draw out his close affinities with the pre-Socratics, especially Parmenides and Heraclitus, and Aristotle. But this viewpoint likewise runs into difficulties because Heidegger is less interested in *what* a historical philosopher actually said than in *how* such thought relates to his own program of "destroying the history of ontology."[5]

Third, others would note that Heidegger was a pupil of Husserl and that his major work was "dedicated to Edmund Husserl in friendship and admiration."[6] But a strict phenomenological assessment of Heidegger's work is dubious, for Husserl repudiated Heidegger's use of his method and thereby raised problems rather than solutions in understanding Heidegger's work. Even though much of *Being and Time* might best be understood within such a framework, Heidegger's later writings make a decided "turn" and therefore the phenomenological method cannot suffice as a thoroughly adequate categorization.

A fourth suggestion, which seems most viable in light of the above, is to approach Heidegger through Heidegger. All of the above suggestions are likely wellsprings of his thought and should be taken into account, but any rigid categorization would limit and prejudge Heidegger's thought. In adopting such an approach, a few biographical points may be most explicative.

BIOGRAPHICAL POINTS

Heidegger was born in 1889 at Messkirch in Baden, in the Black Forest region of Germany. His father was sexton in the

Catholic church, and, being steeped in Catholicism, Heidegger intended to study for the priesthood. But "the teenage boy received the book that was, very largely, to initiate and shape his own intellectual history": Franz Brentano's *On the Manifold Meaning of Being According to Aristotle*. [7] Later, as a student at the University of Freiburg, he abandoned the idea of becoming a priest, and decided to devote his life to philosophy. After learning of Husserl's indebtedness to Brentano's work, he sat under Husserl's training in "phenomenological seeing," only to depart from it as early as his doctoral dissertation on *The Theory of Judgement in Psychologism*. Because of his frail health he was allowed to teach and study at Freiburg during World War I.

In 1923 Nicolai Hartmann was instrumental in bringing Heidegger to Marburg with the rank of professor. Here he befriended Rudolf Bultmann, came into contact with the theology of Karl Barth, thoroughly studied Kierkegaard and Luther, and befriended Karl Jaspers before returning to Freiburg as Husserl's successor. It was while at Marburg that Heidegger composed *Being and Time*, and with its publication in 1927 he seemed to become famous overnight and was soon acclaimed one of Germany's greatest philosophers.

As professor at Freiburg from 1928 until after World War II, Heidegger penned much of his work, the vast majority of which is still unpublished. Having moved from Freiburg to a ski hut in the nearby Black Forest, Heidegger declined honorable invitations to teach at Berlin and explained that he was unable and unwilling to separate himself from his *heimat* because it was an indispensable source of thinking for him. Here he spent most of his remaining years.

The somewhat larger, philosophical time frame in which Heidegger worked is formulated by Joseph Fell.[8] At least four ontological tendencies confronted Heidegger that he would attempt to overcome: (1) Dualism in modern thought between two kinds of Being, the Being of the subject and the Being of the object, was left antithetically defined and, for Heidegger, devoid of any essential relation. (2) The Kantian dualism between the modes of being of the "thing-in-itself" and the "thing-for-us" was problematic because only the latter was held to be knowable, yet man has a desire for access into reality as a whole. (3) In post-Hegelian thought there exists a tendency to regard ontology as necessarily temporal or historical, so that beings and the relations between beings appears different in successive epochs. This was problematic for ontology because Being seems to be no longer specifiable. (4) In post-Kierkegaardian and post-Nietzschean thought, there was the view that both the essence and value of existence were cognitively absent and could not be supplied without faith or will. This posed an acute problem because it suggested that ontology was a function of attitude and decision.

Given these major ontological tendencies and Heidegger's background and influences, he was thrust onto his path in quest of the meaning of Being. His early works, before the "turn" in his thought after *Being and Time,* are characterized by a descriptive approach that philosophically explores man's temporal being in order to focus on Being in its totality and unity. In his later works Being is intuitively approached and mystically apprehended by man who can only "wait" on Being to act in language.

THE EARLY HEIDEGGER:
APPROACHING BEING (TRUTH) THROUGH *DASEIN*

Martin Heidegger's major work, *Being and Time,* attempts to heal a broken ontological totality that he inherits from his philosophical predecessors. He realizes that he stands within the philosophical tradition that goes back through Kierkegaard to Kant and thereby recognizes that one cannot leap outside the confines of finite, "historic" existence. As Kierkegaard declared that he was compelled to content himself with existing,[9] so Heidegger begins his philosophical investigation with an analysis of *Dasein,* which is "not a Thing, not a substance, not an object"[10] but is the kind of Being that belongs to persons.

Dasein is the German expression used to draw attention to man's personal existence, which is of an ontological constitution. This term is usually left untranslated in English discussions of Heidegger's thought because it does not have one simple notion. Literally, it means "Being-there," which identifies it with, yet distinguishes it from, "Being" in general. The question of the meaning of Being was the lifelong theme of Heidegger's work and so here again no simple definition can be offered. What can be said at this point, though, is that Dasein is an *entity* who "is," and the question that is to be worked out is Being—"that which determines entities as entities."[11] In order to discern the meaning of Being, the choice of starting points is not optional. This is because of the existential (and ontological) difference between the interrogation of trees, mountains, and things that merely "are," and the questioning of man who *"exists."* Hence man alone is seen to be the appropriate starting point because he alone has some understanding of, and responsibility for, who he is. Man alone "ex-sists" or "stands-out": "Dasein is an entity for which, in its Being, that Being is an issue."[12] Dasein *alone* asks the fundamental question, "Why is there something rather than nothing?" Dasein *alone* is held to be a unique transcendent possibility in contrast to objects in the world that have no such existential character. If man is understood as a mere objectification of acts, it "is tantamount to depersonalization."[13] Furthermore, the term *Dasein* is meant to express Heidegger's view of man, which understands existence prior to the separation of subject and object. Man as Dasein is not an individual subject that objectively exists in the material world; rather he is a "Being-there" whose essence is found in existential possibilities and not in scientific actualities. Thus the discussion of Being must begin with an analysis of Dasein (called "fundamental ontology") whose Being "must be exhibited in a way of its own, essentially different from the way in which entities are discovered."[14] The goal is to "lay bare" the meaning of Being in the widest sense so that one cannot fail to grasp its "true" significance.

Worldhood as Dasein

The basic state of Dasein is that of "Being-in-the-world," an expression that combines man's ontological essence (Being) and his existential condition (in-the-world), which is held to be the necessary prior condition of man, who can understand himself as a "subject" only if he is *already* a "Being-in-the-world." So the subject-object bifurcation is preempted and such a hyphenated description can begin to offer clues into the rich existential relations that Dasein has at hand. Such relations are held to be far superior to bland, spatial analysis, which can only see man as a thinking subject who is located in the world.

"World" or "worldhood," for Heidegger, does not mean the totality of the things in nature, nor does it mean the environment of man. It is the whole in which man finds himself immersed or "thrown." "World" is not therefore "ontic," i.e., concerned primarily with entities and the facts about them, but is "on-tological," i.e., concerned with the a priori meaning of Being. Heidegger insists that we cannot conceive of Dasein apart from "world" because such a condition is prior to any separation of self from world in the objective or cognitive sense. World is "given" along with Dasein prior to any act of conceptualization and the compound expression "stands for a *unitary* phenome-non."[15] The word *in* in the phrase "Being-in-the-world" is not to be understood spatially, as in the phrase "water in the glass," but as connected with the idea of "dwelling in" or "residing." Here again the relational aspect is crucial, since *possibilities* can issue from *relations*, and in such relations man's Being may be-come "uncovered."

Heidegger views the world as an environment with which man has a practical relationship brought about by "concern." "Con-cern is our relation to things (not persons) insofar as this takes such active forms as using, handling, producing, etc."[16] For example, if man thinks of a lake in regard to his practical con-cerns, he will understand it as a recreation area, as a source of food, or in any other number of ways. When man is related in this "primordial" way to the lake, it has become "ready-to-hand." If the lake is understood merely as a body of water that takes up space, it is being related to in only a minimal way and is only "present-at-hand." From such an analysis the everyday world becomes much more than a number of separate objects. It is suddenly realized as a complex and interdependent whole.

Anthony Thiselton suggests three closely related points that follow from Heidegger's conclusions about practical concern and the ready-to-hand.[17] First of all, the most immediate environ-ment of man reaches out into the larger "world." Heidegger expresses this widening of horizons as he speaks about any item of concern that is ready-to-hand as both in the person's "domes-tic world" and also in the *"public world."*[18] Second, it appears that the early Heidegger comes near to "use" as the meaning of language. He says that a sign (which would include linguistic signs) is something that is ready-to-hand and functions *both* in our immediate environment and in the "world."[19] Third, a sharp contrast is drawn between Heidegger's own view of "world" and that of Descartes, which is the more scientific or objectivist orientation. For example, it is held that often the true meaning of spatial distance is *not* best revealed by scientific calculations, but rather by such phrases as "a good walk," "a stone's throw," or "as long as it takes to smoke a pipe." Such ways of speaking relate to subjectivity and are held to be primordial descriptions of the unitary phenomenon of "world." It is important to note that Heidegger does *not* exclude the notion of scientific objectivity but holds that "certainty" is "something more primitive than scientific knowledge and anchored more firmly to human attitudes and practices in life. . . . To make the Cartesian model of knowledge the *only* one is, in Heidegger's view, not only narrow but also arbitrary."[20] Thus we see that any "commonsense" objective view of reality is curtly rejected, for it is just such an objective view that Heidegger is seeking to get behind and beyond. Thiselton notes the apparent application of this view of "world" in the work of Funk, Via, Crossan, and Fuchs on the parables of Jesus.[21] These writers hold that parables operate at a precognitive or preconceptual level and that consequently one can have a fresh experience of reality that is a vision of what cannot be stated in discursive speech.

Understanding as Dasein

Heidegger's conceptions of understanding and interpretation are also rooted in his approach to Dasein and its world. Understanding is *not* a separate topic in Heidegger's thought. The existential constitution of Dasein, "the Being of the 'there,'" is found to be composed of three conditions: states-of-mind, understanding, and discourse.[22] These three are all found to be "existentially equiprimordial," that is, one condition cannot be descriptively accounted for, or "reduced," in terms of the others. Hence these three are a priori, analytic existentials that uncover the universal structure of human existence. An existential is a mode of human existence that must be *prior* to the fact of an occurrence, because it is held that apart from the existential constitution of Dasein, no *fact* could matter to Dasein. The ultimate existential is called "care," which is finally revealed as the basic unifying factor of human existence. These three terms are important elements in Heidegger's project of uncovering the meaning of Being, but "understanding" is most relevant to our present topic. Therefore brief comments will be made on states-of-mind and discourse, and particular attention will be paid to "understanding."

States-of-mind belong to the essential character of Dasein and they reveal the *actual* (in contrast to the *possible*) mode of existence.[23] Michael Gelven emphasizes what we have already seen, that actuality/possibility "becomes almost a guiding theme," a theme that becomes "rampant"[24] in Heidegger's thought. Prior to the discussion of states-of-mind in *Being and Time*, the modes of authentic and inauthentic existence are discussed. It is pointed out that the inauthentic mode is one grounded in actuality, and the authentic is grounded in possibility. In order to offer a complete philosophy of existence both the actual *and* the possible state of affairs must be taken into account, since both are essential parts of reality. In the human life both of these factors are important, and they light up "the way we find ourselves." States-of-mind disclose a partial meaning of our existence through "moods." Moods can light up our Being-in-the-world in a way that is neither objective nor subjective but comes before the separation of subject and object. Heidegger has already implied that Dasein is not another object in the world, not just another fact of which account must be taken, and if a "mood" is so understood, then it truly can make " 'how one is and how one is faring.' "[25] Moods such as fear, joy, boredom, and anxiety direct our attention to what is inevitable in life and thereby emphasize the actual or the given. Heidegger's belief is that feeling-states "disclose" truths to us. They are *not* "mere feelings" that are divorced from any cognitive, or in this case precognitive, function. Macquarrie discusses this concept with reference to Rudolf Otto's concept of creaturely feeling and the numinous and to Paul Tillich's notion of ultimate concern.[26] Thiselton points out that this principle also relates closely to Robert Funk's claim that the "mood" conveyed by a New Testament narrative or parable "is not tied exclusively to cognition, or to discursive and conceptual language."[27] The particular importance of "mood" is that it necessarily discloses a *truth* about the *actual* world of Dasein. But as we will continue to see, possibility is *more* significant for Heidegger than actuality and hence "understanding" that discloses truth in the mode of the possible is fundamental and essential.

Heidegger's analysis of understanding is assessed by Gelven as one of the most significant sections of *Being and Time*.[28] Its importance is immediately seen because it is held to be not only an existential structure that is equiprimordial with state-of-mind, but understanding is grounded in *possibility*. This of course is held to be existentially superior to state-of-mind's ground, which is actually, because Dasein *has* possibilities before it *knows* possibilities. "Possibility as an *existentiale* is the most primordial and ultimate positive way in which Dasein is characterized ontologically."[29] Understanding is not primarily something that Dasein *does,* but rather it is what Dasein *is. "Understanding is the existential Being of Dasein's own potentiality-for-Being."*[30] So for Heidegger, possibilities become available to the inquirer neither through pure cognition (cognition that does not have a tangible object) nor through experience. Rather, they become available to the inquirer through the *"existence*-structure" of the inquirer himself. "And if Heidegger's account is accurate, a purely cognitive account of epistemology cannot be made because the relation of ideas to facts has been grounded in existence."[31] Gelven enumerates the more salient points of Heidegger's discussion of understanding: (1) The cognitive faculties of understanding are based on and secondary to the existential aspects; (2) understanding operates through a projection of possibilities; and (3) there is an essential link between thinking and being.[32]

This phenomenological analysis is eventually analyzed in Division Two of *Being and Time* on ontological grounds where time is seen to be the determining factor. Here Heidegger seeks to *describe* his interpretation of how one's self-reflection reveals the two modes of existence, but his view is not completed until one's understanding is developed into "interpretation." "In interpretation, understanding does not become something different. It becomes itself. Such interpretation is grounded existentially in understanding."[33] Interpretation is obviously *not* "the acquiring of information about what is understood; it is rather the working-out of possibilities projected in understanding."[34] The term *interpretation,* then, means the function of understanding that makes explicit what we, as existing beings, already *are* simply because we do exist. Again we see that the final ground is in Dasein and implied here again is existential superiority over the metaphysically prior actuality. In regard to "interpreting" a Bible text, one is then concerned with possibilities of meaning for human existence rather than some naked object that is present-at-hand at which "we merely stare."[35] Such an emphasis assesses the traditional historical-critical method of interpreting a text as wholly innocuous. (This point will be commented on in the final evaluation and critique section.)

Because the essence of Dasein is something that rests in possibilities, it can never be pinned down or grasped. Consequently, with Dasein as the ground of interpretation, "interpretation" is an act that consists of relating things in the world to itself and because of the nature of Dasein, "an interpretation is never a presuppositionless apprehending of something presented to us."[36] We come to objects (or texts) with a "pre-understanding" that enables us to come to an understanding, an understanding that is not "limited" by actualities, facts, or grammatical rules. Heidegger goes on to say that "meaning is an *existentiale* of Dasein, not a property attaching to entities, lying 'behind' them, or floating somewhere as an 'intermediate domain'. . . . *Hence only Dasein can be meaningful or meaningless.*"[37] In other words, propositional statements are *not* meaningful in themselves. They must be made explicit in terms of their relationship to the "concerns" of Dasein. This is what Bultmann and Ernst Fuchs presuppose when, for example, they say that a parable can *mean* something to the hearer only when it *grasps* him. Meaning is not something that is seen from a distance, nor is it something that can possibly be independent of the hearer. Rather, a parable has meaning only when the hearer is grasped in an existential "language-event." Gelven identifies the chief characteristics of Heidegger's theory of meaning as follows: (1) Meaning refers to a condition of Dasein, not to words or sentences; (2) meaning takes its ultimate ground from the world as ready-at-hand rather than present-at-hand; and (3) verbal meaning is a derivative form of existential meaning.[38]

Heidegger believes that the mode of the actual (state-of-mind) and the mode of the possible (understanding) lead directly to "discourse" which is equiprimordial with both, but is their unifying ground.[39] The important point here is that all language is grounded not in words themselves nor in abstract considerations about logic, but in *"the sharing of communication between human persons."*[40] The locus of truth is thereby shifted from propositions to the existential source of such propositions. The existential ground is "discourse" or "talk." "Talking is a sharing which is always more than what is represented by the explicit verbalization of word language."[41] This is of utmost importance because it means that a *reader* contributes his own "talk" when he reads a well-written dialogue. The reader is *not* a "viewer" but a participator in understanding what is written.

Truth as Dasein

Brief mention must be made of Heidegger's account of truth, because it crystallizes the entire existential analytic. The traditional conceptions of truth as "correspondence" or "coherence" are held to be *derived* theories about the *criteria* of truth. Heidegger may accept correspondence as the criteria of truth, but exclusively emphasizes what he considers to be the ontological *essence* of truth. In interpreting the essence of truth, the etymology of the Greek word for truth, *aletheia*, is analyzed and the conclusion drawn is that the essence of truth is "a-letheia," taken to mean "unhiddenness." This Heidegger declares to be the primordial, underived meaning of truth. Since "unhiddenness" is an event, it is a relationship of Dasein with itself, *not* of a subject with an object. "Truth" belongs to Dasein, and propositional truth is a derivative form of truth. "Truth," then, is an existential of Dasein and cannot exist independent of it. There is no truth at all without Dasein, and if Heidegger's theory is correct, then truth does not reside only in propositions. Propositional truth is a derived and limited kind of truth, a type of truth that is *not* intimately tied up with human existence, a type of truth that does not have "possibilities" because propositions have no existence of their own. Heidegger's theory of truth *has* all of the above characteristics and therefore his entire analysis of Being can be declared "true" (by *his* definition). Truth becomes a *phenomenon* rather than a matter of propositions, a phenomenon of Dasein that has an entire range of possibilities, all of which are temporal.

This view of truth is further developed in another early work: *On the Essence of Truth*. Here the "original seat" of truth is found to be *not* in the proposition, *not* in human judgment, but "ultimately" in the "standing-open" of Dasein. It is then argued that the essence of truth is freedom, because freedom makes possible the "letting-be" of things-that-are. Truth is continually being created and is *not* attached to any "timeless" property of propositions nor to logic. This discussion brings us out of the area of *Being and Time* and into the realm of Heidegger's later thought. The analytic has been pressed to a place where only *"Gelassenheit der Milde,* that attitude of quiet composure or yieldedness in which the thinker may listen for the quiet voice of Being"[42] can open up the meaning of Being to Dasein.

THE LATER HEIDEGGER:
APPREHENDING BEING (TRUTH) MYSTICALLY

Every great thinker, Heidegger declared, thinks but one thought, and one cannot help believing that he means this maxim to apply to himself. Even though Heidegger constantly points out his unity of thought, there is, at minimum, a marked contrast in style and focus in his writings after *Being and Time*. This distinction is referred to as "the turn" *(die Kehre)*, and is variously assessed as a reversal in thinking by some,[43] whereas others understand it as a mere development of thought.[44] Macquarrie stresses that both the earlier and later thought are part of a single whole,[45] and as Heidegger himself said thirty-two years after the publication of *Being and Time:* "What mattered then, and still does, is to bring out the Being of beings."[46] The *way* in which Being is brought out in the later works is the concern of this section, and as Heidegger begins with a "destruction" of traditional metaphysics before the new foundation is laid, so must our discussion.

Rejection of Traditional Western Metaphysics

Heidegger's forthright rejection of traditional metaphysics is most clearly seen in *An Introduction to Metaphysics*. The work centers on the principal question of metaphysics, "Why are there things rather than nothing?" This ranks as *the* most important question because it is the most far-reaching, deepest, and most fundamental of all questions. It is *the* question because it seeks to arrive at a final or "primal ground" which is found, according to Heidegger, in a leap—"in a leap through which man thrusts away all the previous security, whether real or imagined, of his life . . . without [the leap] there is no asking."[47] It is the leap that "opens up its own source,"[48] the "original" source. Again, then, the theme of existential possibility is upheld as the most essential factor in seeking an answer to this question.

Heidegger notes that this fundamental question finds in the Bible a ready *answer* that is determinative for all times, namely, "In the beginning God created heaven and earth." But it is precisely because the Bible offers an answer, rather than multiple possibilities, that traditional metaphysics excludes itself from addressing this question adequately. The only way the question can be authentically addressed is for one to "be brought into *relation*"[49] (emphasis added) with the question and this is possible only if one ceases to be a believer and takes all the consequences of such a step. If one has an answer, he cannot do "philosophy." Philosophy is seen as "one of the few *autonomous creative possibilities* . . . of being there [Dasein]"[50] (emphasis added). Those few who truly do philosophy are "creators" who threaten "all values" and thereby open up the paths and perspectives of authentic knowledge. Christian philosophy is viewed as "a round square and a misunderstanding,"[51] because it would *use* philosophy to lead one to a belief in God, and this is to misunderstand its true essence, namely, to let it "do something *with us.*"[52] Christian philosophy leads one to "the conceptual world of the Middle Ages"[53] rather than to the primal ground of philosophy. One can leap into an authentic relation with the ground only "through a fundamental poetic and intellectual experience of being"[54] discovered *not* through words and language, but *in* words and language themselves. How is it that one can apprehend what he cannot conceptualize? It is carried out by means of a "psycho-spiritual process"[55] that is most fully developed in *Discourse on Thinking,* a translation of *Gelassenheit.* But before turning to this short work it would be beneficial to delve further into Heidegger's understanding of language, for it is the focus of *Gelassenheit.*

Language

The heart of the problem of Being is seen to be in the fact that the word *Being* has become empty and idle. It is the "highest concept," but it has become "a vapor and a fallacy."[56] Whose fault is this? Heidegger answers that it is not the fault of the word that it remains so empty. Instead the fault lies with us, because "we have fallen out of being."[57] The meaning of the word Being has become a mere vapor, and creative thinking has degenerated with the division of reality into the realm of things and the realm of ideas. This dualism in turn led, in Heidegger's view, to the split of subject and object so that reality became objectified as a "thing." The importance of this point is evident when we see that this is one of the central concerns of the new hermeneutic. "Fuchs and Ebeling share Heidegger's view that a language which is dominated by the Cartesian perspective of subject and object can do nothing other than perpetuate established ways of seeing the world, which only mirror back man's existing con-

cerns and make him the helpless victim of his place in history."[58]
Consequently the theory of language must be stretched so as to
repair the collapse of language. This is accomplished by "a new
coming to speech," in the "language-event."

The language-event lay dormant, Heidegger believes, in
philosophy from Plato to Nietzsche, because language was
viewed only as a bearer of concepts. But, in the pre-Socratics,
Being was not a mere objective entity of thought. It was an
active, dynamic reality. Such "correct thinking"[59] experienced
what objective thinking could never understand. "Correct
thinking" knows the "determinate meaning" of Being, where
"the determinateness of being is *the* power which still sustains
and dominates all our relations to the essent as a whole, to
becoming, to appearance, to thinking, and to the ought."[60]
Again, Dasein in relation with Being proves to be the necessary
link, but alas, it is the link that reveals that the meaning of Being
can be known "only *questioningly.*"[61] How can one know only
questioningly? Only by holding existential possibility above
metaphysical actuality. It is from this vantage point that
Heidegger offers one last step in the quest for Being, a step by
which one can "know," albeit questioningly. In order to
"know," one must "know how to *wait*, even a whole lifetime"[62]
(emphasis added). "To wait" means a waiting in silence that has
cut off all images, concepts, and representations. Language then
"speaks" by "gathering up all things" into a single eloquent
wholeness and as one correctly listens without the limitations of
concepts the world is opened up for understanding. This is
possible because "words and language are not wrappings. . . . It
is in words and language that things first come into being and
are."[63] On this point Heinrich Ott, Ebeling, and Fuchs agree
with Heidegger's thought and apply it to biblical heremeneutics.
They hold that each particular New Testament passage speaks
to the one gospel, although "the gospel itself—there is only
one—remains unspoken."[64] Such an understanding grants
power and Being to words themselves. For Fuchs, the word *God*
is not a matter of human thought or concepts, but of "the meaning of Being and the truth of God in the call of Being. . . . The
language-event which takes place through the New Testament
constitutes not the communication of concepts, but a call or
pledge."[65]

Such a description of the language-event raises the final question that must be addressed, namely, the role of man as "listener." This consideration penetrates into the heart of Heidegger's task, because the entire quest for the meaning of Being has led to this capstone.

Man as Listener: Gelassenheit

In the work *Discourse on Thinking,* Heidegger roundly deplores "calculative" thinking because it is a thinking that offers man only a technical relation to the world. When man thinks this way, he is "a defenseless and perplexed victim at the mercy of the irresistable superior power of technology" and clings "one-sidedly to a single idea" and runs "down a one-track course of ideas."[66] To think this way is to think of things and the world objectively; consequently one is thinking about the actuality of items rather than about possibilities. By contrast, "meditative thinking" frees man from such an outlook. It returns man to the primordial ground of Being that has been lost and it opens a new ground and foundation to man. How does meditative thinking work? "Meditative thinking demands of us that we engage ourselves with what at first sight does not go together."[67] At one and the same time "technical devices" (objectifications of things) are allowed to enter one's daily life, and are left outside. These "things" are nothing absolute themselves "but remain dependent upon something higher."[68] Things are no longer viewed in an objective way, rather one "views" what is *not* present, a type of phenomenal illusionism; this "gives us a clear vision,"[69] rather than a meaningless relation. Stated another way, Heidegger explains: "I would call this comportment toward technology which expresses 'yes' and at the same time 'no,' by an old word, *releasement toward things (die Gelassenheit).*[70] The "old" sense of this word, *Gelassenheit,* is that of the German mystic Meister Eckhart.

Although Heidegger points out a difference between his use of the word and Eckhart's (for Eckhart it is the casting off of sinful self-seeking, for Heidegger one casts off "subject-ness" and "object-ness"), he distinguishes two "moments" of releasement as Eckhart does. The first moment is negative: a separation from things, a willing not to will. The second moment is positive: a simple openness to Being that "lets Being be," just as Eckhart speaks of "letting God be God." For Eckhart, one lets God be God through *Gelassenheit* and lives without asking "why," and so too for Heidegger Dasein must be without "why" because Being is a groundless ground. All it can do is let Being be, free of reason's categories, principles, and concepts. To ask why would be to seek a "technological" or "calculative" answer. Only when man thinks meditatively is his "essential nature"[71] saved, for "he is a meditative being."[72] If meditative thinking is not kept alive man dies. To lose track of meditative thinking means "to warp, confuse, and lay waste our nature."[73] But, "if releasement toward things and openness to the mystery awaken within us, then we should arrive at a path that will lead to a new ground and foundation. In that ground the creativity which produces lasting works could strike new roots."[74]

Two further points add to this discussion. First, meditative thinking is exemplified in "What Is Metaphysics?" Heidegger points out that science is concerned with what is. "'Nothing' is absolutely rejected by science and abandoned as null and void."[75] To explore *possibilities*, to uncover the meaning of metaphysics, Heidegger addresses the question "What about Nothing?" Here logic is ruled out because it answers that this question is impossible. But, Heidegger argues, with reason's "help" one can go into "the higher category of the Negative."[76] As such, reason itself is dependent on Nothing, and Nothing must be "given" in advance of anything that "is." "Nothing" becomes "an original part of essence" and it "shows itself." As Dasein carries out such an example of meditative thinking, it projects into Nothing, thereby getting beyond what merely "is," and thereby transcending what "is." It can have a vision of what is hidden. Being is something "other" than everything that "is" as long as one does not shut off his ears "to the soundless voice which attunes us to the horrors of the abyss."[77] Being is experienced in Nothing. Thus Being and Nothing hang together, and Hegel's proposition is held to be correct: "Pure Being and pure Nothing are thus one and the same."[78] Because Being is wholly without qualities and because no conceptually meaningful term can designate its true nature, "Nothing" can be equivalent, for it too has no determinate characteristics and is therefore nothing in particular. Such a "reconstruction" of reality is claiming that through ultimate ignorance one apprehends truth. This is the "truth" of metaphysics that one comes to understand when he thinks meditatively rather than calculatively.

Second, when the question is raised as to the object of pure releasement *(Gelassenheit)*, Heidegger answers that it has no object. As Being and Nothing are identical, it is realized that "Nothing is neither an object nor anything that 'is" at all."[79] How then does one think "meditatively"? He courageously "expends" himself, puts aside all images and representations, and engages in a nonrepresentational thinking of Being. How is final access to Being gained? Dasein is essentially powerless except to surrender its will[80] and let Being be. "Philosophy is only set in motion by leaping . . . into the ground possibilities of being as a whole. For this leap the following things are of crucial importance: firstly, leaving room for what-is-in totality; secondly, letting oneself go into Nothing. . . ."[81] In such an endeavor, Heidegger warns us, "thinking is not a means to gain knowledge. Thinking cuts furrows into the soil of Being."[82]

Thiselton points out three aspects of this perspective that Fuchs and Ebeling take up in their approach to the New Testament:[83] (1) As Heidegger believes that language arose out of the wonder evoked in man by Being, so Fuchs believes that the language-event is bound up with the experience of wonder. (2) Ebeling declares that man's task is to realize that "the subject-matter of language *itself* comes to speech *through* language."[84] (3) Texts are accorded rights over against the reader or listener. But of course texts have a "voice" of their own that lives apart from dead objectivity and grammar.

EVALUATION AND CRITIQUE: AN EVANGELICAL RESPONSE

In order to critique the effect Heideggerian thinking poses for the doctrine of inerrancy, the working definition offered by Paul Feinberg is most helpful: *"Inerrancy means that when all facts are known, the Scriptures in their original autographs and properly interpreted will be shown to be wholly true. . . ."*[85] Inerrancy is thereby defined in terms of truth, and truth is defined in terms of "correspondence."[86] The correspondence theory of truth is a corollary of epistemological dualism, which is consistent with metaphysical realism. Metaphysical realism seems to me to be a necessary and consistent approach to reality that is harmonious with biblical revelation. It is within these parameters that the following comments are made.

Language and Meaning

Dasein alone is meaningful or meaningless, argues Heidegger. Subsequently, the priority of the "worldhood" of Dasein over the subject-object distinction is apparent in the hermeneutics of Bultmann and Fuchs. Bultmann holds that objectivity can only mean "a knowledge appropriate to the subject,"[87] and so a truly "objective" interpretation of a text must never stop with grammatical analysis. He and his followers hold that the meaning of the Bible is a new revelation to each succeeding generation as the text is demythologized. Fuchs claims that the word of Jesus grasps the hearer "deep down," at a level prior to the lifeless concepts of subject and object. If the Heideggerian proposal is accepted, it follows that there is *no* one, clear, objective meaning of a text. If this constituted "meaning," then the subjectivity/possibility of the individual reader would be silenced and such a process would be viewed as empty and useless. But is it empty and useless? Is it useless to hold that there is one correct meaning of a text that resides in the original author's intention, which is cemented into propositional statements? If meaning does not terminate with what the author himself intended, then a text has a different meaning in every culture, in every historical setting, and for every individual reader. When meaning is torn from propositions and dropped into the lap of Dasein who noncognitively waits for Being to eventfully reveal itself as itself, the nonentity, qualityless *Being* speaks, as language speaks in Dasein who is used by Being to voicelessly speak. This' effectively makes all meaning (and interpretation) temporal and relative, and one correct meaning of a text is both undesirable and impossible. Cut off from the life of its author, semantic autonomy is off and running its own whimsical course.

In response to this view, it seems to me that *meaning* (which does not change) must be represented in the author's text, and the *significance* (the existential import for the reader) must content itself with a secondary role.[88] As E. D. Hirsch lucidly points out, the semantic autonomy advocated by Heidegger effectively banishes the author from his text when meaning is sought.[89] When the author becomes irrelevant in the hermeneutical task, *all* validity is eventually lost in judging an interpretation's accuracy. "If the meaning of a text is not the author's, then no interpretation can possibly correspond to *the* meaning of the text, since the text can have no determinate or determinable meaning."[90]

If a difficult biblical passage were cited, where more than one interpretation is possible due to a lack of cultural givens neces-

sary for understanding an old text, still the Heideggerian viewpoint is not thereby demonstrated. The goal of a *valid* interpretation is not futile just because a certain text is ambiguous. "Certainty is not the same thing as validity, and knowledge of
ambiguity is not necessarily ambiguous knowledge."[91] Heideggerian objections congregate on such historical reproductions of
what a text meant. To assert that what a text meant in a past age
can never be known is to theorize about what is not capable of
empirical confirmation or falsification. Ultimately such an assertion rests on faith, and one simply accepts or rejects the claim.
For the adherent of biblical inerrancy, its rejection is obvious.

Language and Thinking

In his introduction to three lectures entitled "The Essence of
Language," Heidegger formulates the issue: "to gain an experience with language." In order to gain this experience one must
think "correctly" by listening in silence until language addresses
him. Man suddenly steps backward and language comes to the
fore. Language speaks by pointing, and man is used by language
in order to bring the voiceless saying to sounding. Language
becomes a mystical message from the ineffable voice of Being.
The unsayable cannot be said, only felt. The final goal of interpretation consists in its disappearing, along with the interpreter. The letting be of language is the letting be of Being. Being
is not a concept but it directs "all saying into a growing dumb in
the presence of a happening that transcends all that is sayable in
its indeterminateness and undeterminableness."[92] This view of
language is transposed into theology by both Bultmann and Tillich. They treat the Bible "as a collection of culturally conditioned myths, which for us can function only as symbols of
nonverbal pressure that God exerts on the human spirit by
evoking experiences of mystical, emotional, and ethical insight."[93] It is necessary to make several basic responses to such a
viewpoint.

If Being may be known subjectively, this does not mean that it
is known without inference or the mediation of representative
ideas. If epistemological dualism is true, on which the correspondence theory of truth depends, on which the doctrine if inerrancy depends, then *every* reality is known through the mediation
of such representative ideas, else it is not known at all.

Even a subjective or inner knowledge must be mediated by the

categories of thought. In fact, there would be no personal encounter of Being that does not involve inference by an application of the categories. How could one recognize his experience as
an experience of Being unless it were represented in thought by a
coherent concept with categorical structure? To have a determinate experience of Being, from which Heidegger seems to speak,
implies that one has isolated Being in thought from other objects
of experience. But such a process is both rational and inferential,
and therefore self-defeating.

Suppose it is granted that Heidegger is correct; it cannot be
concluded from an experience that Being is knowable only in this
way. This is the case for the following considerations: (1) Such a
conclusion would be an inference and would by its own admission be devoid of any knowledge of Being. (2) The experience
itself could not be stated, because any statement about it would
be an inference and thereby deny its own basis. (3) Could such a
person with the *Gelassenheit* experience of the meaning of Being
be spoken of as having an experience at all? All that Heidegger
could assert is that such an experience is unintelligible. This does
seem to be the case in Heidegger's program, but is this a satisfac-
tory basis for knowledge and truth? If all difficulties could be
overcome, how could one discern between a false and a true
experience of Being? Either reason and correspondence must be
introduced here, or chaos rules.

Mysticism and Thinking

Heidegger holds that although at the level of *appearance* one
distinguishes separate, individual objects that are real enough,
these differences are not ultimate. At the absolute level of reality
(Being) there is only undifferentiated oneness, a unitary
phenomenon of the whole. Such a monistic view of reality may
be referred to as *phenomenal illusionism*,[94] since it takes the objects
of experience as they appear (phenomena) to be ultimately illusory. Only when one "lets Being be" does an object move out of
"concealedness" into the light of "unconcealedness," where it is
understood as "itself." It is interesting to note here that although
Heidegger has attempted to get behind the traditional dualism of
subject-object to a unitary phenomenon, he has in effect created
his own dualism: items that are merely "ontic" and those that
are "ontological." The principal point here, though, is that
Heidegger has moved the locus of truth away from judgments

(Kant) to primordial understanding and fundamental "mood."
The criticisms in the preceding section would argue that there is
no such thing as "primordial understanding" as a mode of
knowing, but that as Heidegger's project stands, it bears distinc-
tive parallels with Eastern mysticism.

In Chinese Taoism all conceptual knowledge is held to be
inadequate in understanding reality at the absolute level, for it
can only see definite objects with determinate qualities. Concepts become worse than useless in apprehending "reality" and
the conceptual viewpoint is transcended by direct, intuitive
awareness. This amounts to holding that through ultimate ignorance alone one apprehends truth. Its claim is that it is a no-view
viewpoint of reality in that reality is apprehended as it is in itself.
All of these points can easily describe Heidegger's work, and
Stuart Hackett suggests four critical responses to such a position:
(1) A no-view viewpoint is itself a viewpoint because it stands in
contrast to the view, or views, it purports to leave behind.
Therefore it is not "system independent" in its report of Being as
it is in itself. (2) Even if objective truth is only an approximation,
one is misunderstanding the human situation to expect more.
(3) Indeterminate, unqualified Being *is* literally nothing, but, on
the other hand, if Being can be differentiated from the way
reality appears, then Being must have determinate qualities that
involve that difference. (4) If a proponent of such a view argues
that Being is different not by possessing qualities but by being
devoid of all qualities, then how could a person be conscious of
such an indeterminate reality?[95]

From another direction, Heidegger's alternative to epistemological dualism reduces ultimately to self-contradiction.
The "unitary phenomenon," which is supposedly preconceptual,
is merely a form of epistemological monism: the primordial
understanding of an object, which is its Being, and the Being
itself are numerically identical, but the object is real apart from
such knowledge of it. This monism is open to the following objections: (1) Heidegger begins with the "preconceptual" facts of
consciousness and then attempts to find correlates for these facts
in the real, external world. But when a perception is said to be
identical with the Being of the object, it is unintelligible if not
false. The only knowledge of the external world in particular
springs ultimately from perceptions, but if the percept and the
Being of the object were numerically one, there would never be

any reason for saying so; not even Heidegger's claim that Western metaphysics went astray after Plato is a possible excuse. (2) Heidegger's position cannot be salvaged by asserting that the percept and object are only partially the same, partially different. For prior to such a critical determination, the whole percept may be numerically distinct from the object. Also, the fact that one can critically consider the percept to determine its relation to the object implies at once that percept and object are distinct. (3) If the "preconception" were identical with the Being of the item, no experience of qualities would be possible at all—which is obviously ridiculous.

It is instructive at this juncture to note that the comparison of Heidegger with Eastern categories of thinking, and with mysticism in general, is not without warrant. In *On the Way to Language* Heidegger draws attention to a connection between his "way" and the Tao:

> The word "way" probably is an ancient primary word that speaks to the reflective mind of man. The key word in Laotse's poetic thinking is *Tao,* which "properly speaking" means way.[96]

Taoism became an essential ingredient in the Buddhism brought to China in A.D. 520 and in "Who is Nietzsche's Zarathustra?" Heidegger mentions Buddhism in connection with the question of overcoming the will.[97] Even more telling is the comment in which Heidegger recognizes a kin and ally of the mystic in the way he thinks: "The most extreme sharpness and depth of thought belongs to genuine and great mysticism."[98] Last, there is the tantalizing remark of William Barrett in the preface to his anthology of the works of D. T. Suzuki, the leading exponent of Zen Buddhism in the Western world:

> A German friend of Heidegger told me that one day when he visited Heidegger he found him reading one of Suzuki's books: "If I understand this man correctly," Heidegger remarked, "this is what I have been trying to say in all my writings."[99]

All this serves to make the point that if Heidegger's "way" is in the final analysis mystically based, then such an objectively founded doctrine as biblical inerrancy will find no compatibility.

The Danger of Heidegger's Path

Even if one disagrees with the above criticisms of Heidegger's "way," there remains a grave danger inherent in *Gelassenheit,*

especially if it is detached from a religious matrix.[100] Paul
Hühnerfeld writes, "Meister Eckhart would never have taken
the mystical step if he had believed that he was leaping into
Nothingness instead of into the arms of God."[101] For Eckhart,
God is a plenum of Being, goodness, and intelligibility. But for
Heidegger, the situation is radically different. Heidegger's Being
is by no means fatherly, loving, benevolent, or "intelligible."
Gelassenheit goes hand in hand with anxiety, a notion expressed in
"What Is Metaphysics?": "For awe dwells close by to essential
anxiety as the terror of the Abyss."[102] The abyss is the ground of
Being, which is the "groundless play of Being." It is unintelligible, it admits of no explanation, and it is simply inscrutable.
"Heidegger has virtually undermined all possibility of hope. For
there can be no 'rational basis' for hope . . . nor can there be the
hope which is founded on love . . . Heidegger's 'Being' cannot be
determined personalistically."[103] Dasein cannot will "the
Event" to come to pass; there is nothing in "the Event" to love,
but much to fear. There is much to fear because it is releasement
to a truth that is untruth. So it is that Heidegger aptly called his
thinking a "sacrifice,"[104] and in his der Spiegel interview said,
"Only a god can save us. . . . I cannot help."[105]

EPILOGUE

Norman L. Geisler

Norman L. Geisler

EPILOGUE

T HERE ARE, OF COURSE, many other thinkers who have contributed to the presuppositions accepted by modern errantists. One notable example is the process theology flowing from Alfred North Whitehead. This, however, is a topic for another book.[1]

It is important here to note that the philosophies discussed in this volume indeed contribute to the intellectual "air" that twentieth-century errantists breathe. Many of these influences can be detected in the writings of the contemporary continental theologian G. C. Berkouwer and in his American counterparts, Jack Rogers and Stephen T. Davis.

PHILOSOPHICAL INFLUENCES ON
BERKOUWER'S VIEW OF SCRIPTURE

In Berkouwer's earlier work on Scripture,[2] he held the historic orthodox view of the inspiration and inerrancy of Scripture.[3] Then, after reading Karl Barth, he changed his view and wrote his *Holy Scripture.*[4] Since the Kierkegaardian influences on Barth are well-known, we have here perhaps the link between the neoevangelical (errantist) view of Scripture and Kierkegaard (see chap. 5).

There are other philosophical influences on Berkouwer; the perceptive reader can discern them from his own words. It is not

231

through the influence of Hume's anti-supernaturalism that he
wrote: *"God's word has not come to us as a stupendous miracle* that shies
away from every link with the human in order thus to be truly
divine"[5] (emphasis added). Again, Berkouwer says he "does not
wish to interpret the God-breathed character [of the Bible] in an
abstract *supernaturalistic and 'miraculous' manner"*[6] (emphasis
added). Thus, he adds, the Word of God (Scripture) "is not
known to us in the outlines of a *supernatural miracle* lifted out of
time and human weakness . . . but in the human form of word
and writing"[7] (emphasis added). Why this shying away from the
supernatural? Is this not evidence of the naturalistic influence on
our intellectual culture due to the writings of men like Hobbes,
Spinoza (chap. 1), and Hume (chap. 2)?

Berkouwer is quite clear in following the Barthian position
(influenced by Kierkegaard) that the words of Scripture are not
themselves a revelation but merely a *record* and witness to the
revelation. In short, he speaks against the orthodox view (once
held by himself) of verbal inspiration. He says, "Even conservative theologians have often had difficulty with the term 'verbal
inspiration.'" He quotes approvingly one who says, "The phrase
'verbal inspiration' is one to which so great ambiguity attaches
that it is now very commonly avoided by careful writers."[8] If the
Bible is not God's revelation in words, what is it? According to
Berkouwer, "Holy Scripture is the revelation, that is, the only
instrument 'by which the revelation of God in Christ can be
known'"[9] (emphasis added). He speaks, then, of Scripture as
"the normative *witness* to this revelation"[10] (emphasis added).
The human words of Scripture are "the way of the *reliable testimony* of God"[11] (emphasis added). Of course, as one can easily
see, "reliable [human] testimony" *about* God is very different
from an infallible and inerrant Word *of* God.

The influence of higher criticism, which began with Hobbes
and Spinoza and was given further impetus through the left-wing
disciples of Hegel (see chap. 4) is also evident in Berkouwer. His
insistence on separating the words of Jesus and those of Scripture
indicates an influence of modern form and/or redaction criticism. Berkouwer wrote, "An intelligible distinction can be made
between believing in Scripture and believing in the word that
Jesus had spoken."[12] In fact the Bible is only human words[13]
that are *taken into service* by the Holy Spirit.[14] Sometimes these
words are in error. For example, the apostle Paul "did not in the

least render timeless propositions concerning womanhood."[15] This is Berkouwer's analogue to Rudolf Bultmann's demythologizing of the Scripture, which reflects the philosophy of Heidegger (see chap. 8). (In accord with Berkouwer's denial of the absolute divine authority of what the apostle Paul affirmed about the role of women, another errantist, Paul Jewett (in *Man as Male and Female*) concluded that the apostle Paul was *wrong* in what he affirmed about the husband being the wife's "head" [1 Cor. 11:3]). Other influences of Bultmann on Berkouwer are evident. He rejects, for example, the biblical presentation of "the three-decker universe"[16] and speaks of attending to the "Word in the midst of many words, to its intent and purpose."[17] This is akin to Bultmann's search for the existential "kernel" beneath the human mythological "husk" of Scripture. In point of fact, Berkouwer even defends Bultmann's use of "myth," arguing that we "cannot directly take up a position against Bultmann's theological concern with demythologizing. . . ."[18]

In order to defend his view, Berkouwer retreats to both a relativistic and an intentionalistic view of truth.[19] In line with the relativism of Nietzsche (see chap. 6) and other modern thinkers, Berkouwer denies that the Scriptures express absolute truth. Besides his claim that the "Scripture subjected itself to the fate of all writing"[20] which involves error, Berkouwer says, "It [the Bible] comes to us in the midst of an overwhelming multiformity of human witnesses, of *human questions* and answers, *of skepticism* and trust, of faith and unbelief. . ."[21] (emphasis added). Indeed, Berkouwer boldly proclaims, "God did not reveal himself with a number of profound ideas or timeless truths . . ."[22] (emphasis added). This skepticism and relativity of truth view is reflective of both David Hume and Friedrich Nietzsche (see chaps. 2 and 6). The skepticism, relativism, and error of human words used in the service of God is no problem for Berkouwer. For him "this divine taking-into-service . . . *does not erase the weakness of the human word nor its limitations*"[23] (emphasis added). He asks, "Does this human aspect not *limit and relativize the Word of God?*"[24] (emphasis added).

The early influence of the separation of the scientific and the "spiritual" aspects of Scripture seen in Hobbes and Bacon (see chap. 1) are manifest in Berkouwer. Berkouwer quotes Herman Bavinck with approval: "The authors of Holy Scripture apparently did not know anything more than their contemporaries concerning all these sciences, such as geology, zoology, physiology, and medicine." Neither, he adds, was that necessary, "because *they did not offer scientific theories . . .*"[25] (emphasis added). Why not? Because, says Berkouwer, "it was not the purpose of Scripture to offer revealing information on that level."[26] Thus we are free to speak of "innocent inaccuracies"[27] in the Bible. For "the purpose of Scripture is not to orient us concerning the composition of the cosmos in its created parts, nor to inform us scientifically about the 'composition of man.'"[28]

Clearly Berkouwer, under the influence of existentialism springing from Kierkegaard and Heidegger, rejects the correspondence view of truth for a functional, pragmatic, intentional one. This will be amplified in the discussion of Rogers below. It will suffice here to document the point. Truth does not reside in the *affirmation* of the author in Scripture, but in the "*intent* of the author"[29] behind Scripture. Berkouwer rejects "the concept of error in the sense of incorrectness. . . . If erring is formalized in such a way, it cannot later be related to truth in a biblical sense." For in the Bible "what is meant is . . . a *swerving from the truth* and upsetting the faith (2 Tim. 2:18)"[30] (emphasis added). To speak, then, of inerrancy is wrong. For "the formalization of inerrancy virtually destroys this intention," Berkouwer insists.[31]

PHILOSOPHICAL INFLUENCES
ON JACK ROGERS'S VIEW OF SCRIPTURE

In his book *The Authority and Interpretation of the Bible*, Rogers frankly admits the influences of Berkouwer on his errancy view of Scripture,[32] but he also bought into Kant, Kierkegaard, Edmund Husserl, Heidegger, Wittgenstein, and even Whitehead. Rogers recognizes the influence of Kant on Barth[33] and admits Berkouwer changed his view on Scripture after studying Karl Barth.[34] Likewise, Rogers recognizes the influence of Kierkegaard on Barth,[35] with whom Rogers also acknowledges influence by way of Bavinck through Berkouwer on his own intentionalist (functional) view of truth.[36] "Intentionalism" springs from the philosopher Husserl, who, though not acknowledged by Rogers, played a significant role in shifting the focus from words to intentions. This misdirection was addressed by linguistic philosophers (see chap. 7). Rogers speaks approvingly of Heidegger's attack on "objective thinking"[37] in favor of a more subjective (existential) one of "salvation through union with God."[38] Throughout his book Rogers reflects a conventionalistic view of the relativity of language (a la Wittgenstein; see chap. 7). We have already noted the influences of Heidegger on Bultmann (or their similarities) (see chap. 8). Rogers in turn sympathizes or identifies with a good deal of Bultmannian thought. Like Bavinck and Berkouwer, Rogers focuses on "the divine content of Scripture, not on its human form."[39] He commends men like Abraham Kuyper and Bavinck because "they reaffirmed . . . the saving content, not the supernatural form of Scripture." By this he hopes with Bultmann "to recognize a center and a periphery to the message, as opposed to the mechanical model of scholasticism, which tended to treat every verse of the Bible as of equal importance."[40] By this Rogers hopes to avoid the orthodox view "that Scripture had to come in what seems to us a perfect form."[41] Herein, says Rogers, "is a way that distinguished between the central saving message of Scripture and all of the difficult surrounding material that supports the message."[42]

From the previous citations one can see how Rogers would justify the use of higher criticism of Scripture. This becomes evident in Rogers' (mis)understanding of "accommodation." He considered B. B. Warfield's rejection of the notion that accommodation may include error as an "overreaction."[43] By separating human fallible form from divine infallible content, Rogers hoped to gain a "freedom of exegesis."[44] These hopes are reminiscent of Hobbes, Bacon, and Spinoza, who likewise believed themselves defenders of the "essential" truth of Christianity by sacrificing the human form.

Rogers, like some of his philosophical ancestors, rejected the infallibility of Scripture in the scientific sphere. He wrote plainly, "The Bible was not a textbook of science or an academic tract."[45] Rogers believes that the biblical authors "reflect views of life, history, and the cosmos which were then current."[46] Also A. A. Hodge is criticized for believing "it was a purpose of the Bible to convey scientific matters. . . ."[47] Rogers is not really consistent on this matter, since he desires to exlude physical science from inerrant revelation but, strangely enough, he wishes to retain social sciences. He says, "The use of 'salvation' to designate the primary purpose of Scripture in this study should not be taken to exclude, for example, social and ethical concerns."[48]

The most dominant theme of Rogers' book—his function-

over-form thesis—is deeply indebted to a number of philosophers (Kant, Kierkegaard, William James, et al.). Like Berkouwer, Rogers does not understand biblical truth as that which
corresponds to the facts, to reality (a correspondence view of
truth). Rather, he sees truth as intentional, functional, or pragmatic. He approvingly quotes Berkouwer's definition of "error"
as "a swerving from the truth" and contends we should understand "error in the biblical sense of sin and deception. . . ."[49] He
identifies meaning with function, referring to "the function, the
meaning of the gospel. . . ."[50] With Berkouwer, Rogers speaks of
"a religious pragmatic" and of "a 'functional' view of Scripture." He believes that for Calvin and Berkouwer, "religious
knowledge was either personal, relational knowledge, or it was
not considered worthy of the name knowledge."[51] The Kierkegaardian similarities are obvious to those acquainted with the
Danish thinker. Rogers commends "Forsyth, [who] returned to
the functional authority of Scripture. . . ."[52]

Of course, Rogers denies propositional revelation in the style
of the post-Kantian, post-Kierkegaardian existentialists. Hodge
is criticized for believing "that the words as well as the thoughts
of the Bible were inspired. . . ."[53] Warfield, too, is chastized by
Rogers for holding that "the authority of Scripture is shown to
inhere even in its vocables, its tenses, its numbers, and its forms
of speech as God's Words."[54] He believes we should place our
"concentration on the message rather than the words,"[55] that is,
"in the *thought* of the biblical writers and not in the form of their
words"[56] (emphasis added). Rogers does not elaborate on just
how one can separate thought from words. He is sure, however,
that, as Berkouwer said, "*Behind* this connection of message and
words is the power of the Spirit."[57] For Rogers the true meaning
of Scripture, then, is not *in* the words of Scripture, as Paul
affirmed,[58] but *behind* them. Here again we are faced with
philosophies foreign to the affirmations of the New Testament
and with the nearly unanimous body of orthodox Christians
down through the ages until relatively recent times.[59]

Philosophical Influences
on Stephen T. Davis's View of Scripture

With the prefatorial blessing of Clark Pinnock, who has been
in recent decline from his earlier inerrancy position, Stephen
Davis launches a clear-cut attack on the doctrine of biblical

inerrancy in his book *The Debate About the Bible*. [60] Despite the fact that Davis acknowledges that he cannot really *prove* an error in the Bible,[61] he believes there are many errors. He attempts to list some. His *reason* (?) for believing some things are errant is illuminating. He concludes that the command to kill the Canaanites contradicts moral teaching found elsewhere in the Bible.[62] Why? Davis answers: "I speak for no one except myself, but *I believe that killing innocent people is morally wrong*"[63] (emphasis added). Elucidating further on the killing of the Canaanites, Davis writes, "I frankly find it difficult to believe that it was God's will. . . ."[64] What, then, is Davis's grounds for affirming the Bible is in error here? His own *moral sentiment*. Where did this moral determination of what is true and what is false in Scripture come from? The names of Spinoza (see chap. 1) and Kant (see chap. 3) will come to the mind of the careful reader.

What is of more than passing interest is that Davis (and other errantists) seem willing and able to go beyond their own separation of the infallible moral teaching of the Bible from the fallible scientific teaching, and actually condemn the Bible for some of its moral pronouncements. Davis writes, "The Bible is infallible, as I define that term, but not inerrant. That is, there are historical and scientific errors in the Bible. . . ."[65] Besides the fact that errantists never tell us exactly where the alleged line between moral and scientific teaching is, they wander over it themselves. Rogers, for example, spoke of the Bible as infallible in social and interpersonal matters,[66] but Paul Jewett claimed the Bible was wrong when it spoke of a wife's interpersonal relation to her husband.[67] Davis says, "There are historical and scientific errors in the Bible," and adds, "I have found none on matters of faith and practice."[68] However, he speaks confidently of Paul's sexism and even of Jesus' mistaken belief about the time of His second coming.[69] But are not these issues moral and doctrinal? And if the Bible is not infallible in doctrinal and moral matters, then what is left?

This epilogue is by no means exhaustive of the deleterious influences of philosophy on modern errantists. It is intended only to be suggestive of some of the more significant ones. It is plain that the intellectual "air" breathed by contemporary errantists is filled with philosophical pollutants. One cannot help but wonder what serious effects these pollutants will have on the health and life of the church of Jesus Christ.

NOTES

Notes on the Preface

[1]Benedict De Spinoza, *The Chief Works of Benedict De Spinoza*, trans. R. H. M. Elwes, vol. 1, Introduction, *Tractatus Theologico-Politicus, Tractatus Politicus* (London: George Bell, 1883), p. 166.

[2]Stephen T. Davis, *The Debate About the Bible* (Philadelphia: Westminster, 1977), p. 139.

Notes on Chapter 1

[1]There are, of course, ancient philosophical roots to modern biblical errancy; see my "Philosophical Presuppositions of Biblical Errancy" in *Inerrancy* (Grand Rapids: Zondervan, 1979), pp. 308–11. Contrary to Rogers, who mistakenly blames Aristotle (through Aquinas and Turretin) for the rise of inerrancy, it is really more Plato and the Platonic-Alexandrian school of allegorizing Scripture to get at its higher spiritual or symbolic meaning who are really the source of the problem (see Jack Rogers, *The Authority and Interpretation of the Bible* [New York: Harper & Row, 1979], esp. pp. 35, 44, 172–73).

[2]Francis Bacon, *The New Organon* (New York: Bobbs-Merrill, 1960), Book One, LXX.

[3]Ibid., CXXVII.

[4]Ibid., CXXIV.

[5]Ibid.

[6]Ibid., LXXIII.

[7]Thomas Aquinas, *Summa Contra Gentiles*, I, 4, 3–5.

[8]Thomas Aquinas, *Summa Theologica*, II–III, 2, 10.

[9]Bacon, *New Organon*, Book One, LXV, and Book Nine. One contemporary opponent of inerrancy speaks of Bacon's influence on his successors as follows: "The virtuosi [prominent seventeenth-century scientists] followed Bacon's lead, making science and religion separate spheres with distinct tasks." In the final analysis this is what Rogers himself does (see Rogers, *Authority and Interpretation of the Bible*, p. 225; cf. pp. 26–28, 251, 287).

[10]Ibid., Book One, LXV.

[11]Harry Rimmer read the modern wave theory of light into Job 38:7, which speaks of stars "singing." See *The Harmony of Science and Scripture* (Grand Rapids: Eerdmans, 1952), p. 127.

[12]Thomas Hobbes, *Leviathan* from *Great Books of the Western World* (Chicago: Encyclopaedia Britannica, 1952), chap. 1.

[13]Ibid., p. 49.

[14]Ibid., p. 269.

[15]Ibid., p. 54.

[16]See A. J. Ayer, *Language, Truth and Logic* (New York: Dover, n.d.), chap. 1.

[17]Hobbes, *Leviathan*, p. 80.

[18]Ibid., p. 83.

[19]Ibid., p. 165.

[20]Ibid., p. 71.

[21]Ibid., p. 70.

[22]Ibid., p. 70–71.

[23]Ibid., p. 70.

[24]Benedict De Spinoza, *The Rationalists*, hereafter referred to as *Ethics* (Garden City, N.Y.: Doubleday, 1960), p. 247. Benedict De Spinoza, *The Chief Works of Benedict De Spinoza*, trans. R. H. M. Elwes, vol. I, *Introduction, Tractatus Theologico-Politicus, Tractatus Politicus;* hereafter referred to as *Tractatus* (London: George Bell, 1883), p. 81.

[25]Spinoza, *Ethics*, p. 210.

[26]Spinoza, *Tractatus*, p. 194.

[27]Ibid., p. 165.
[28]Ibid., p. 166.
[29]Ibid., p. 167.
[30]Ibid., p. 190.
[31]Ibid., p. 172.
[32]Ibid., pp. 196–97.
[33]Spinoza, Ethics, pp. 322, 327.
[34]Ibid., p. 212.
[35]Spinoza, Tractatus, p. 92.
[36]Ibid., p. 83.
[37]Ibid., p. 96.
[38]Ibid., p. 87.
[39]For the documentation of this point, which is a correction of the mistaken statement in the Encyclopedia of Philosophy, s. v. "Spinoza," vol. 7, p. 531, that it "was not discovered for publication until the late eighteenth century," I am indebted to Dr. John Woodbridge.
[40]Spinoza, Tractatus, p. 126.
[41]Ibid., p. 128.
[42]Ibid., p. 147.
[43]Ibid., p. 150.
[44]Ibid., p. 155.
[45]Ibid., p. 159.
[46]Ibid., p. 171.
[47]Ibid., p. 170.
[48]Spinoza, Ethics, p. 24; Tractatus, p. 93.
[49]Stephen T. Davis, The Debate About the Bible (Philadelphia: Westminster, 1977), p. 139.
[50]For two recent books on the archaeological support of Scripture, see Archaeology and the Bible, Donald J. Wiseman and Edwin Yamauchi (Grand Rapids: Zondervan, 1979), and the latter's Stones and the Scriptures (Philadelphia: Lippincott, 1972).
[51]The fact that errantists have cast the defense of their view in terms of an inductive approach to the phenomena as opposed to what they call a "traditional" or "deductive" approach is ample testimony to the long-range effects of Bacon's inductivism. See W. Sanday, "Retrospect and Results: The Traditional and Inductive Views of Inspiration Compared," Inspiration: Eight Lectures (London: Longmans, Green, 1903); and Dewey M. Beegle, The Inspiration of Scripture (Philadelphia: Westminster, 1963).
[52]The whole question of methodology and inerrancy is a fascinating one. Some have argued for a basically deductive approach (B. B. Warfield in The Inspiration and Authority of the Bible [Philadelphia: Presbyterian and Reformed, 1970], p. 201–2.), some for an adductive approach (Arthur Holmes, "Theological Method and Inerrancy" in Bulletin of the Evangelical Theological Society, vol. 11, no. 3 [Summer 1968]). James I. Packer expounds a kind of retroductive approach ("Hermeneutics and Biblical Authority," Themelios, 1 [Autumn 1975]: 3–12). In reflecting on these approaches it seems to me that there is an element of truth in each of them. The doctrine of inspiration is based on an inductive study of Scripture, which yields two truths: (1) the Bible is God's Word and (2) God cannot err. The latter truth adduces—the Bible is "God-breathed." From these truths, inerrancy is deduced. If God cannot err, then the Bible cannot either. However, this inerrancy model is "filled in" or "modified" retroductively as one examines the data (phenomena) of Scripture in the light of the model.
[53]See John Wenham, Christ and the Bible (Downers Grove, Ill.: InterVarsity, 1973), chap. 1.
[54]The word myth is used five times in the New Testament, always as something to be rejected (1 Tim. 1:4; 4:7; 2 Tim. 4:4; Titus 1:14; 2 Peter 1:16). In the last passsage Peter declares, "We did not follow cleverly invented stories when we told you about the power and coming of our Lord Jesus Christ."

Notes on Chapter 2

[1]René Descartes, *A Discourse on Method*, Meditations IV, V.

[2]Benedict De Spinoza, *The Chief Works of Benedict De Spinoza*, trans. R. H. M. Elwes, 2 vols. (New York: Dover, 1951), 1:87.

[3]Herbert of Cherbury, *De Veritate*, trans. Meyrick H. Carre (Bristol: Arrowsmith, 1937), pp. 289–307.

[4]See J. L. Neve and O. W. Heick, *A History of Christian Thought*, 2 vols. (Philadelphia: Muhlenberg, 1946), 2:63–64; Colin Brown, *Philosophy and the Christian Faith* (Downers Grove, Ill.: InterVarsity, 1968), pp. 78–80.

[5]David Hume, *An Enquiry Concerning Human Understanding*, sec. 12, "Of the Academical or Skeptical Philosophy," pt. 3.

[6]Ibid., sec. 10, "Of Miracles," pt. 1.

[7]Ibid.

[8]Ibid., pt. 2.

[9]Ibid.

[10]Ibid., sec. 12, pt. 3.

[11]John Herman Randall, Jr., *The Making of the Modern Mind*, rev. ed. (Boston: Houghton Mifflin, 1940), pp. 293, 553–54.

[12]Wilbur M. Smith, *The Supernaturalness of Christ* (Boston: Wilde, 1954), p. 142.

[13]David F. Strauss, *A New Life of Jesus*, 2nd ed., 2 vols. (London: Williams and Norgate, 1879), 1:199–201.

[14]Friedrich Schleiermacher, *The Christian Faith*, ed. H. R. Mackintosh and J. S. Stewart, 2 vols. (New York: Harper & Row, 1963), 1:178–84.

[15]Albert Schweitzer, *The Quest of the Historical Jesus*, trans. W. Montgomery (New York: Macmillan, 1971), pp. 51–53.

[16]Ibid., p. 154.

[17]Ernst Renan, *Life of Jesus* (London: Mathieson, n.d.), pp. 147–55.

[18]Otto Pfleiderer, *Philosophy and Development of Religion*, 2 vols. (Edinburgh: Blackwood, 1894), 1:5–6.

[19]Adolf Harnack, *What Is Christianity?* trans. Thomas Bailey Saunders, 3rd and rev. ed. (London: Williams and Norgate, 1912), pp. 25–31.

[20]See *Enquiry*, sec. 10, pt. 1.

[21]Rudolf Bultmann, "New Testament and Mythology," in *Kerygma and Myth*, ed. Hans Werner Bartsch (New York: Harper & Row, 1961), pp. 4–5, 10; Rudolf Bultmann, *Jesus Christ and Mythology* (New York: Scribner, 1958), pp. 14–18.

[22]Paul Tillich, *Systematic Theology*, 3 vols. (Chicago: University of Chicago Press, 1971), 1:115–18.

[23]John A. T. Robinson, *Honest to God* (Philadelphia: Westminster, 1963), pp. 11–18, 64–68.

[24]Lawrence Burkholder, Harvey Cox, and Wolfhart Pannenberg, "A Dialog on Christ's Resurrection," *Christianity Today* 12, no. 14 (12 April 1968): 5–9.

[25]Immanuel Kant, *Critique of Pure Reason*, Introduction, pt. 4.

[26]Auguste Comte, *Course of Positive Philosophy*.

[27]Ludwig Wittgenstein, *Tractatus Logico-Philosophicus* (1922).

[28]Moritz Schlick, *General Theology of Knowledge* (1922).

[29]A. J. Ayer, *Language, Truth and Logic* (New York: Dover, 1946), p. 35.

[30]Ibid., pp. 5ff., 33ff.

[31]Ibid., pp. 31, 54.

[32]Ibid., pp. 115–16.

[33]Ibid., pp. 33ff., 107–12.

[34]Antony Flew, "Theology and Falsification," *New Essays in Philosophical Theology*, ed. Antony Flew and Alasdair MacIntyre (New York: Macmillan, 1955), pp. 96–99.

[35]Brown, *Philosophy and the Christian Faith*, p. 168.

[36]Cf. Paul M. Van Buren, *The Secular Meaning of the Gospel* (New York: Macmillan, 1963), pp. 14–15.

[37]For an outstanding compilation of such treatments by linguistic analysts, see John Donnelly, ed. *Logical Analysis and Contemporary Theism* (New York: Fordham University Press, 1972).

[38]*Enquiry*, sec. 10, pt. 1.

[39]C. S. Lewis, *Miracles* (New York: Macmillan, 1947), p. 105.

[40]For instance, see William Hordern, *A Layman's Guide to Protestant Theology* (New York: Macmillan, 1955), p. 37.

[41]Such an apologetic will not be attempted in this chapter. For validation of two such arguments, see Gary Habermas, *The Resurrection of Jesus: An Apologetic* (Grand Rapids: Baker, 1980), esp. chaps. 1–3.

[42]It is not our purpose here to decide whether the Jansenist miracles actually occurred or not. We are only concerned with Hume's reaction when purported miracles admittedly fulfill his own criteria.

[43]For Hume's evaluation of his first three criteria with regard to the Jansenist miracles, see *Enquiry*, sec. 10, pt. 2.

[44]Ibid.

[45]Hume's historical opus is *The History of England*, 6 vols. (London: Gilbert and Revington, 1848).

[46]Lewis, *Miracles*, pp. 105–6.

[47]David Hume, *An Abstract of A Treatise of Human Nature* (Cambridge: Cambridge University Press, 1938, from the 1740 edition), pp. 14–16.

[48]See Alastair McKinnon, "'Miracle' and 'Paradox,'" *American Philosophical Quarterly* 4 (1967):309, for instance.

[49]Patrick Nowell-Smith, "Miracles," *Hibbert Journal* 48 (1950): 354–60. This essay is reprinted in Flew, *New Essays*, pp. 243–53.

[50]See *The Encyclopedia of Philosophy*, s.v. "Miracles," by Antony Flew; also Antony Flew, *Hume's Philosophy of Belief* (London: Routledge and Kegan Paul, 1961), pp. 207f.

[51]Lewis, *Miracles*, p. 105.

[53]For a good treatment of this issue, see Richard Swinburne, *The Concept of Miracle* (London: Macmillan, 1970), pp. 26–32.

[53]*Enquiry*, sec. 10, "Of Miracles," pt. 1.

[54]Ayer, *Language, Truth and Logic*, Introduction (written in 1946), pp. 5–26.

[55]Brown, *Philosophy and the Christian Faith*, p. 138. For a brief statement of several philosophical problems in logical positivism, see David Elton Trueblood, *Philosophy of Religion* (New York: Harper and Bros., 1957), pp. 195–202.

[56]Ayer, *Language, Truth and Logic*, pp. 15–16.

[57]See Habermas, *Resurrection of Jesus*, for one such approach.

Notes on Chapter 3

[1]John Gerstner, *Reasons for Faith* (Grand Rapids: Baker, 1967), p. 9.

[2]Clark Pinnock, *Biblical Revelation* (Chicago: Moody, 1971), p. 130.

[3]Ibid., p. 12.

[4]Francis Schaeffer, *How Should We Then Live?* (Old Tappan, N.J.: Revell, 1976), p. 162.

[5]Francis Schaeffer, *Escape From Reason* (Chicago: InterVarsity, 1968), p. 33.

[6]An excellent discussion of Pietism and Wolffianism and their conflict in Königsberg can be found in Theodore Green's "Historical Context and Religious Significance of Kant's *Religion*," included in his translation of Kant's *Religion Within the Limits of Reason Alone* (New York: Harper & Row, 1960).

[7]*Critique of Pure Reason*, trans. Norman Kemp Smith (New York: St. Martins, 1965), p. 41.

[8]Ibid., p. 65.
[9]Ibid., p. 93.
[10]Ibid., p. 409.
[11]Ibid., p. 410.
[12]Ibid., p. 415.
[13]*Critique of Practical Reason*, trans. Lewis White Beck (Indianapolis: Bobbs-Merrill, 1956), p. 48.
[14]Ibid., p. 162.
[15]See, for example, the discussions in *Critique of Practical Reason*, p. 31, or *Fundamental Principles of the Metaphysics of Morals*, trans. Thomas Abbott (Indianapolis: Bobbs-Merrill, 1949), sec. 2.
[16]I cannot deal with Kant's arguments in detail; however, numerous discussions of his ethical religion are available. See, for example, Stephen Körner, *Kant* (Baltimore: Penguin Books, 1955), chap. 7, for a popular account.
[17]*Critique of Practical Reason*, p. 132.
[18]Ibid., p. 122.
[19]See *Critique of Pure Reason*, pp. 500ff.
[20]*Critique of Practical Reason*, p. 130.
[21]See Kant's *Religion Within the Limits of Reason Alone*, pp. 23–24. Page references are to the translation by Theodore Greene and Hoyt Hudson (New York: Harper & Row, 1960).
[22]Ibid., p. 39.
[23]Ibid., p. 36.
[24]Ibid., pp. 37–38.
[25]Ibid., p. 36.
[26]Ibid., p. 40.
[27]Ibid., pp. 48, 49.
[28]Ibid., p. 46.
[29]Ibid., p. 48.
[30]Ibid., p. 56.
[31]Ibid., p. 57.
[32]Ibid., p. 54.
[33]Ibid., p. 55.
[34]Ibid., p. 54.
[35]Ibid., p. 53.
[36]Ibid., p. 78.
[37]Ibid., p. 69.
[38]Ibid., p. 52.
[39]Ibid., pp. 66–69.
[40]Ibid., p. 67.
[41]Ibid., p. 132.
[42]Ibid., p. 102.
[43]Ibid., p. 105.
[44]Ibid., p. 94.
[45]Ibid., p. 103.
[46]*Critique of Judgment*, trans. James Meredith, from *Great Books of the Western World* (Chicago: Encyclopaedia Britannica, 1952), p. 89.
[47]*Religion*, p. 108.
[48]Ibid., p. 120.
[49]Ibid., p. 109.
[50]The following is discussed in *Religion*, pp. 106–7. Note also p. 158, where Kant says that anything more than rational religion is *illusion*.
[51]Ibid., p. 121.
[52]Ibid., p. 115.
[53]Ibid., p. 106.

246   NOTES

[54]Ibid., pp. 106, 144.
[55]Ibid., p. 110.
[56]Ibid., p. 130.
[57]Ibid., p. 142.
[58]Ibid., p. 142n.
[59]Ibid., p. 175.
[60]Ibid., p. 155.
[61]See, for example, Ogden's "What Sense Does It Make To Say, 'God Acts in History'?" in *Journal of Religion* 43, 1 (January 1963), 3.
[62]See Ogden's "The Reality of God," in *The Reality of God and Other Essays* (New York: Harper & Row, 1966).
[63]This is most clear in Ogden's recent *Faith and Freedom* (Nashville: Abingdon, 1979).
[64]See Ogden, "On Revelation," in *Our Common History as Christians* (New York: Oxford, 1975).
[65]*Religion*, p. 3.
[66]"The Challenge to Protestant Thought," *Continuum* 6, 2 (Summer 1968), 237.
[67]For a contemporary critique of this notion see J. L. Austin, *Sense and Sensibilia* (New York: Oxford, 1962).
[68]The arguments of recent phenomenological epistemologies are helpful at this point, though not at others. See, for example, Maurice Merleau-Ponty, *Phenomenology of Perception* (New York: Humanities, 1962). The relevant chapter, "What Is Phenomenology?" is reprinted in *Philosophy Today, No. 3*, ed. Jerry Gill (New York: Macmillan, 1970).
[69]A helpful summary of this argument can be found in Bruce Aune's *Rationalism, Empiricism, and Pragmatism* (New York: Random, 1970), chap. 2.
[70]See especially Whitehead's *Process and Reality* (New York: Macmillan, 1929), p. 246.
[71]The following are some additional works to consult on Kant. The best general overview of Kant's philosophy is W. S. Körner, *Kant* (Baltimore: Penguin Books, 1955). On his philosophy of religion see James Collins, "Functions of Kant's Philosophy of Religion," *Monist* 60, 2 (April 1977), 159; Allen Wood, *Kant's Moral Religion* (Ithaca: Cornell, 1970); as well as many commentaries on the *Critique of Practical Reason;* and F. E. England, *Kant's Conception of God* (London: Allen and Unwin, 1929). The best comments on Kant's *Religion* are those included in the Harper Torchbooks edition (1960), Theodore Greene, "The Historical Context and Religious Significance of Kant's *Religion,*" and John Silber, "The Ethical Significance of Kant's *Religion.*" Critical remarks on Kant from a conservative viewpoint can be found in virtually any general discussion of philosophy of religion, but see especially Alvin Plantinga, *God and Other Minds* (Ithaca: Cornell, 1970); Stuart Hackett, *The Resurrection of Theism* (Chicago: Moody, 1957); John Carnell, *Introduction to Christian Apologetics* (Grand Rapids: Eerdmans, 1950); Norman Geisler, *Philosophy of Religion* (Grand Rapids: Zondervan, 1974); and Herman Dooyeweerd, *A New Critique of Theoretical Thought* (Philadelphia: Presbyterian and Reformed, 1969). A more positive assessment of Kant can be found in Stephen Evans's recent *Subjectivity and Religious Belief* (Grand Rapids: Eerdmans, 1978).

Notes on Chapter 4

[1]G. W. F. Hegel, *Geschichte der Philosophie*, in *Hegels sämtliche Werke*, Jubiläumsausgabe, ed. Hermann Glockner, 26 vols. (Stuttgart: Frommanns Verlag, 1959), p. 610.
[2]G. W. F. Hegel, *Phänomenologie des Geistes* (Hamburg: Felix Meiner, 1952), pp. 63–75. English translation: *Hegel's Phenomenology of Spirit*, trans. A. V. Miller (Oxford: Clarendon, 1977), pp. 46–57.
[3]Ibid., p. 66; Miller, p. 49.
[4]Ibid., pp. 67–71; Miller, pp. 49–52.
[5]Ibid., pp. 70–129; Miller, pp. 58–103.

[6]Ibid., p. 19; Miller, p. 9.

[7]G. W. F. Hegel, *Enzyklopädie der philosophischen Wissenschaften*, in *Werke*, ed. Eva Moldenhauer and Karl Markus Michel (Frankfurt: Suhrkamp, 1970), vols. 8–10. English translation: *Encyclopedia of Philosophy*, trans. Gustav Emil Mueller (New York: Philosophical Library, 1959).

[8]G. W. F. Hegel, *Wissenschaft der Logik* (Hamburg: Felix Meiner, 1963), 1:31; English translation: *Hegel's Science of Logic*, trans. W. H. Johnston and L. G. Struthers (New York: Humanities, 1929), p. 60.

[9]G. W. F. Hegel, *Vorlesungen über die Philosophie der Religion*, in *Werke*, 17:285–99.

[10]Hegel, *Enzyklopädie*, 10:394; *Phänomenologie*, p. 564. Mueller, p. 287; Miller, p. 591.

[11]G. W. F. Hegel, "Glauben und Wissen," *Jenaer Schriften 1801–1807*, in *Werke*, 2:432.

[12]Hegel, *Philosophie der Religion*, pp. 194–203.

[13]Ibid., pp. 196–98.

[14]Ibid., p. 195.

[15]Ibid., p. 199.

[16]Ibid., pp. 199–201.

[17]Ibid., p. 201.

[18]E.g., in *Enzyklopädie*, 10:374; Mueller, p. 281.

[19]Bruno Bauer, *Die Posaune des jüngsten Gerichts über Hegel den Atheisten und Antichristus* (Leipzig: published anonymously, 1841), p. 148.

[20]Bruno Bauer, *Hegels Lehre von der Religion und Kunst* (Leipzig: published anonymously, 1842), p. 59.

[21]Ludwig Feuerbach, *The Essence of Christianity*, trans. George Eliot (New York: Harper & Row, 1957), pp. 1–32.

[22]Ibid.

[23]Ibid., p. 211.

[24]Ibid., pp. 209–11.

[25]Ibid.

[26]D. F. Strauss, *The Life of Jesus Critically Examined*, trans. George Eliot, ed. Peter C. Hodgson (Philadelphia: Fortress, 1972).

[27]Ibid., pp. 57–59, 86–87.

[28]Ibid., pp. 77–81.

[29]Ibid.

[30]F. C. Baur, *Ferdinand Christian Baur on the Writing of Church History*, ed. and trans. Peter C. Hodgson (New York: Oxford, 1968), pp. 21–22.

[31]Ibid.

[32]Peter C. Hodgson, *The Formation of Historical Theology: A Study of Ferdinand Christian Baur* (New York: Harper & Row, 1966), pp. 207, 212.

[33]Ibid., p. 205.

[34]E.g., ibid., pp. 191–92.

[35]Hegel, *Enzyklopädie*, 10:394; Mueller, p. 287.

[36]G. W. F. Hegel, "Wie der gemeine Menschenverstand die Philosophie nehme, dargestellt an den Werken des Herrn Krug," in *Jenaer Schriften*, 2:188–207.

Notes on Chapter 5

[1]Many fine studies of Sören Kierkegaard's life are available. The most complete is the two-volume study by Walter Lowrie, *Kierkegaard* (New York: Harper, 1962).

[2]Alasdair MacIntyre, "Kierkegaard," in *Encyclopedia of Philosophy* (New York: Macmillan, 1972), 4:339.

[3]Sören Kierkegaard, *Repetition* (Princeton: Princeton University Press, 1941), pp. 3–4.

[4]*Encyclopedia of Philosophy*, p. 357.

[5]Sören Kierkegaard, *The Concept of Dread* (Princeton: Princeton University Press, 1944), p. 77.

[6]Quoted by Walter Lowrie in Introduction, Sören Kierkegaard, *Either/Or* (Princeton: Princeton University Press, 1959), 2:xiii.

[7]Henry Chadwick, "Lessing," in *Encyclopedia of Philosophy*, p. 445.

[8]Sören Kierkegaard, *Concluding Unscientific Postscript* (Princeton: Princeton University Press, 1941), p. 85.

[9]Ibid., p. 61.

[10]Ibid., pp. 60-61.

[11]Niels Thulstrup, "Commentator's Introduction," Sören Kierkegaard, *Philosophical Fragments*, 2nd ed. (Princeton: Princeton University Press, 1962), p. 1.

[12]*Postscript*, p. 88.

[13]Immanuel Kant, "Fundamental Principles of the Metaphysics of Morals," in *Kant's Critique of Practical Reason and Other Works on the Theory of Ethics*, trans. Thomas Kingsmill Abbott, 3rd ed. (London: Longmans, Green, 1883), p. 38.

[14]*Postscript*, p. 226.

[15]*Either/Or*, 1:71.

[16]Ibid., 1:76.

[17]Ibid., 1:254.

[18]Ibid., 1:313.

[19]Ibid., 1:305.

[20]Ibid.

[21]Ibid., 1:85.

[22]Ibid., 2:88.

[23]Romans 7:19.

[24]Sören Kierkegaard, *Stages on Life's Way*, trans. Walter Lowrie (Princeton: Princeton University Press, 1940), p. 430.

[25]*Postscript*, pp. 494-95.

[26]Sören Kierkegaard, *Fear and Trembling* (New York: Oxford University Press, 1939), p. 62.

[27]*Postscript*, p. 412.

[28]Romans 7:24.

[29]*Postscript*, pp. 505-8.

[30]Ibid., p. 506.

[31]Sören Kierkegaard, *Fear and Trembling and Sickness Unto Death* (Princeton: Princeton University Press, 1941), pp. 145, 153, 155.

[32]*Concept of Dread*, p. 38.

[33]*Sickness Unto Death*, p. 153.

[34]Sören Kierkegaard, *Point of View for My Work as an Author*, trans. Walter Lowrie (New York: Oxford University Press, 1939), p. 82.

[35]Sören Kierkegaard, *Training in Christianity* (New York: Oxford University Press, 1941), p. 39.

[36]*Postscript*, p. 44.

[37]Ibid., p. 29.

[38]Ibid.

[39]*Sickness Unto Death*, p. 213.

[40]Ibid.

[41]*Fear and Trembling*, p. 75.

[42]*Sickness Unto Death*, p. 150.

[43]*Training in Christianity*, p. 79.

[44]Sören Kierkegaard, *Journals and Papers*, 7 vols. (Bloomington: Indiana University Press, 1978), no. 2911.

[45]Ibid., no. 210.

[46]Ibid., no. 203.

[47]*Postscript*, p. 25.

[48]*Fragments*, p. 99.

[49]*Postscript*, p. 510.

50*Fragments*, p. 115.
51Josiah Thompson, "The Master of Irony," in *Kierkegaard: A Collection of Critical Essays* (Garden City: Doubleday, 1972), p. 161.
52*Postscript*, Introductory Essay, p. xviii.
53*Journals and Papers*, no. 214.
54*Postscript*, p. 511.
55Cf. Thompson, pp. 256ff.
56*Journals and Papers*, no. 208.
57*Postscript*, p. 193.
58*Journals and Papers*, no. 2870.
59Ibid., no. 209.
60*Postscript*, p. 201.
61Ibid., p. 116.
62*Fragments*, p. 108.
63Ibid., p. 56.
64*Postscript*, p. 290.
65Ibid., p. 339.
66Sören Kierkegaard, *Journals* (New York: Oxford University Press, 1938), 1:412.
67Sören Kierkegaard, *For Self Examination* (New York: Oxford University Press, 1941), p. 200.
68*Postscript*, p. 186.
69Ibid., p. 187.
70The Athanasian Creed reads: ". . . Jesus . . . was begotten from the Father before all ages, God from God, whole from whole, sole from sole, complete from complete, king from king, Lord from Lord, Living Word, Living Wisdom, True Light, Way, Truth, Resurrection, Shepherd, Door, Unchangeable and Immutable; invariable image of the deity. . . . and was made man, . . ."
71*Training*, p. 131.
72*Postscript*, pp. 194, 195.
73*Training*, p. 143.
74Hugh Ross Mackintosh, *Types of Modern Theology* (London: Nisbet, 1949), p. 244.
75*Training*, p. 142.
76H. V. Martin, *The Melancholy Dane* (New York: Philosophical Library, 1950), p. 70.
77*Training*, p. 143.
78Ibid., p. 9.
79Ibid., p. 67.
80*Fragments*, p. 116.
81Ibid., p. 128.
82Ibid., 130.
83Ibid., p. 73.
84Ibid., p. 76.
85*Journals and Papers*, no. 2898.
86*Postscript*, p. 182.
87Ibid., p. 31.
88Ibid., p. 30.
89Georg Wilhelm Friedrich Hegel, *Lectures on the Philosophy of Religion* (London: Kegan Paul, 1895), 3:126.
90*Journals*, no. 1258.
91Ibid., no. 1090.
92Karl Barth, *The Epistle to the Romans* (London: Oxford University Press, 1933), p. 38.
93Ibid., p. 10.
94Karl Barth, *Credo* (London: Hodder and Stoughton, 1936), p. 186.
95Ibid., p. 186.
96Barth, *Romans*, p. 99.
97Rudolf Bultmann, *Kerygma and Myth* (New York: Harper & Row, 1961), pp. 37ff.

[98]Paul Tillich, *Protestant Era* (Chicago: University of Chicago, 1948), p. 82.
[99]Ibid.
[100]Reinhold Niebuhr, *Nature and Destiny of Man* (London: Nisbet, 1949), 1:176.
[101]Bultmann, *Kerygma*, p. 117.
[102]Ibid., p. 35.
[103]Ibid., p. 39.
[104]Ibid.
[105]Ibid.
[106]Ibid., p. 42.
[107]C. S. Lewis, *Christian Reflections* (Grand Rapids: Eerdmans, 1967), pp. 152ff.
[108]Harold Lindsell, *The Battle for the Bible* (Grand Rapids: Zondervan, 1976), p. 31.
[109]Richard Quebedeaux, *The Young Evangelicals* (New York: Harper & Row, 1974), p. 4.
[110]*Journals and Papers*, no. 2877.
[111]Ibid., no. 2898.
[112]*Postscript*, p. 30.

Notes on Chapter 6

[1]See "The Chicago Statement on Biblical Inerrancy," in *Inerrancy*, ed. Norman L. Geisler (Grand Rapids: Zondervan, 1979), pp. 493–502; see esp. the section "Infallibility, Inerrancy, Interpretation," pp. 500–1.
[2]H. Van Riessen, *Nietzsche*, ed. David H. Freeman (Philadelphia: Presbyterian and Reformed, 1960), pp. 9, 15.
[3]The parable of *The Madman* can be found in Walter Kaufmann's *Nietzsche: Philosopher, Psychologist, Antichrist* (New York: Meridian, 1966), p. 81.
[4]Kaufmann's book is cited in note 3; Karl Jaspers, *Nietzsche* (Tucson: University of Arizona Press, 1965).
[5]Jaspers, *Nietzsche*, p. 56. For a detailed view of Nietzsche's life, the influences of friends, a detailed chronology, etc., see Terry L. Miethe, *Friedrich Nietzsche and the Death of God: The Rejection of Absolutes*, published in limited edition by the author, 1973; 104 pages.
[6]Jaspers, *Nietzsche*, pp. 88–89.
[7]Kaufmann, *Nietzsche*, p. 91; Jaspers, *Nietzsche*, p. 271.
[8]Kaufmann, *Nietzsche*, pp. 28, 41, 42, 44.
[9]Norman L. Geisler, *Philosophy of Religion* (Grand Rapids: Zondervan, 1974), chap. 3.
[10]Ibid., pp. 52–53.
[11]Thomas J. J. Altizer, *The Gospel of Christian Atheism* (Philadelphia: Westminster, 1946), pp. 25, 90.
[12]Jaspers, *Nietzsche*, pp. 434–35.
[13]Ibid., p. 167.
[14]Walter Kaufmann, *The Portable Nietzsche* (New York: Viking, 1968), p. 594.
[15]Ibid., p. 595.
[16]Ibid., p. 584, from *The Antichrist*.
[17]Friedrich Nietzsche, *The Genealogy of Morals* (New York: Doubleday, 1956), pp. 168–69.
[18]Jaspers, *Nietzsche*, p. 242.
[19]Kaufmann, *Portable Nietzsche*, p. 198.
[20]Nietzsche, *Genealogy of Morals*, p. 166.
[21]Ibid., p. 288.
[22]Kaufmann, *Portable Nietzsche*, p. 142.
[22]Ibid., pp. 581–82.
[24]Friedrich Nietzsche, *Beyond Good and Evil* (New York: Random, 1966), pp. 68–69.
[25]Kaufmann, *Nietzsche*, pp. 83–84.

26Kaufmann, *Portable Nietzsche,* p. 294.
27Jaspers, *Nietzsche,* p. 158.
28Kaufmann, *Portable Nietzsche,* pp. 46–47. Here Nietzsche tells us what truth is to
him. See also pp. 52–53.
29Nietzsche, *Beyond Good and Evil,* pp. 75–76.
30Kaufmann, *Nietzsche,* p. 291.
31Ibid., p. 289.
32Ibid., pp. 294–95.
33Kaufmann, *Portable Nietzsche,* p. 618.
34Nietzsche, *Genealogy of Morals,* p. 281.
35Nietzsche, *Beyond Good and Evil,* p. 86.
36Karl Jaspers, *Nietzsche and Christianity* (Chicago: Regnery,1963), p. 5.
37Jaspers, *Nietzsche,* p. 121.

Notes on Chapter 7

1W. Donald Hudson, *Wittgenstein and Religious Belief* (New York: St. Martin's, 1975),
p. 8.
2It is for this reason that I have called Wittgenstein's philosophy as a whole noncognitivism. Noncognitivism, generally speaking, means that one's utterances are not assertions of facts and are thus neither true nor false. Noncognitivism is relevant especially to
ethics and epistemology. I am not using it in relation to all of Wittgenstein's views.
However, since his theory of language in the *Tractatus* and the *Investigations* results in
certain kinds of sentences being noncognitive, it seemed to be an appropriate label for my
study.
3I am assuming here that any analytic statement that is noncontradictory is true, and
any such statement that is contradictory is false. As for synthetic propositions, I am
assuming that they are to be verified or falsified by empirical means. In general, I am
operating with a correspondence theory of truth. For a thorough handling of the concept
of biblical inerrancy see Paul D. Feinberg, "The Meaning of Inerrancy," in *Inerrancy,* ed.
Norman L. Geisler (Grand Rapids: Zondervan, 1980). After setting forth various possible
definitions, Feinberg defines biblical inerrancy in terms of truth and presents his case for
doing so.
4Hudson, *Wittgenstein,* pp. 13–14.
5Ludwig Wittgenstein, *Tractatus Logico-Philosophicus* (London: Routledge & Kegan
Paul, 1971), 4.01, p. 63. Hereafter cited as *Tractatus.*
6Ibid., 1.1, p. 31.
7Ibid., 1.2, p. 31.
8Ibid., 2, p. 31. In this edition *Sachverhalt* is rendered "atomic fact," but that leaves the
question as to the meaning of an atomic fact. By atomic fact, Wittgenstein seems to mean
a state of affairs that is elementary in nature. See also Hudson, *Wittgenstein,* p. 20; George
Pitcher, *The Philosophy of Wittgenstein* (Englewood Cliffs, N.J.: Prentice-Hall, 1964), pp.
19–20; and Norman Malcolm, "Wittgenstein, Ludwig Josef Johann," *Encyclopedia of
Philosophy,* ed. Paul Edwards (New York: Macmillan, 1972), 8:330. These three interpret
it to have the meaning I've mentioned.
9*Tractatus,* 2.021, p. 35.
10Pitcher, *Philosophy of Wittgenstein,* p. 19.
11*Tractatus,* 2.01, p. 31. See also 2.0272, p. 37.
12Ibid., 2.03, p. 37.
13Ibid., 2.061, p. 37. See also 1.21, p. 31.
14Ibid., 2.02, p. 35.
15Ibid., 2.021, p. 35.
16Ibid., 2.0272, p. 37.

[17]Ibid., 2.0271, p. 37.
[18]Ibid., 2.014, p. 35. See also 2.0121 and 2.0122.
[19]Ibid., 2.0141, p. 35.
[20]Hudson, *Wittgenstein*, p. 20.
[21]*Tractatus*, 2.06, p. 37.
[22]Ibid., 1.12, p. 31.
[23]Ibid., 3.202, p. 47.
[24]Ibid., 3.203, p. 47.
[25]Ibid., 3.22, p. 49.
[26]Ibid., 3.26, p. 49.
[27]Ibid., 4.22, p. 89.
[28]Ibid., 3.21, p. 47.
[29]Ibid., 4.21, p. 89.
[30]Ibid., 3.3, p. 51.
[31]Ibid., 4.221, p. 89.
[32]Ibid., 4.2211, p. 89.
[33]Ibid., 2.13, 2.131, 2.14, and 2.15, p. 39.
[34]Ibid., 2.15, p. 39.
[35]Ibid., 4.03, p. 69.
[36]Ibid.
[37]Pitcher, *Philosophy of Wittgenstein*, p. 78.
[38]*Tractatus*, 3.1432, p. 47.
[39]Ibid., 2.151, p. 39. See also 2.18.
[40]Ibid., 5.631, 5.632, 5.633, p. 151.
[41]Ibid., 6.41, p. 183.
[42]Ibid., 6.421, p. 183.
[43]Ibid., 6.432, p. 187.
[44]Ibid., 6.54, p. 189.
[45]Ibid., 5.5561, p. 147.
[46]Ibid., 5.6, p. 149.
[47]Wittgenstein says that "the totality of true propositions is the total natural science (or the totality of the natural sciences)" (4.11). This definitely helps to demonstrate the limits of the world and of language. Only true propositions of natural science are about the world. True and false propositions of natural science set the limits of language, because even false ones are about possible states of affairs *in the world*. Of course, if all that can be said is something about natural science, then statements about theology, ethics, and metaphysics are obviously unsayable.
[48]*Tractatus*, 7, p. 189.
[49]Ibid., 6.522, p. 187.
[50]Ibid., 4.12 and 4.121, p. 79.
[51]Ibid., 5, p. 103. See also 5.3, p. 119.
[52]Ibid., 5.3, p. 119.
[53]Pitcher, *Philosophy of Wittgenstein*, p. 57. See *Tractatus*, 4.4 and 4.41.
[54]*Tractatus*, 4.46, p. 97.
[55]Ibid., 4.463, p. 99.
[56]Ibid., 4.031, p. 69.
[57]Ibid., 2.21, p. 43.
[58]Ibid., 2.221, p. 43.
[59]Ibid., 2.222, p. 43.
[60]Ibid., 2.223, p. 43. Sections 2.221, 2.222, and 2.223 are about the closest Wittgenstein comes in the *Tractatus* to giving a theory for verification of propositions.
[61]Ibid., 4.26, p. 91.
[62]Ibid., 5.5151, p. 135.
[63]Ludwig Wittgenstein, *Notebooks 1914-1916*, ed. G. H. von Wright and G. E. M. Anscombe (Oxford: Basil Blackwell, 1961), entry for 5.6.15.

⁶⁴*Tractatus*, 4.116, pp. 77, 79.

⁶⁵A similar kind of rejection in inerrancy could come from Wittgenstein's claim that propositions about the world have no necessity. He writes, "A necessity for one thing to happen because another has happened does not exist. There is only *logical* necessity" (6.1222, p. 163). When he speaks of *logical* necessity, he is referring to the necessity of analytic propositions. It should be obvious that given Wittgenstein's comments in 6.1222, one cannot say that just because the Bible was inspired by the work of the Holy Spirit, it *must* also be inerrant. As he says, just because one thing happens does not mean that anything else must of necessity occur. It is interesting and important to note that there are those who would make just this kind of point, viz., inspiration does not entail inerrancy. See, for example, Clark Pinnock, "Three Views of the Bible in Contemporary Theology," in *Biblical Authority*, ed. Jack Rogers (Waco: Word, 1977), p. 64. I am not arguing that Pinnock, or anyone else on the contemporary scene, has come to this position because of an adherence to Wittgenstein's views. My point is only that Pinnock has arrived at the same conclusion that would be necessitated on this matter, *if one were to apply Wittgenstein's views*.

⁶⁶I should add that few, if any, evangelical errantists would go so far to reject inerrancy. This is quite a radical way to do so. Nonetheless, the point is that one *could* use Wittgenstein's views to reject inerrancy in the way mentioned.

⁶⁷See Antony Flew, "Theology and Falsification," in *The Philosophy of Religion*, ed. Basil Mitchell (London: Oxford University Press, 1971).

⁶⁸Ludwig Wittgenstein, *Philosophical Investigations* (New York: Macmillan, 1968), sec. 7, p. 5e. Hereafter cited as *Investigations*.

⁶⁹Ibid., sec. 23, p. 11e.

⁷⁰Ibid., sec. 19, p. 8e.

⁷¹Ibid., sec. 23, pp. 11e–12e.

⁷²In particular, Wittgenstein came to hold that there are no such things as simple objects and that the words *simple, complex*, and *composite* vary in meaning, depending on the language-game, so one cannot specify one common meaning for each concept, let alone try to apply them to language as a whole. Moreover, Wittgenstein came to see that words in a proposition do not name objects in the world. See *Investigations*, secs. 27, 39, 41, and 47 for these ideas.

⁷³*Investigations*, sec. 43, p. 20e.

⁷⁴Ibid., sec. 23, pp. 11e–12e.

⁷⁵Ibid., sec. 11, p. 6e.

⁷⁶Ludwig Wittgenstein, *Lectures and Conversations on Aesthetics, Psychology and Religious Belief*, ed. Cyril Barret (Oxford: Basil Blackwell, 1966), pp. 61–62. It is for this reason that Wittgenstein would say that propositions of religious belief are, factually and empirically speaking, nonsensical.

⁷⁷Ibid., p. 60.

⁷⁸Ibid., pp. 56–57.

⁷⁹Ibid., p. 56.

⁸⁰Ludwig Wittgenstein, *On Certainty*, ed. G. E. M. Anscombe and G. H. von Wright (New York: Harper & Row, 1972), sec. 559, p. 73e. See also *Investigations*, p. 226e.

⁸¹*On Certainty*, sec. 370, p. 48e. See also *On Certainty*, sec. 411, p. 52e as well as secs. 111–12, 234–35, 337, 446, 512, and 514.

⁸²Ibid., sec. 519, p. 68e.

⁸³Ibid., sec. 115, p. 18e. See also *On Cetainty*, secs. 341, 450, and 625.

⁸⁴Ibid., sec. 257, p. 34e.

⁸⁵*Investigations*, p. 224e.

⁸⁶Ibid., p. 223e. See also *Investigations*, secs. 202 and 206 for Wittgenstein on trying to obey a rule privately.

⁸⁷Ibid., sec. 303, p. 102e.

⁸⁸Ibid., sec. 293, p. 100e.

⁸⁹Ibid., sec. 304, p. 102e.

[90]Ibid., sec. 290, p. 99e.

[91]Ibid., sec. 258, p. 92e.

[92]Ibid., sec. 337, p. 108e. See also *Investigations*, sec. 358, p. 113e.

[93]Ibid., sec. 641, pp. 164e–65e.

[94]Ibid., sec. 580, p. 153e.

[95]Ludwig Wittgenstein, "The Blue Book," in *The Blue and Brown Books* (New York: Harper & Row, 1965), pp. 24–25. See also Carl Wellman, "Wittgenstein's Conception of a Criterion," *Wittgenstein and the Problem of Other Minds,* ed. Harold Morick (New York: McGraw, 1967), p. 158.

[96]"Blue Book," p. 51. See also R. Sundara Rajan, "Wittgenstein's Conception of Criterion," *Journal of the Indian Academy of Philosophy* 6 (1967) :46.

[97]*Investigations*, sec. 350, p. 111e.

[98]Ibid., sec. 65, p. 31e. See also *Investigations*, secs. 66–67, 77, and 165 for examples of the many comments Wittgenstein makes that illustrate this anti-essentialism theme.

[99]See, for example, *Investigations*, secs. 69–71, 76–77.

[100]*Investigations*, sec. 84, p. 39e.

[101]See Harold Lindsell, *The Battle for the Bible* (Grand Rapids: Zondervan, 1976), chap. 9, for examples of some instances in which some evangelicals have handled alleged errors in such a way.

[102]I personally think the response to make is that the move is legitimate. Even in a case where one resolves a historical or scientific discrepancy by presenting historical or scientific *facts,* he employs the "use strategy." My reason for making this claim is that his decision to answer the objection by means of presenting historical or scientific facts shows that he has *previously* decided that the statement in question is being *used* to teach history or science and therefore presenting historical and/or scientific facts would be appropriate to meet the charge of error. Moreover, even the *errantist* employs the "use strategy," whether he recognizes it or not. His demand that every alleged historical and/or scientific error be answered by presenting historical and/or scientific evidence shows his presuppositions about the *use* of all such statements. Both the errantist and the inerrantist *by their practice* seem to recognize the legitimacy of employing the notion of use. Consequently, I do not see that the inerrantist can be faulted for employing the "use principle" to resolve alleged errors in particular cases. One may dislike *on a given occasion* the appeal to the writer's intended use as a means of resolving a given difficulty, but that does not make it illegitimate to do so. The notion of use should not be eliminated altogether from discussions of errancy or inerrancy of the propositions of Scripture. Anyway, as I have mentioned, one could not eliminate the notion even if he tried.

[103]See, for example, R. B. Braithwaite, "An Empiricist's View of the Nature of Religious Belief," in *Philosophy of Religion.* After denying that statements of religious belief are being used either to assert something about the empirical world or to express an emotion, Braithwaite claims that such propositions are being used conatively, i.e., to express the *intention* of the asserter to act in a particular way specified in the assertion.

[104]William K. Wimsatt, Jr., and M. C. Beardsley, "The Intentional Fallacy," in *An Introduction to Literary Criticism,* Marlies K. Danziger and W. Stacy Johnson (Boston: D. C. Heath and Company, 1967). See also Suzanne K. Langer, *Feeling and Form: A Theory of Art* (New York: Scribner, 1953), and Suzanne K. Langer, *Philosophy in a New Key: A Study in the Symbolism of Reason, Rite, and Art* (Cambridge: Harvard University Press, 1951), for elaboration of these ideas.

[105]*Investigations*, secs. 75–77.

[106]Ibid., sec. 88, p. 41e.

[107]For exposition and explanation of these ideas see Braithwaite, "An Empiricist's View."

Notes on Chapter 8

[1]John Macquarrie, *Martin Heidegger* (Richmond: John Knox, 1968), preface.
[2]Ibid.
[3]Paul D. Feinberg, "The Meaning of Inerrancy," in *Inerrancy*, ed. Norman L. Geisler (Grand Rapids: Zondervan, 1979), p. 294.
[4]Martin Heidegger, *Discourse on Thinking*, trans. John M. Anderson and E. Hans Freund (New York: Harper & Row, 1966), p. 54.
[5]Martin Heidegger, *Being and Time*, trans. John Macquarrie and Edward Robinson (New York: Harper & Row, 1962), pp. 41–49.
[6]Ibid., p. 5.
[7]George Steiner, *Martin Heidegger* (New York: Viking, 1978), p. 16.
[8]Joseph Fell, *Heidegger and Sartre* (New York: Columbia University Press, 1979), pp. 23–27.
[9]Sören Kierkegaard, *Concluding Unscientific Postscript*, trans. David F. Swenson and Walter Lowrie (Princeton: Princeton University Press, 1944), p. 190.
[10]Heidegger, *Being and Time*, p. 73.
[11]Ibid., p. 25.
[12]Ibid., p. 236.
[13]Ibid., p. 73.
[14]Ibid., p. 26.
[15]Ibid., p. 78.
[16]Macquarrie, *Martin Heidegger*, p. 61.
[17]Anthony C. Thiselton, *The Two Horizons: New Testament Hermeneutics and Philosophical Description with Special Reference to Heidegger, Bultmann, Gadamer, and Wittgenstein* (Grand Rapids: Eerdmans, 1980), pp. 156–58.
[18]Heidegger, *Being and Time*, p. 100.
[19]Ibid., p. 114.
[20]Thiselton, *Two Horizons*, p. 159.
[21]Ibid., p. 160.
[22]Heidegger, *Being and Time*, p. 203.
[23]Ibid., pp. 172–73.
[24]Michael Gelven, *A Commentary on Heidegger's 'Being and Time'* (New York: Harper & Row, 1970), p. 76.
[25]Heidegger, *Being and Time*, p. 173.
[26]John Macquarrie, *Studies in Christian Existentialism* (London: SCM, 1966), pp. 30–42.
[27]Thiselton, *Two Horizons*, p. 163.
[28]Gelven, *Commentary on Heidegger's 'Being and Time,'* p. 83.
[29]Heidegger, *Being and Time*, p. 183.
[30]Ibid., p. 184.
[31]Gelven, *Commentary on Heidegger's 'Being and Time,'* p. 89.
[32]Ibid., p. 90.
[33]Heidegger, *Being and Time*, p. 188.
[34]Ibid., pp. 188–89.
[35]Ibid., p. 190.
[36]Ibid., pp. 191–92.
[37]Ibid., p. 193.
[38]Gelven, *Commentary on Heidegger's 'Being and Time,'* p. 99.
[39]Ibid., p. 104.
[40]Thiselton, *Two Horizons*, p. 168.
[41]Gelven, *Commentary on Heidegger's 'Being and Time,'* p. 104.
[42]Thiselton, *Two Horizons*, p. 176.
[43]See Marjorie Grene, *Martin Heidegger* (London: Bowes & Bowes, 1957), p. 117; and Karl Lowith, *Heidegger, Denker in durftiger Zeit* (Gottingen: Vandenhoeck and Ruprecht, 1960), p. 7.

[44]See Werner Brock, "An Account of 'The Four Essays'," in *Existence and Being* by Martin Heidegger (London: English Vision, 1968), p. 134.

[45]John Macquarrie, "Heidegger's Earlier and Later Work Compared," *Anglican Theological Review* 49 (1967): 7.

[46]Martin Heidegger, *On the Way to Language*, trans. P. D. Hertz (New York: Harper & Row, 1971), p. 30.

[47]Martin Heidegger, *An Introduction to Metaphysics*, trans. Ralph Manheim (New Haven: Yale University Press, 1959), pp. 5-6.

[48]Ibid., p. 6.

[49]Ibid., p. 7.

[50]Ibid., p. 9.

[51]Ibid., p. 7.

[52]Ibid., p. 12.

[53]Ibid., p. 13.

[54]Ibid., p. 14.

[55]Ibid., p. 29.

[56]Ibid., p. 36.

[57]Ibid., p. 37.

[58]Thiselton, *Two Horizons*, p. 335.

[59]Heidegger, *Introduction to Metaphysics*, p. 194.

[60]Ibid., p. 202.

[61]Ibid., p. 206.

[62]Ibid.

[63]Ibid., p. 13.

[64]Heinrich Ott, "What Is Systematic Theology?" in *New Frontiers in Theology: I. The Later Heidegger and Theology*, ed. James M. Robinson and John B. Cobb, Jr. (New York: Harper & Row, 1963), p. 87.

[65]Thiselton, *Two Horizons*, p. 336.

[66]Heidegger, *Discourse on Thinking*, p. 53.

[67]Ibid.

[68]Ibid., p. 54.

[69]Ibid.

[70]Ibid.

[71]Ibid., p. 56.

[72]Ibid.

[73]Ibid., p. 54.

[74]Ibid., p. 57.

[75]Martin Heidegger, "What Is Metaphysics?" in *Existentialism: From Dostoevsky to Sartre*, ed. Walter Kaufmann (New York: New American Library, 1975), p. 244.

[76]Ibid., p. 245.

[77]Ibid., p. 261.

[78]Ibid., p. 255.

[79]Ibid., p. 251.

[80]Heidegger, "Conversation on a Country Path about Thinking," in *Discourse on Thinking*, p. 61.

[81]Heidegger, "What Is Metaphysics?", p. 257.

[82]Heidegger, *On the Way to Language*, p. 70.

[83]Thiselton, *Two Horizons*, p. 342.

[84]Ibid.

[85]Feinberg, "Meaning of Inerrancy," p. 294.

[86]Ibid., p. 295.

[87]Rudolf Bultmann, *Essays, Philosophical and Theological* (London: SCM, 1955), p. 255.

[88]See E. D. Hirsch, Jr., *Validity in Interpretation* (New Haven: Yale University Press, 1967); and Walter C. Kaiser, Jr., "Legitimate Hermeneutics," in *Inerrancy*, ed. Norman L. Geisler, pp. 117-47.

[89]Hirsch, *Validity in Interpretation*, pp. 1–23.

[90]Ibid., pp. 5–6.

[91]Ibid., p. ix.

[92]Otto Pöggeler, "Heidegger's Topology of Being," in *On Heidegger and Language*, ed. Joseph J. Kockelmans (Evanston: Northwestern University Press, 1972), p. 114.

[93]James I. Packer, "The Adequacy of Human Language," in *Inerrancy*, ed. Norman L. Geisler, p. 202.

[94]Stuart C. Hackett, *Oriental Philosophy: A Westerner's Guide to Eastern Thought* (Madison: University of Wisconsin Press, 1979), p. 58.

[95]Ibid., pp. 63–64.

[96]Heidegger, *On the Way to Language*, p. 92.

[97]Martin Heidegger, "Who Is Nietzsche's Zarathustra?" trans. Bernd Magnus *Review of Metaphysics* 20 (1967): 424.

[98]Martin Heidegger, *Der Satz vom Grund* (Pfullingen: Verlag Gunther Neske, 1965), p. 71.

[99]William Barrett, ed., *Zen Buddhism: Selected Writings of D. T. Suzuki* (Garden City: Doubleday, Anchor, 1956), p. xi.

[100]John D. Caputo, *The Mystical Element in Heidegger's Thought* (Oberlin: Oberlin Printing Company, 1978), pp. 245–54.

[101]Paul Hühnerfeld, *In Sachen Heidegger: Versuch über ein deutsches Genie* (Munich: Paul List Verlag, 1961), p. 125.

[102]Heidegger, "What Is Metaphysics?" in *Existence and Being*, p. 355.

[103]Caputo, *The Mystical Element in Heidegger's Thought*, pp. 248–49.

[104]Heidegger, "What Is Metaphysics?" in *Existence and Being*, p. 359.

[105]"'Only a god can save us': *Der Spiegel's* interview with Martin Heidegger," *Philosophy Today* 20 (1976): 277, 279.

Notes on the Epilogue

[1]See the projected ICBI book on theology and inerrancy edited by Gordon Lewis and Bruce Demorest, Moody.

[2]*Het probleem der Schriftkritiek (The Problem of Biblical Criticism)*, 1938 (not translated into English). For a brief but excellent evaluation of Berkouwer by an admiring student see Carl Bogue, *A Hole in the Dike* (Cherry Hill, N.J.: Mack, 1977).

[3]See Jack Rogers and Donald K. McKim, *The Authority and Interpretation of the Bible: An Historical Approach* (New York: Harper & Row, 1979), pp. 406–7.

[4]Ibid., p. 427.

[5]See G. C. Berkouwer, *Studies in Dogmatics: Holy Scripture*, trans. Jack B. Rogers (Grand Rapids: Eerdmans, 1975), p. 145.

[6]Ibid., p. 170.

[7]Ibid., p. 207.

[8]Ibid., p. 157.

[9]Ibid., p. 161.

[10]Ibid., p. 163.

[11]Ibid., p. 147. See also pp. 163, 265.

[12]Ibid., p. 166.

[13]Ibid., pp. 143, 203.

[14]Ibid., p. 145.

[15]Ibid., p. 187.

[16]Ibid., p. 182.

[17]Ibid., p. 184.

[18]Ibid., p. 254.

[19]See article by Norman L. Geisler, "The Concept of Truth in the Inerrancy Debate," *Bibliotheca Sacra* (October 1980).

[20]Berkouwer, *Holy Scripture*, p. 199.
[21]Ibid., p. 167.
[22]Ibid., p. 245.
[23]Ibid., p. 206.
[24]Ibid., p. 240.
[25]Ibid., p. 178.
[26]Ibid., p. 181.
[27]Ibid., p. 245.
[28]Ibid.
[29]Ibid., p. 244.
[30]Ibid., p. 181.
[31]Ibid., p. 182.
[32]See Rogers, *Authority and Interpretation of the Bible*, pp. 426–27.
[33]Ibid., pp. 406–7.
[34]Ibid., p. 427.
[35]Ibid., pp. 410–11.
[36]Ibid., p. 393.
[37]Ibid., p. 71.
[38]Ibid.
[39]Ibid., p. 391.
[40]Ibid., p. 399.
[41]Ibid., p. 429.
[42]Ibid., p. 436.
[43]Ibid., p. 342.
[44]Ibid., p. 392.
[45]Ibid., p. 26.
[46]Ibid., p. 251.
[47]Ibid., p. 287.
[48]Ibid., p. xxiv, n. 12.
[49]Ibid., p. 431.
[50]Ibid., p. 435.
[51]Ibid., p. 434.
[52]Ibid., p. 398.
[53]Ibid., pp. 304–5.
[54]Ibid., p. 337.
[55]Ibid., p. 20.
[56]Ibid., p. 30.
[57]Ibid., p. 430.
[58]See 1 Corinthians 2:13, "*Words* . . . taught by the Spirit . . ." and 2 Timothy 3:16, God-breathed out the *writings*.
[59]See the excellent historical study by H. D. McDonald, *Theories of Revelation: An Historical Study: 1700–1960* (Grand Rapids: Baker, 1979), esp. pp. 196–99.
[60]Stephen T. Davis, *The Debate About the Bible* (Philadelphia: Westminster, 1977).
[61]Ibid., p. 95.
[62]Ibid., pp. 96–98.
[63]Ibid.
[64]Ibid., p. 97.
[65]Ibid., p. 115.
[66]Rogers, *Authority and Interpretation of the Bible*, xxiv, n. 12.
[67]Paul Jewett, *Man as Male and Female: A Study in Sexual Relationships from a Theological Point of View* (Grand Rapids: Eerdmans, 1979).
[68]Davis, *Debate About the Bible*, p. 115.
[69]Ibid., p. 116.

BIOGRAPHICAL INDEX

SUBJECT INDEX

A posteriori, 58, 83
Accommodation, 235
Aesthetic stage, 109-12
Agnosticism, 59-62
Analytic and synthetic statements, 35, 37
Anthropology
of G. W. F. Hegel, 85ff.
of Immanuel Kant, 61ff.
Atheism, of Nietzsche, 147
Atomic impressions, 77-78
Authority and Interpretation of the Bible, The (Rogers), 234

Being and Time (Heidegger), 208
Beyond Good and Evil (Nietzsche), 151
Bible
and Absolute Spirit, 87-89
allegorical interpretation of, 19
authority of, 127
as containing God's Word, 16
and contradictions, 16
functional view of, 13-14, 235-36
as history, 117-19
and moral criteria for authenticity, 17-18
as nonpropositional revelation, 16-17
and science, 21, 233ff.
as a witness to God's Word, 232
Bibliology
of Francis Bacon, 13-14
of G. C. Berkouwer, 232-34
of Ludwig Feuerbach, 91
of G. W. F. Hegel, 87-89, 97-98
of Thomas Hobbes, 15-16
of David Hume, 30
of Immanuel Kant, 62-72
of Sören Kierkegaard, 116-19, 122
of Friedrich Nietzsche, 155-56
of Jack Rogers, 235-36
of Benedict Spinoza, 7, 16-18

Categorical imperative, 61
Causality, 29
Christ. *See* Jesus Christ.

Christianity
attacks on, in Nietzsche's writings, 150-56
deistic views of, 27
Concern, concept of, in Heidegger's thought, 210-11
Concerning Natural Religion (Hume), 29
Criticism
biblical, 11, 127
historical, 125
influence of Deism on, 27
Critique of Judgment (Kant), 68
Critique of Practical Reason (Kant), 60
Critique of Pure Reason (Kant), 57

Dasein, 208-15
Dawn of Day, The (Nietzsche), 138
De Veritate (Herbert of Cherbury), 26
Debate About the Bible, The (Davis), 237
Deduction, 16
and induction, 12, 28
Deism, 26-27
Demythologizing, 126-27
Dialectic
of G. W. F. Hegel, 82-85
of Sören Kierkegaard, 107-8
Discourse on Thinking (Heidegger), 219
Documentary hypothesis, 11

Either/Or (Kierkegaard), 110
Empiricism, 25
atomic impressions, 77-78
epistemology of, 27-28
Encyclopedia (Hegel), 85, 96
Enlightenment, 25, 53
Enquiry Concerning Human Understanding, An (Hume), 30
Epistemology
of René Descartes, 26
of G. W. F. Hegel, 83ff.
of Martin Heidegger, 208ff.
of Thomas Hobbes, 14ff.
of David Hume, 28-30
of Immanuel Kant, 57-62
of Sören Kierkegaard, 107ff.